HEALTHY BABY
TOXIC WORLD

Melody Milam Potter Ph.D.
Erin E. Milam

New Harbinger Publications, Inc.

List of Advisors

Jerry T. Davis, D. O.: Family Medicine (Lake Worth Medical Center, Fort Worth, Texas); Physician Training (North Texas Health Science Center, Fort Worth, Texas)

Nancy Didriksen, Ph.D.: Environmental Health and Neuropsychology (Clinical Behavioral Health, Inc., Richardson, Texas); Adjunct Professor: Graduate School in Clinical Psychology; (University of North Texas, Denton, Texas)

John L. Laseter, Ph.D., BCFE, BCFM: Clinical and Forensic Toxicology (AccuChem Laboratories, Richardson, Texas; Chief Executive Officer)

Frances McManemin, Ph.D.: Clinical Health Psychology and Behavioral Medicine (Meridian Behavioral Health Services, Dallas, Texas); Adjunct Professor: Graduate School in Clinical Psychology (University of North Texas, Denton, Texas)

Publisher's Note

This publication is designed to provide accurate and authoritative information in regard to the subject matter covered. It is sold with the understanding that the publisher is not engaged in rendering psychological, financial, legal, or other professional services. If expert assistance or counseling is needed, the services of a competent professional should be sought.

Distributed in the U.S.A. by Publishers Group West; in Canada by Raincoast Books; in Great Britain by Airlift Book Company, Ltd.; in South Africa by Real Books, Ltd.; in Australia by Boobook; and in New Zealand by Tandem Press.

Copyright © 1999 by Melody Milam Potter and Erin E. Milam
New Harbinger Publications, Inc.
5674 Shattuck Avenue
Oakland, CA 94609

Cover design by Blue Design
Edited by Kayla Sussell
Text design by Michele Waters

Library of Congress Catalog Card Number: 98-68754
ISBN 1-57224-139-X Paperback

All Rights Reserved

Printed in the United States of America on chlorine-free paper with soy ink

New Harbinger Publications' Website address: www.newharbinger.com

01   00   99

10   9   8   7   6   5   4   3   2   1

First printing

To Katie and Ramsey, and the babies to come, who deserve a clean world in which to grow.

Contents

Acknowledgments

No book can be written without the help and support of others. We want to sincerely thank the following friends and associates who have given their time and contributed their help and cooperation in the creation of this manuscript: Warren Lane of the U.S. Environmental Protection Agency, who provided us with invaluable information; Dr. Ernest Harrell, Chairman of the University of North Texas graduate program in psychology, for answering neurological questions; Ann Brooks, Carol Riley, Janna Ferguson, James Austin, Coy Bowen, and Michael Tribble of the North Texas Health Science Center Library who cheerfully helped us with resources; Rebecca Moore, who provided us with information on infant stimulation; Pat Springer, who researched legal information; Beth Laseter, who helped facilitate information transfer; Doug Seba (formerly of the EPA), who suggested resources; Dr. Joel Robert Butler and Dr. Frank Lawlis, who have been sources of unending inspiration; and our editors at New Harbinger, Kayla Sussell, Catharine Sutker, and Kristin Beck, who worked with us cheerfully and enthusiastically. Ms. Sussell deserves special recognition for going out of her way to present this troubling material in a positive and helpful way.

We especially want to acknowledge our literary agent, Natasha Kern, for her encouragement, her willingness to believe in us and teach us, her unfailing enthusiasm for our work, and her efforts in getting this book to the public.

Special thanks to Laura Conner of Natasha Kern Literary Agency for her contribution of a cover concept that is both positive and appealing. Our appreciation to Kirk Johnson of New Harbinger's marketing department for his efforts in producing the book cover.

In addition we want to thank our families for supporting us and allowing us to take time away from family responsibilities. Thanks to Charlotte Hennington, Sherry Middleton Moore, and Robert C. Moore II for keeping the baby while we studied, researched, and wrote the manuscript, and for their continued love and support. Thanks to our spouses, Bobby J. Potter and Christopher Moore, who gave us unfailing support, prepared their own meals, and took the pressure off us while we worked. Extra thanks to Bobby Potter for helping with some of the more tedious research.

Our sincere appreciation goes to some very busy professionals, including our advisors, who contributed their time and energy to reviewing this book, providing research, and advising us on technical points. Dr. Frances Mcmanemin deserves extra thanks for spending untold hours going over the book and making suggestions.

Portions of this book first appeared in articles written by Dr. Melody Milam Potter and Erin E. Milam for the Alternative Medicine Forum on America Online. We want to thank the staff of the Alternative Medicine Forum for their help and encouragement.

Introduction

"What do you want, a boy or a girl?"

After answering that question you probably added, "... but I really don't care as long as it's healthy!"

Having a baby can be the most exciting event in your life. Your baby is an extension of you and will share love and happy moments with you for a lifetime. But bringing a child into this world can also be a little scary. This little human must learn from you how to survive and flourish on our ever-changing planet and she or he will be fully dependent on you for a very long time. Naturally, you want to do what's best for your baby and to make decisions that will help her/him develop in the healthiest way possible.

Everyone knows we live in an incredibly toxic world. All you have to do is switch on the television set to figure that out. The news media blasts us with information about toxins and chemical spills daily. Warning labels pop up on many of the items we purchase. It's hard to know what's really safe to use and what should be avoided. Especially where your baby's development is concerned.

Even so, you can provide an optimal, healthy environment for your baby by making some simple and inexpensive choices at the right time. The time between the moment of conception and age two represents a critical period in your child's development. The growing baby's systems are still being built and need all their strength just to make the baby. A baby's systems cannot tolerate chemicals the way that an adult body can. In fact, a baby's toxic defense systems remain undeveloped until sometime around age two. During this period of rapid development, exposure to synthetic chemicals, pesticides, solvents, household cleaners, even pollutants in air, food, and water, can cause serious damage to your baby. Potential problems range from physical birth defects or mental slowness to less obvious disorders such as learning disabilities. Disorders like these, resulting from disrupted development, may be permanent or will require considerable effort for your child to overcome. Your unborn baby depends on your judgment and your body for protection. Later, when the baby arrives in the world, your knowledge must continue to protect her/him from substances that would injure or slow natural growth.

As a parent, you maintain the greatest control over your baby's world. We believe that knowledge represents strength, especially when you must make decisions concerning your baby. How you control your environment from the time you conceive until your baby completes his/her development will make a crucial difference in the baby's health physically, intellectually, and emotionally. Your baby will benefit in a major way from any steps you take to provide a natural, nontoxic environment during periods of rapid fetal and infant development. Knowing how synthetic chemicals affect your developing infant will give you the power you need to protect the baby's health and will improve the chances of unobstructed, normal developmental progress.

We do not think you can start too soon. Or too late for that matter. It is never too late for your child to benefit from a clean, natural lifestyle. Any action you take at any stage of your child's development will help the infant body recover from previous exposures and begin to develop healthily. Even if you begin to practice environmental safety measures after your child's infancy, these practices will still confer benefit, so if you have an older child, don't despair. Your child's body will take advantage of improvements made in his/her environment at any age. However, the best defense you have against the effects of synthetic chemicals is to reduce your child's exposure from this moment on, no matter what age.

Our Criteria for Warning You

The last thing we want to do with this book is to frighten parents unnecessarily. In fact, our goal is to increase parents' control over the outcome of pregnancies by giving them information and options. However, we must make it clear that the study of effects on human development from environmental substances and conditions is an area of science that has been gravely neglected in the past. Much of the information comes from animal studies and from reports of children born after their pregnant mothers suffered accidental exposures.

For many chemicals there are as many studies reporting "no effect" as there are those that report "significant effects."

The amount of confusion in evaluating the research is staggering. Health experts often disagree, so for some chemicals we did not find complete concurrence regarding their effects on fetal development. Where significant conflict among experts exists, we have noted that. In many cases, government environmental agencies present an ambiguous picture regarding a chemical's developmental effects. Governments must balance the extreme weight of the chemical pollution in their societies against the need for health safety, so they often must attend to substances that cause the most obvious problems. Chemicals causing developmental disorders that do not show up for years rarely get the attention of regulatory agencies. Last, but not least, there is the financially motivated lobbying of the chemical companies that often downplays the health effects of their products in their efforts to maintain their commercial advantage with consumers.

We, therefore, had to establish some general rules to determine which toxins or chemical categories would warrant a warning in this book, the goal being to educate but not to panic a future parent. Here are the criteria we tried to follow (a substance must meet at least one):

- Were there existing human or animal studies that showed developmental (neurological, behavioral, or birth defects), or reproductive effects (including preterm births, low birth weight, or spontaneous abortion) for a substance? In most cases, if a substance causes birth defects or reproductive effects, it can potentially damage the fetus in more subtle ways that affect brain function.

- Were there controversial opinions in the health industry about the substance? Controversy presents a red flag that usually indicates valid concerns.

- Was the toxin fairly common in daily life? Could it contribute significantly to the total daily chemical exposure, or did it affect a large number of people? Many chemicals, when combined, can interact to increase their toxic effects or simply overload the body's detoxification system so that toxins remain in the body longer.

- Were there reports of accidental exposure that seemingly resulted in developmental disorders, reproductive effects, or birth defects?

- Was the chemical known to cross the blood-brain barrier, the placental barrier, or have neurological, carcinogenic, or mutagenic effects?

- Was the chemical or substance in a class with or similar to other substances known to cause developmental effects?

If these criteria seem conservative, we certainly hope they are. Our intention is to take a *conservative approach* where the health and happiness of your baby is concerned. We encourage you to do the same.

Of Rats and Humans

Most developmental research has been performed on animals—usually rats, mice, or other rodents. Sometimes primates such as monkeys are employed in research studies. Using small animals has been a regrettable but necessary part of evaluating the potential damage of toxic substances to our babies, and ourselves. Naturally, scientists question whether rat studies apply to humans. After all, rats, although they are mammals, are not humans.

Certainly we can't, and we wouldn't even if we could, line up pregnant mothers, dose them with toxic chemicals, and check their babies for developmental problems or birth defects. Doing so would be unconscionable. Consequently, for useful information we must depend heavily upon animal studies and accidental exposures.

Accidental chemical exposures, while informative, provide results that are uncontrolled. There is no way to determine what other factors may have interfered or actually caused the described symptoms. So, while they are a good step above guessing, accidental case studies fall into the category of uncontrolled research that may or may not be considered valid and trustworthy.

Animal studies, although usually well-controlled, may be faulty in that animals often process toxins somewhat differently than humans do. The effects produced in one species may not occur in another. For instance, rats have much better immune systems than humans and so toxins may not affect them as much. Researchers must use much greater quantities of a chemical to test effects on rats. That leads us to the conclusion that if a substance injures a rat's babies, it may very well hurt a developing human child. A scientist interviewed on a recent television show said it succinctly, "Would you want to give your kid something that killed a rat?" To this question we respond with a resounding "No," and we feel that warning you about negative developmental effects in rats and other animals serves the purpose of this book.

What seems to be the case with rat studies (we are using the term "rat" generically to include most research animals) is that, because of their superior immune systems, what will hurt a rat will probably hurt a human. However, the reverse may not be true. What helps a rat may not help a human. This has been demonstrated in many cancer research studies where a potential cancer cure resulted in significant recovery in rats but showed disappointing results in humans.

On the other hand, a substance that produces no teratogenic (developmental disrupting) effects in a lab rat may still harm a human. A dramatic case in point is thalidomide, a drug which tested fine in animals but caused limb deformities in babies when used as an antianxiety agent by pregnant women in the 1950s. In the 1990s, rats still provide the best indicators of potential human response that we have.

There are other problems inherent in the use of animals for teratogenic research. First, in the real world no chemical exists in isolation. Tests on rats usually involve the administration of a single chemical to the animal. In life, we tend to receive multiple chemicals which can interact. Second, teratogenic effects in humans often fail to show up until a child enters school and must perform academic tasks. It's really hard to test rat babies for learning disabilities, language skills, and dyslexia. (They just hate taking all those tests!) When we look for teratogenic effects in an animal we can see only effects that pertain to a rat, not always a human. Therefore, many studies that fail to show effects in rats are just not sensitive enough to determine delayed effects on humans. This is the case with most studies on teratogenic effects.

Good news from the scientific community tells us that new research methods are being developed which, in future studies, will apply directly to humans and, in some cases, will make using animals unnecessary (Hood 1990).

These techniques will often involve the use of human tissue in the place of live animals and thus will be more applicable to humans. Assessing toxicity may include use of human blood serum or human placentas. We intend to update this book regularly to include the new information forthcoming from this research.

How to Use This Book

We suggest you read every chapter of this book to get an idea of how chemicals affect your baby's development and the many areas of life chemicals can affect. If you are curious about a chemical mentioned in a table or a paragraph, look it up in the Guide to Common Chemicals in chapter 12 to learn what kind of chemical it is, its aliases, where it is found, and what its developmental effects may be.

Simple Solutions

Every chapter has at least one section entitled "Simple Solutions." (Some chapters have many such sections.) These sections address the question: "What can I do to protect my baby and myself from this chemical?" Our answers are aimed at providing you with easy-to-implement solutions. There are steps you can take to protect your baby's health and your own. There are many preemptive actions you can perform to safeguard your own environment. In spite of the growing toxicity of many ordinary, everyday products, you are not helpless. Read and implement the suggestions we make in the "Simple Solutions" sections and take heart.

Once you have finished reading, use the book as a reference manual. Read labels on products you intend to purchase. Then look up the chemicals in this book or in one of the resources we have provided in the appendix before making your decision.

Although there is no way that a single publication can adequately provide complete information on all the chemicals that can affect development, portions of this book describe how to look at a chemical name and recognize the base word from which it is derived. That way you can avoid some of the really damaging substances.

Chapters 1 and 2 discuss the benefits of providing your developing baby with a safe environment and show how your baby's brain and other sensitive systems develop. Chapter 3 describes how you can reduce your body's load of stored chemicals before and after you conceive and tells you how to remain relatively chemical-free during your pregnancy.

We will show you how to provide a clean, safe environment for your baby during your pregnancy in chapters 4 through 8, and from birth through the first few years of life with discussions on breastfeeding, healthy foods, clothing, and nursery products in chapters 9 and 10. From the sidebars that appear throughout this book you will learn what chemicals to avoid and why, how they affect your baby, and how to prevent them from interfering with your baby's healthy growth.

Are you worried that you haven't done enough? Chapter 11 gives you ways to help your baby develop to its full potential even if it has experienced a less than perfect fetal life. The Guide to Common Chemicals and Developmental Effects at the end of chapter 12 provides a reference with which to identify commonly encountered substances that can affect your baby's development.

This book offers you options, lots of them. You can choose methods to protect your baby that you can realistically afford in terms of finances, energy, and time. Remember, any action you take will help your baby prepare for a healthy and happy life, and the more you can do, the better.

How to Grow a Healthy Baby

Every parent expects to give birth to a bright, happy, healthy baby who sees and hears well, breathes and sleeps well, eats and eliminates well, walks on time, talks on time, learns social rules willingly, gets the usual quota of colds and childhood illnesses, and basically behaves just like every baby should. In addition, parents hope to provide their baby with the best opportunity possible to become successful in our competitive society. They want their baby to be the brightest, most coordinated, healthiest, and happiest child he or she can be, to perform well in school, grow up, get a good job, leave home eventually, and rear his or her own healthy children. Parents want normal children with the potential to excel.

Unfortunately, the present generation of children appears to be subject to an extraordinary increase in learning disabilities, allergies and sensitivities, local epidemics of birth defects, and aberrant, violent behaviors not always explainable by "poor parenting." Hearing daily reports on TV about the poor performance of children in today's schools, vicious gang behaviors, and the wide range of pediatric health concerns amid greatly improved health techniques, we all find ourselves asking, "What is wrong with our world today?" And too many parents find themselves living the heartbreak of rearing a child who falls short of healthy, happy, and smart without even considering that the cause may be synthetic chemicals or toxic conditions.

In the past, parents depended on the media for information about toxic hazards. They built their limited knowledge from bits and pieces found in parenting magazines, television news shows, and radio programs that reported on a single research study or a group of studies based on a single toxic issue. Parents then developed a false sense of security thinking they were well-informed. Because there is no readily available central information source about infant development and common toxins, parents often forget the material they hear, or they convince themselves that most of it is media sensationalism. In fact, the media has not even scratched the surface of the real and present dangers.

Until the last few years the information about toxic effects on the development of babies has been sparse and scattered. Only recently have scientific studies accumulated to the point that a general picture of the threats to our children's development could be drawn. And the only available information has been written by and for biochemists and medical specialists in a language that requires a degree in chemistry or medicine to interpret. We want to help you put this information together in a meaningful way that helps you to help your child.

One woman we know has a mentally challenged son. After his birth, when it became obvious that he had problems, she asked the doctor, "What caused this?" The doctor, a well-meaning, but misguided, professional, told her, "You didn't make a good nest for him." We think that response was unintentionally cruel. That woman would have done anything she could have done to prevent her child from suffering toxic consequences during her pregnancy. And, in fact, that child grew into a young man who holds down a good job today and functions well in society because his mother worked so hard at providing him with an enriched environment during his early years.

Most people don't know about the issues discussed in this book. If they had known about them they would have dealt with them. One concern we had in writing this book is that some parents may look back and feel regrets about children they have already reared. Don't do that. Regrets are useless; just realize that if you had known these facts, you would have done things differently.

Do not feel guilty for what you are unable to do to clean up your baby's world. This book is full of information, choices, and options. Feeling guilty and worrying only makes for more "self-stress." Instead, you can pat yourself on the back for every step you take to protect your baby from toxic conditions. No one can maintain a perfectly chemical-free environment. That is impossible in today's world. Synthetic chemicals are everywhere and will be for generations to come. Your goal is a chemical-reduced lifestyle that will permit your baby to develop a healthy body and emotional state.

This chapter gives you basic guidelines for providing a healthy, nontoxic environment during your baby's fetal development. Guarding your own health and nutrition during pregnancy and breast-feeding, maintaining a low-stress lifestyle, and keeping your baby's total chemical exposures to a minimum are the subjects included. You will learn why avoiding chemicals during pregnancy is so important and how Mother Nature does her part to help your baby overcome the effects of toxic chemicals.

Birth Defects and Developmental Disorders

What is the difference between birth defects, developmental defects, and developmental disorders? There is no formal distinction among these terms. A developmental disorder includes any problem that originates from disrupted development. However, in terms of general usage, the term defect is most often used to describe obvious structural damage in the body, something that can be seen with the eye or with laboratory equipment. Such defects include abnormal heart openings, malformed limbs, or spina bifida.

The term disorder, in general, refers to more subtle functional damage like an improperly functioning system or an organ that may appear complete and fully formed, yet functions inefficiently or ineffectively. Disorders include conditions such as hyperactivity or behavioral dysfunction where the brain fails to control inappropriate impulses, or dyslexia where the brain fails to perceive information properly.

Here are some important definitions that you will need as you read this book:

- **teratogen**: anything that interrupts or disrupts fetal development

- **teratology**: the study of anything that interrupts or disrupts fetal development

- **behavioral teratology**: anything that interrupts or disrupts fetal development in such a way as to cause behavioral, intellectual, or mental disorders

Developmental disorders then are simply conditions that occur from faulty development of the brain, the immune system, or other organs causing them to work improperly. These disorders can only rarely be observed at birth and tend to manifest later when the child begins to communicate verbally or to attend school.

Developmental disorders often occur at much higher rates than observable birth defects. For learning disabilities alone, there are estimates as high as 30 percent in the U.S. as opposed to birth defects that occur at a rate of 2 to 3 percent. In some parts of Africa and Poland, observable birth defects approach 100 percent and the more subtle developmental disorders have never been measured (personal communication, 1998, Dr. John Laseter, international biochemical and environmental consultant).

What Are Developmental Disorders?

Environmental factors can play a part in the development of the following disorders and conditions. This list is incomplete but will expand as the scientific community learns more about teratology and, specifically, behavioral teratology.

- Hyperactivity
- Reproductive dysfunction
- Developmental delays
- Impaired social adaptation
- Sudden Infant Death Syndrome
- Attentional deficits
- Reduced intellectual functioning
- Aggressive behavior
- Criminal behavior
- Poor motor coordination
- Dyslexia
- Poorly functioning organs or systems
- Learning disabilities
- Cancer in childhood and later life
- Sexual dysfunction
- Immune dysfunction or disorders
- Sleep disturbances
- Cancer in subsequent generations
- Autism
- Speech or language problems
- Low birth weight
- Spontaneous abortion
- Obvious birth defects
- Chemical sensitivity in child and later generations
- Sensory deficits

- Poor math or computational ability
- Schizophrenic disorders
- Emotional disorders

The Causes of Developmental Disorders and Birth Defects

An ongoing mystery surfaces from the vast amount of literature on this subject. Experts agree that no one knows what causes 85–90 percent of all birth defects and 60–70 percent of all developmental disorders. They do acknowledge that the developing fetus is extremely vulnerable to chemicals, drugs, and other insults or trauma.

At the same time, a huge amount of research exists that identifies chemical after toxic chemical as teratogenic (damaging to the fetus). We found citations going back to 1959 where researchers specifically noted that, although damage from toxic chemicals in the early weeks of pregnancy caused major defects in the physical structure of the fetus and often resulted in spontaneous abortion, exposure to those same chemicals later in the pregnancy were likely to cause the baby's brain or organs to function poorly. This more subtle trauma was said, even then, to manifest as learning problems, mental disorders, and defects in intelligence. Today we call those problems learning disabilities, Attention Deficit Disorder (ADD), hyperactivity, behavior disorders, and impaired intellectual functioning.

Few researchers study these more subtle effects of chemicals. They are hard to measure since they can't be easily determined in animals and they don't show up in humans often until school age. So, they are often ignored.

Genetics and the Environment

Developmental disorders can result from genetic or environmental influences or a combination of the two. For instance, some disorders are a result of mutated genes passed on from the parent to the baby. The disorder already exists in the family and the baby inherits the predisposition for that disorder. Whether the baby develops the disorder or not can depend on the baby's environment. Often, the predisposition in the genetic code must be triggered by environmental factors in order to manifest. Sometimes, even in the absence of a predisposition, an environmental stressor, such as chemicals, emotional stress, and poor nutrition, occurs in enough strength and at an important enough stage of development to cause a disorder (Spreen, Risser, and Edgall 1995).

Consider the following quotes from Reproductive and Developmental Hazards (Welch 1993) a bulletin published by the United States Department of Health and Human Services:

"Many chemical agents are suspected of causing adverse reproductive or developmental effects; however, strong evidence exists for only a few." (Most researchers suggest that this is mainly because too little research exists on specific substances.)

"Only a handful of the thousands of chemicals currently in use are regulated because of their potential to produce adverse reproductive effects. Many substances that threaten to damage reproduction may do so at exposure durations or levels lower than the permissible exposure limits set to protect against other effects. Reproductive toxicity, however, has seldom been the major consideration in the decision to ban a substance."

"Chemical exposures should be strictly controlled or eliminated for all females of reproductive age."

According to the scientific evidence that is available, a significant part of the unidentifiable sources of developmental disabilities can be related to environmental chemicals (Hood 1990). The substances and conditions noted in this book are known to have developmental repercussions and avoiding them will, at the very least, eliminate them as potential sources of developmental disorders.

Even when a predisposition for a disorder does exist, if you protect your baby from environmental effects, the disorder may never develop. In fact, in a family where a genetic predisposition for a physical ailment such as diabetes or a mental disorder such as depression exists, as a rule, only a few individuals in the next generation actually develop the disorder. This may be due to the absence of environmental influences strong enough to trigger the disorder.

Even genetic disorders can be caused by the environment. Some environmental factors, such as toxic chemicals and radiation, have the power to change genes in damaging ways. Once mutated, genes are altered forever and can be handed down to the next generation, and the next. Scientists are discovering that many chemicals that cross the placenta are *mutagenic* (any agent that tends to increase the frequency or extent of mutation is called a *mutagen*).

Some Mutagenic Chemicals

- PCBs (polychlorinated biphenyls)
- Chromium
- PBBs (polybrominated biphenyls)
- Chloromethyl methyl ether
- Vinyl chloride
- Benzidine
- Alpha-naphthylamine
- Benzene
- Ethylene oxide
- Arsenic
- Formaldehyde
- Mineral oils (some)
- EDB (ethylene dibromide)
- DBCP (dibromo chloropropane)

This list was adapted from *Occupational Health: Recognizing and Preventing Work-Related Disease* (1995) edited by B. Levy and D. Wegman.

The Link Between Toxins and Developmental Disorders

Most developmental disorders come from subtle structural alterations in the brain or other organs or systems. The toxic effects of chemicals on brain tissue show the same types of structural damage, sometimes very diffuse and widespread. This suggests that chemical exposures can cause a variety of disorders.

For instance, heavy exposure to solvents in adults causes widespread deterioration of brain tissue, changes in neurotransmitter (brain chemicals), imbalances, enlargement of brain cavities, and shrunken brain lobes. Prolonged pesticide exposure results in similar neurological damage. We discuss below a few specific developmental disorders to show how this type of brain damage can translate into specific disorders.

Hyperactivity and Attention Deficit Disorder. ADHD children experience a decrease in the activity and balance of brain chemicals due to poor biochemical development. They often have poor development of the frontal lobes of the brain and reduced blood flow in those areas.

Criminal or aggressive behavior, poor behavioral control. Violent offenders with no childhood history of neglect or mistreatment often have abnormal functioning in the frontal lobes of the brain. (Deckel, Hesselbrock, and Bauer 1996; Moller, et al., 1996). Thrill-seeking criminals especially show brain dysfunction (Kuruøglu, et al., 1996; Raine, et al., 1998). Recent studies show that prenatal smoking is related to criminal behavior in offspring. Researchers concluded that CNS damage was involved (Brennan, Grekin, and Mednich 1999; Rantakallis, et al. 1992).

Sudden Infant Death Syndrome. Many SIDS babies show delayed brain myelination (sheathing around brain cells) and immature brain cells. The brain stem and cerebellum, the areas of the brain that control respiration, are often damaged. Also, brain cells that control the stress response often appear altered (O'Rahilly and Muller 1996; Kelmanson 1995).

Tourette's syndrome. Tourette's syndrome appears to result from a genetic predisposition combined with damage caused by disturbances in brain chemistry.

Reduced intellectual functioning. Low IQ and intellectual impairment is often related to reduced brain size, diffuse brain damage, and reduced brain surface (Morgane, et al. 1992).

Dyslexia and learning disabilities. Individuals with these disorders often show abnormalities in brain chemistry, abnormal convolutions (folds) in the brain, dysfunction in the brain's parietal lobes, and a lack of symmetry in the temporal lobes (Spreen, Risser, and Edgall 1995).

Immune dysfunction and chemical sensitivity. In immune dysfunction, the thymus gland's immune response regulators often show poor development. This gland undergoes rapid development during the first two years of life making it susceptible to toxins in infancy. Exposure to chemicals like DES and benzo[a]pyrene during fetal life makes animals more susceptible to infection because of compromised immune functions.

Autism. Autism can arise from abnormal nerve cell organization in the various organs and lobes of the cerebral cortex, the outer thinking layer of the brain (Waterhouse, Fein, and Modahl 1996; Shields, et al., 1996; Mountz, et al., 1995). Because autistic individuals do not usually procreate, experts believe that if genetic damage is responsible, it likely occurs from metabolic or environmental influences (Rutter, Graham, and Yule 1970). The brain damage seen in autism, such as immature nerve cells and brain features that disappear after birth, usually occurs during prenatal, and, to a lesser extent, postnatal development (Bauman and Kemper 1985).

Depression. The brains of serious depressives often show lesions in the white matter of the brain. The prefrontal and temporoparietal brain cortex also responds poorly to neurotransmitter release. A genetic component likely interacts with an environmental factor.

Speech or language problems. These disorders often are due to immature brain cells, lesions in the language areas of the brain, myelin deficiencies, and interference with fetal brain development. Genetic tendencies may contribute.

Schizophrenia. The brains of schizophrenics show enlarged brain cavities and altered activity in the prefrontal and temporal lobes, especially in the brain structures that control emotion. Researchers have concluded these changes result from incorrect positioning of brain cells during the third stage of prenatal brain development (Seidman 1983; Raz, et al., 1988; Bogerts 1997; Chua and McKenna 1995).

These types of brain damage can occur from toxic exposure. In fact, a single toxin can have varying effects. It may cause different effects at different stages of fetal development, depending on what system or what brain organ is developing at the time. The effects also vary depending upon other toxins present in the body, the nutritional status of the mother and fetus, and of course, genetic predisposition and alcohol or drug intake.

Low Birth Weight, Spontaneous Abortion, and Preterm Birth

Many studies on the developmental effects of chemicals show a relationship to preterm birth, low birth weight, or spontaneous abortion, rather than to "birth defects" or "developmental disorders" as such. These effects provide important signs that fetal damage is occurring. For instance, spontaneous abortion, or miscarriage, often occurs when the fetus has suffered major insult and cannot survive in the womb.

Since the baby develops as a whole, low birth weight can indicate that systems other than the size of the baby have been frustrated also. Both infant mortality and observable birth defects are related to low birth weight. Preterm births are often associated with later developmental problems. Therefore, when a chemical is seen to be related to one of these pregnancy consequences, we must assume that other, later, effects are also possible.

Many teratogens have been associated with preterm births but the way that chemicals influence the process is not clear. However, because a hormonal signal coming from the fetus initiates labor, and we know that various chemicals simulate or disrupt hormones, synthetic chemicals may play a role in early delivery. The baby's hypothalamus and a hormone called ACTH cause the secretion of cortisol, a steroid that moves through the placenta to the mother signaling the beginning of labor.

Everyday life stress, emotional stress, and anything else that causes physical stress, including synthetic chemicals, may also increase cortisol production and be implicated in early deliveries (Upledger 1996; Spreen, Risser, and Edgall 1995).

Hormone Disruptors in Development

Hormones are natural substances in our bodies that control growth, sexual functions, stress reaction, digestive processes, metabolism, and brain development. Many synthetic chemicals can mimic hormones in the body. A tiny exposure to one of these chemicals can trigger a full hormonal response. In some cases, stimulation of only 1 percent of a nerve's receptors can produce a full cascade of hormonal responses.

Hormones circulating in your body and your developing baby's brain play a crucial part in the development and function of his/her brain, reproductive organs, and sexual orientation. Since hormones regulate most body processes, a chemical hormone impostor can create endless havoc if encountered during baby's delicate fetal development. In fact, improper levels of hormones or the presence of hormone impostors during pregnancy can produce offspring who have improperly formed genitals or who lack adequate hormonal preparation of brain areas that control sexual behavior. In a male, this can result in testes that don't descend properly at puberty or in confusion in sexual identity (Colborn 1990).

Synthetic pesticides disrupt the baby's progress in a number of ways. First, they can block the action of the normal hormone. For example, a synthetic pesticide may occupy the normal hormone's position on a nerve cell that stimulates the growth of the baby's genitals. The natural hormone is blocked, and the chemical molecule cannot stimulate the nerve cell appropriately. It can occupy the position but since it doesn't fit properly, it can't trigger the correct growth response. So genital growth does not occur as programmed. A male baby may have small, malformed, or nonfunctional ovaries, testicles, or the presence of abnormal secondary sex characteristics such as prominent breasts. Animals given regular doses of some pesticides during fetal development often show these effects or exhibit altered sexual functioning later on. For example, roosters in these experiments act and look like hens. During critical developmental stages, getting the right message to fetal cells in the proper sequence and in the proper amount makes the difference whether your baby progresses according to genetic instructions.

A synthetic hormone can also unbalance hormone levels in the body. Some substances such as DDT, a hormone mimic, elevate the total hormone level. However, DDT's metabolic derivative, DDE, lowers hormone levels. So, when DDT enters the body, it first raises the hormone levels out of range. Then, after it breaks down into DDE, the levels plummet dangerously.

Known and Suspected Hormone Disruptors

Many pesticides	Benzenes
Phthalates	Breakdown products of pesticides
Dioxins	Benzo(a)pyrene
Furans (pollutants like dioxins that come from industrial processing)	Metals such as lead, cadmium, and mercury
PCBs	Pyrethrins and Permethrin
PBBs	Many solvents
Styrenes	Phenols

Hormone mimics also interfere with the enzymes responsible for breaking them down for elimination. These hormone impostors accumulate instead of being excreted. Even small changes in the amount of hormone or hormone impostors in the mother's or newborn's bloodstream can disrupt development by altering the stimulation of brain cells. Thus, the developing baby's brain may receive messages from synthetic chemicals that confuse the developing brain cells and ultimately result in disorders such as hyperactivity, aggressive behavior, or sexual dysfunction.

In our polluted world, most of us carry multiple toxic chemicals in our bodies that perform the actions described above. These substances are known hormone disruptors and our bodies often contain levels of these chemicals several thousand times higher than normal hormone levels should be.

"Acceptable Levels" Are Not Acceptable for Your Baby

Why should you even worry about your baby's chemical exposure?

Aren't noxious chemicals controlled by regulatory agencies that protect us from harmful substances? Well, yes and no. Government agencies have limited the use of some chemicals in food, water, and air to an "acceptable level" for human use. Evaluating safety limits for synthetic chemicals usually involves determining how much of the chemical is required to produce death, cancer, or obvious birth defects. However, since such chemicals are rarely tested on humans, most of the decisions made for synthetic chemical approvals are based on animal data. Animals in various stages are exposed to the chemical and the results are simply projected for a larger animal, the adult male human. Regulators then use this information to calculate a dose which, for a 150-pound adult male, avoids those consequences.

That's why synthetic chemicals, when used as directed and in a conscientious manner, can still cause subtle damage to babies in the form of learning disabilities, reduced IQ, and behavioral problems. Lower doses of these chemicals can produce this type of subtle developmental disorder while larger amounts often create more obvious birth defects. Thus "acceptable chemical levels" are often nothing more than educated guesses which do not take a conservative approach for a five-ounce fetus or developing infant. Acceptable levels often fail to take into account combinations of chemicals, multiple daily exposures to a single chemical, chemicals already stored in the mother's body, the sensitivity of developing tissue to chemicals, or the many levels of harm that fall short of death and mutation.

Daily Exposures

During an ordinary day, we take in combinations of hundreds of chemicals through food, water, and air. And, in daily food consumption, a single toxic substance, such as a food preservative, may be ingested from several different sources. In one 24-hour period, a pregnant mother or baby can easily take in more than the acceptable daily level of a single chemical and combine that with multiple doses of several other chemicals. These chemicals may then interact to produce totally unpredictable results or they may overload the body's detoxification system so that more toxic chemicals stay in the body longer.

Small, frequent exposures from chemicals used regularly inside the home or yard may be even more harmful to a baby than a single heavy exposure. Heavier exposures quickly trigger body defenses to eliminate the danger, while small amounts of a frequently used substance may go relatively unnoticed. Unchallenged, these toxic substances can pass into the fetus while the mother's detoxification system largely ignores or deprioritizes them.

Even with heavy chemical exposures, the body works rapidly to eliminate the substance but then slows down as the toxic concentration in the blood drops. This means two things: first, in a heavy exposure the body tries to remove the largest part of a toxin and leaves the remainder to be removed at a slower rate. Second, if the exposure is low, as may happen with "acceptable" pesticide use, the body assigns the chemical a low priority status so that it remains in the blood for an extended period. In the meantime, it can cross freely into the fetus. During pregnancy, a mother's minor chemical exposure may result in the baby receiving an extended exposure while the mother's body removes the toxin at a leisurely pace.

Synergistic Effects

Chemicals can interact with one another to increase toxic effects. These "synergistic" effects mean that the less-than-toxic doses of separate chemicals combine to produce toxic effects hundreds of times greater than expected (Hood 1990; Lee 1985).

The job of the body's toxic response system is to change the toxic chemical into a harmless substance that can be excreted from the body. One synthetic chemical may multiply the effects of another if one of them prevents this transition. When people drink alcohol and take tranquilizers, the combination of the two can be deadly even when the amount of alcohol and tranquilizers separately remain within safe limits.

Your Body: What Mother Nature Never Knew

Mother Nature never anticipated the possibility that humans would become so clever at creating harmful chemicals. So when she designed the pregnant body to ensure an abundance of nourishment and oxygen for the developing baby, she never realized these design elements would make a mother far more susceptible to chemicals and more likely to transfer those substances to her baby. The discussions below describe some of the physical changes that your body experiences during a pregnancy. Chapters 3 through 10 will tell you how to overcome the increased risks.

Greater ventilation. During pregnancy, you take in larger volumes of air and experience higher levels of ventilation in your lung tissue, the goal of which is to provide more oxygen to your baby. Blood flow to the lungs is also increased. These alterations enhance the absorption of inhaled chemicals by as much as an additional 40 percent, making it important that you strictly limit your inhalation exposure (Denker and Danielsson 1987).

Placental acid balance. All fluids in your and your baby's bodies have a pH or acid level. Your baby's acid level is slightly different from yours to draw nutrients across the placenta. Because the baby has higher acid levels than you do, more alkaline chemicals (including narcotics and anesthetics) travel across the placenta and stay on the fetal side to lower the acidity and maintain a balance. Early in your pregnancy, during the first few weeks, just the opposite is true. Your baby's acid level is lower than yours so that acid chemicals (valproic acid, salicylic acid, thalidomide) are attracted to the baby's side of the placenta. This balance-seeking can lead to an accumulation of alkaline chemicals or acid chemicals depending on the time of exposure (Nau 1986; Scott and Nau 1987).

Altered blood composition. During pregnancy you will have lower blood concentrations of the proteins that attach to toxins and move them out of your body. That increases the chemicals available to your baby. You can remedy this situation by making sure you get plenty of antioxidants from the foods you eat. Antioxidants tie up toxins and move them out of the body through the urine (Nau 1986).

Reduced gastrointestinal activity. Because your intestines move more slowly and food remains in your stomach longer, ingested chemicals absorbed through your gastrointestinal system have more opportunity to reach your baby (Mattison 1990).

Altered circulation. Blood flow to your hands increases six fold during pregnancy, so chemicals you handle can be absorbed at a rate up to six times greater than before conception. You should avoid handling chemicals with your bare hands and quickly wash off any chemical that contacts your skin (Mattison 1990).

Increased body fat. Maternal body fat increases about 25 percent during pregnancy. Since toxins are stored in fat tissue, chemical storage in your body can increase (Hyyten 1980).

Increased estrogen levels. Estrogen levels increase up until about the sixth month of pregnancy, before leveling off. Recent research suggests that the toxicity of estrogen-like chemicals, like some pesticides, is enhanced by increased estrogen. Similar substances potentiate or facilitate one another. Because these estrogen mimics act like female hormones, the presence of higher estrogen levels increases their effects (Mathews and Devi 1994).

One helpful bodily change does take place in pregnancy. That is, the increased blood flow and filtration through the kidneys facilitates elimination of chemicals (Krauer 1987). You can take advantage of this opportunity by drinking plenty of water to move chemicals out of your body.

Your Baby's Development: How Nature Protects Your Baby

Here is the good news. Your baby's developing body has some adaptive mechanisms that help to overcome effects from synthetic chemicals. For instance, even though the brain is not a particularly adaptable organ, there are some safety factors built into its programming. Within certain limits, your baby's developing brain may compensate for some negative effects that may occur both prenatally and after birth. This may explain why the results of even extreme chemical exposures on an unborn child may be subtle, such as dyslexia, or limited to certain brain areas, like a speech disorder, rather than resulting in severe birth defects. That a baby's developing brain shows some resilience to outside influences such as chemicals is crucial because the brain controls all body systems.

Your baby's developing brain may fight toxic effects in several ways. If a brain area is in a period of slow growth, then a single, high-level chemical exposure may have only a subtle effect. If a brain area is growing quickly, then a long-term, low-level exposure may not do much damage. If some cells are damaged, the brain can often choose to continue growth for a longer period, or nearby brain cells may take over the job of the damaged ones; or like a growing highway system, healthy cells may compensate by building more connections to other brain cells (Isaacson and Jenson 1992).

This rule applies to systems other than the brain as well. The length of time various areas of the brain and other systems require for development is discussed in chapter 2.

Unfortunately, the problem we face with your baby's toxic exposure falls into the "we-don't-exactly-know-what's-going-on" category. In so many cases no one knows exactly what effect a specific chemical exposure will have on the baby or whether the baby's body will be able to overcome the effects. Since we can't look into your baby's body to see what's happening, conservatively avoiding as many chemicals as possible during periods of intensive development makes good sense.

Mother Nature struggles to protect a baby by keeping the effects of developmental damage to a minimum. These are survival mechanisms pure and simple. Multiple backup systems are in place to insulate a baby from serious injury. However, Mother Nature can do only so much, and while she may be able to patch up some damage, a baby may still suffer subtle effects. In this day of keen competition and high aspirations, you want to avoid even minor dysfunctions that could place your child at a disadvantage mentally or physically.

How You Can Protect Your Baby

Nature has provided your baby with one more safety net, you, a parent who wants to provide an optimal environment for the baby's development. If this sounds like a tough job, don't worry, it's not. There are literally dozens of ways to accomplish this goal and protect the baby while he or she grows in your womb, and, later, to keep your baby safe in the nursery.

 *Simple Solutions For Protecting Your Baby*

Watch your health and nutrition. The old adage that a baby takes what it needs from its mother's body no matter what the mother's condition is simply not true. During pregnancy, a malnourished mother transports fewer and lower-quality nutrients to her growing baby, so that the baby lacks body-building materials when they are needed the most.

Sufficient nutrition helps to protect your baby's body from toxic effects. A poorly nourished mother has difficulty eliminating chemicals. Thus the fetus incurs even greater risk when the mother uses or is exposed to chemicals. Harmful substances stay in a malnourished mother's body longer and continue to circulate through the placenta to her baby for longer periods. A malnourished infant, during pre- or postnatal development, can experience a buildup of dangerous chemicals in her/his body and may suffer damage to any system in active development.

A mother who eats plenty of food can suffer from malnutrition if her diet consists of junk food or protein-deficient meals. A pregnant vegetarian woman we know noticed that the growth of her leg hair had slowed so much that she needed to shave her legs only every two weeks. She was protein-deficient. Once she added meat to her diet, normal hair growth resumed.

Caution

Nutritional deficits in the mother during pregnancy and in the baby from birth to age four or five cause low brain weight due, in part, to a significant reduction in brain cells and/or cell connections. A mother's malnutrition during pregnancy causes a reduced number of cells in her baby's brain often leading to intellectual or neurological disorders. Extensive rehabilitation during the child's first year and a half must then be done to keep the damage from becoming permanent.

Adequate protein. If you avoid meat during pregnancy, you must pay careful attention to meeting your protein needs. You may need to increase your intake of eggs, beans, dairy products, and other partial proteins to ensure that your baby has the necessary nutrients needed for development and that your own body can protect your baby adequately. If you avoid milk products, you will probably need to take calcium and Vitamin D and B12 supplements. Discuss your nutritional needs with your physician.

Some Vegetarian Protein Sources

The following are partial proteins. Combine at least two of these to make a whole protein.

- Legumes (peas, beans, and some clovers)
- Seeds and nuts
- Peanuts
- Sunflower seeds
- Pecans
- Whole grains
- Walnuts
- Cashews
- Whole grain bread
- Corn
- Dairy (milk and cheese products)
- Cornmeal
- Whole grain cereals
- Brown rice
- Whole grain pasta
- Eggs

Adequate amounts of carbohydrates, fat, vitamins, and minerals. Pregnant and nursing mothers also need adequate carbohydrates, fat, vitamins, and minerals. You will want to eat whole grain products, such as 100 percent whole wheat bread or oat bran cereals, and several daily portions of fresh fruits and vegetables. Most doctors prefer expectant mothers take a vitamin/mineral supplement since the lack of some nutrients, such as folic acid, can cause serious birth defects like spina bifida. Iron, the one nutrient that a mother will sacrifice to her baby, may need to be supplemented in required doses. Mothers often can have low iron stores because of menstrual blood loss prior to pregnancy and/or previous breast-feeding.

Pregnant mothers need to be especially cautious about getting plenty of minerals and vitamins from natural sources. Mineral foods include milk, grains, green leafy vegetables, and seafood. Vitamin-rich foods are liver, vegetables, and fruits.

Try to watch your fat intake and weight gain. Your total fat intake should not exceed 30 percent of the food you eat daily and should not fall much lower than 20 percent. Many toxic chemicals are readily dissolved in fat, and eating a high-fat diet allows them to remain in your body where they eventually threaten the fetus. The body requires fat to function normally, however, and too little fat in the diet can cause the body to break down fat tissue, a situation that can release toxins that have been stored in fat tissue. Therefore, a moderate level of fat in the diet reduces the additional storage of chemicals while preventing the release of chemicals previously stored.

Weight gain. Although a certain amount of weight gain is healthy and desirable for the fetus's health, gaining too much weight can increase the storage of synthetic chemicals in your body. A weight gain of about thirty pounds is the average for a full-term pregnancy. However, your ideal weight gain depends on your weight before pregnancy. The National Academy of Science recommends weight gain according to the woman's prepregnancy weight. An underweight or teenage female or a woman carrying twins should gain approximately 28 to 40 pounds, a woman of normal weight, 25 to 35 pounds, and an overweight woman, 15 to 25 pounds. Not only will you feel better during your pregnancy if you control your weight gain, but labor will be easier, and you won't have so much weight to lose after the baby is born. As you will see in chapter 3, losing large amounts of weight after delivery can pollute breast milk.

Keep stress levels low. Pregnancy can be a stressful time. Your body and lifestyle are changing and your emotions may sometimes seem out of control. Try to manage your stress levels to provide a calm environment during your baby's fetal and postnatal development. That doesn't mean your baby can't experience any stress or that an occasional argument between you and your spouse will cause irreparable harm. It means that the environment around your baby should be generally peaceful. Even during your pregnancy your baby can hear you speak and can experience your stress through stress hormones that circulate in your bloodstream.

Stress-related hormones behave just like toxic chemicals to the fetus. Natural hormones like norepinephrine and cortisol, released when you or your baby become upset, present little problem when the upset ends quickly. However, persistently stressful situations cause these substances to remain in the bloodstream long enough to affect your baby's brain development. And high stress levels can increase the release of stored toxins into your bloodstream where they can pass over to your baby. Stress effects on the developing fetus and infant are discussed in detail in chapter 6.

Maintaining low stress also allows your body to eliminate synthetic chemicals more efficiently, thus protecting your baby. Relaxation techniques can increase by as much as four times the amount of chemicals you eliminate. Stress management techniques such as moderate exercise and relaxation will help restore your body's defenses when you are under unusual stress. Controlling your stress may mean that you must cut back your work hours, change jobs, reduce your contact with stressful people, or make healthier choices in the way you live. Only you can make those decisions, but we want to encourage you to do whatever it takes to provide some emotional comfort for yourself and your baby during this crucial time.

Reduce your baby's "total load." Reducing your baby's total chemical load is what this book is all about. If you can keep your baby's total load to a minimum, in most cases, she/he will develop as nature intended. Understanding the concept of total load will also keep you from wanting to zip yourself or your baby into a protective bubble.

The mother's immune and metabolic systems form a team to rid her body of chemicals and other foreign substances. In the case of the unborn fetus, the mother's body takes on this job for the baby. We like to visualize the mother's body as a rain barrel. During normal everyday interaction with the environment many different substances collect in the barrel. These include such things as indoor air pollution, impure water, chemically contaminated food, and stress hormones. Continued exposure to different chemicals or to a significant amount of a single substance can fill the barrel so that the body cannot get rid of them. When the barrel overflows, symptoms are produced. In other words, when the total load of chemicals and stress becomes more than the body can handle, the body or the brain sustains damage from the effects. In the case of the developing baby, these symptoms may take the form of a birth defect or a brain dysfunction because the baby fails to develop properly.

Caution

According to many experts, no level of chemical exposure can be considered absolutely safe for the developing fetus (Brown 1983; Anselmo 1987). However, in today's world, a chemically free environment would be impossible to maintain.

The real key to reducing your baby's total chemical load involves finding effective ways to reduce each substance that goes into your barrel. When enough material has been eliminated so that your barrel is not full (your immune system functions well), you will better tolerate exposure to toxic substances and you will create a safer environment for your baby. Because knowing what you or your baby has been exposed to is sometimes difficult to figure out, and avoiding chemical exposure may be impossible at times, the best plan is to keep your barrel as empty as possible by avoiding or eliminating those chemicals you can control.

Your body, if healthy, can manage some level of chemicals without any difficulty. If your toxic control systems are not overloaded by chemicals or stress and are working well, they can do a reasonable job of protecting your body. However, while your body is cleaning toxins out of your system, your baby can be exposed to chemicals as they await elimination in your blood stream. This makes it crucial that you avoid chemicals whenever possible.

Remember, your baby's toxic control systems remain immature and unable to function adequately from conception until well into childhood, so he/she remains dependent upon your body for chemical control. Maintaining a safe environment while your baby's defenses mature allows his/her body to prepare for dealing with chemicals and disease in the future. By keeping the chemicals in your baby's surroundings at a low level you are buying her/him time enough to develop fully and without interference.

Reduced Toxic Load Protects Your Baby from Infection

Babies who grow in a chemically reduced environment have more resources to fight off infections and viral diseases even when exposed to germs. Early in the 1900s the medical profession was split over the cause of infection. One faction claimed disease was caused by microorganisms, while the other protested that disease was the result of a weakened immune system. The second theory was rejected in favor of the first.

Bioaccumulation

Bioaccumulation occurs when synthetic chemicals accumulate in your body and your baby's body during repeated low-level exposures. How much is stored depends on the elimination rate of the chemical and the amount absorbed by the body. Some chemicals cannot be eliminated quickly enough before the next exposure and so a buildup occurs. A chemical with a slow elimination rate, like the PCBs found in refrigerants and electrical supplies, is never successfully eliminated and each successive exposure adds to the total amount already stored in body fat. Bioaccumulation can occur from something as simple as small amounts of pesticides from food or water.

Bioaccumulation causes your body to experience chemical exposures twice, the first time when you take in the chemical and the second time when the fat cells storing the chemical are used by the body for energy. Every time your fat cells are broken down for use, the stored toxins are released into the bloodstream.

Today we know that the second theory is also accurate. Most germs that cause infectious disease are frequently carried by the body in a harmless condition. However, when the body becomes weakened, these microorganisms multiply and invade healthy tissue. Infants and the elderly are especially vulnerable to flu epidemics and other diseases since they have ineffective immune systems. Babies who have heavy chemical loads may not be able to fight off germs and can develop faulty immune systems that lead to allergies, repeated infections, and lots of visits to the doctor.

Why Your Doctor May Not Warn You About Chemicals

Before and during pregnancy and for the first few years after your baby's birth, seeing a physician on a regular basis can help prevent many health problems. A doctor may be able to spot and treat a medical problem before it makes permanent changes in your baby's health. Your doctor, however, may or may not caution you about synthetic chemicals and may not press you to provide a natural environment for your baby. Most of the information in this book comes from research studies and reports buried in embryology and toxic biochemistry textbooks not readily available to the general public, or even to many health professionals. Bear in mind that unless they have a special interest in environmental medicine or ecological issues, many obstetricians and pediatricians remain unaware of the extent of the dangers common chemicals present to your baby.

You may very well find yourself in the position of having to educate your doctor about these issues. Many doctors still allow toxic pesticides to be sprayed in their offices. It's okay to offer your doctor reading materials, like this book, on chemical hazards. You will also want to discuss your concerns with your doctor about any significant chemical exposure you or your baby experiences.

There are some physicians who specialize in chemical exposure. You can ask your doctor for a referral especially if you work in conditions that expose you to chemicals on a daily basis or if you have concerns about exposures that you can't control.

New Research in Progress

In the last few years, worldwide awareness about the effects of chemicals on children has increased dramatically and has initiated changes for child safety. In some countries, to continue to sell their products, chemical companies must now submit new research evidence demonstrating the safety of their products. The goal is to reduce health-threatening chemicals in products like baby foods and in the environment. For instance, over the next ten years in the U.S., commercial infant foods must adhere to a new level of safety.

This long-awaited turnaround in attitude has delighted medical scientists who have, for years, been warning about some of the most common chemicals permeating our food and water. Although the most publicized dangers usually involve effects on wildlife and the ozone layer, researchers have documented the nasty effects of these so called "safe" chemicals on the fetus and infant. In fact, much of what you will learn in this book about babies and synthetic chemicals has been known by the scientific community for years. Most human teratogens, substances that we now know interfere with fetal development, were long ago predicted to be harmful to human beings by animal studies but these were often ignored by government entities who have the power to affect our lives.

While new information about chemicals will eventually improve the chemical toxicity problem, it will have a rather minor impact on your baby's total chemical experience for a long time to come. Again, even though your government may try to create safe conditions for your baby, the authorities can't control your baby's daily life the way that you can.

Your Baby's Development

Fetal Development

Your baby's development actually begins during your own fetal life, when your own egg cells form. At the beginning of your life, your egg cells number in the millions. By the time you reach adulthood, only 300 will have survived the body's culling process. Each month one of these eggs will be called upon to mature and move toward the fallopian tubes in hopes of meeting and joining with a sperm cell. If you avoid chemical exposures, that will give your eggs their best chance of developing healthily as they mature in preparation to form a baby.

Your baby's father's contribution, the sperm cell, will have seventy-four days until it grows into a mature sperm cell and is fully able to penetrate your egg cell and join with it to create a living being. Therefore, mens' reproductive cells are subject to environmental effects for a much shorter time than women's ova. However, during the nearly eleven-week period while the sperm develop and mature they, too, can be altered by chemical exposures (Upledger 1996; Spreen, Risser, and Edgall 1995).

Weeks One and Two

Conception begins when a sperm enters the egg. The fertilized egg follows its genetic orders and moves into the uterus to find a nest in the uterine wall. Any trauma that occurs during weeks one to two will simply terminate the pregnancy by preventing implantation of the fertilized egg or by affecting the embryo so that it dies and moves out of the body. If implantation is successful, the fertilized egg divides forming a placental connection to the uterus by establishing blood circulation. The embryo divides into three layers which become the brain, the muscles, and the organs. Rapid growth takes place as cells take on the characteristics of their genetically programmed functions. The amniotic sac forms by creating a cavity around the embryo. During these first two weeks and approximately six additional weeks, your genes orchestrate the basic formations of your baby's organ systems and tissues. Any insult during this time can result in defective structures easily observable at birth, conditions that often require surgical or medical intervention.

Week Three

Week three begins the critical period for the development of the eye and ear which continues through weeks eight and nine. The major body organs begin to form. The cardiovascular system and the first blood cells are produced, a primitive heart is formed, and circulation begins. An umbilical cord connects the tiny embryo, which remains unrecognizable as a baby, with a primitive placenta. Tissues that will grow into muscles and bones begin to unfold from the middle embryonic layer.

The origin of a brain and spinal cord is generated from the top layer of the embryo. A small group of cells moves to the head of the embryo and forms a structure that gives rise to the spinal cord. This structure releases a chemical that generates the development of the brain, spinal cord, and nerve centers.

Cells in the neural tube, the originator of the brain and spinal cord, reproduce at a rate of 250,000 per minute to produce the embryo's brain. Insult at this time can interfere with the delicate network of cells and connections that form the basic brain structures. Because these are the building blocks of the brain, any alterations in these basic structures can interfere with subsequent development.

These cells in the neural tube hold the plans for the entire nervous system. If they encounter no interference, they migrate to other locations in the baby's body and follow the plans for making connections and developing functions. Their instructions have been programmed into the genes, the DNA structures that guide development and create a baby that looks like you and your spouse.

Week Four

During week four the lens of the eye begins its development which continues through week eight. All major organs and structures begin developing including the digestive system, lower and upper limb buds, liver, gallbladder, stomach, intestines, thyroid, pancreas, and lungs. The beginnings of jaws, and limb buds make an appearance. Temporary kidneys start to function.

This week sees closure of the neural tube forming the spinal column, the failure of which can result in neural tube defects such as spina bifida.

Note that deficiencies in calcium, protein, zinc, and folic acid that are present in the mother may contribute to these disorders as well as chemical exposures.

Week Five

Mouth, nostrils, and esophagus begin formation in week five. During this period, a major heart valve is completed; upper limbs and tiny primitive hands appear. Permanent kidneys replace the temporary ones.

Developmental Periods for Major Organs and Systems

	Critical Periods (Major Birth Defects)	Sensitive Periods (Developmental Disorders)
Brain	3–16 weeks	15 weeks to age 2 years
Heart	3–6 weeks	6–8 weeks
Arms and legs	4–5 weeks	5–8 weeks
Ear	3–9 weeks	9–16 weeks
Eyes	3–8 weeks	8–full term
Upper lip	5–6 weeks	6–8 weeks
Teeth	6–8 weeks	8–full term
Palate	6–9 weeks	9–13 weeks
External genitalia	7–13 weeks	13–full term
Immune system		8 weeks–early childhood

Adapted from Moore and Persaud 1998.

The main parts of the brain are now present and the tiny embryo shows evidence of a functioning brain through reflex movements that respond to touch. Brain structures continue to grow rapidly and the pituitary gland (the master gland) begins formation. The brain grows capillaries thus establishing the beginnings of the blood-brain barrier.

Week Six

By week six, foot buds and toe rays appear while eye muscles, external ears, upper lip, trachea and larynx, bronchial tubes, and intestines are all in active growth. Joints like the elbow and wrists, knees and ankles form. Baby teeth, palate, and facial muscles are present. Muscle contractions begin, a diaphragm appears, and the miniscule heart, which has by now undergone its gross development, divides into four chambers.

Week six also sees the differentiation of brain cells into specialized areas. The olfactory lobes (governing the sense of smell) and the pituitary gland begin operating.

Week Seven

External genitalia, internal sex organs, testes, ovaries, and nipples begin to form during week seven. Limbs and fingers grow and differentiate. The baby's elbows are functioning. Cartilage, connective tissue, bone (growth continues until late teens), eyelids, nose, tongue, and the semicircular canal inside the ears make their appearance.

Nerve cells in the retina of the eye are actively developing. Brain waves appear, and the baby can turn its head and upper body in response to touch.

Approximate Critical Periods for Brain Development

Exposure to teratogenic substances or conditions may produce damaging effects or block development of specific brain structures during the specified periods.

Implantation failure or death of embryo	Pregnancy weeks 1–2
Abnormal brain or severe neurological disorders	Pregnancy weeks 3–6
Developmental disorders, minor structural defects, fewer brain cells, inaccurate, delayed, or ceased placement of brain cells	Pregnancy week 7–full term

Minor development disorders, faulty myelination, delayed or reduced formation of nerve cell connections	Birth–18 months, possibly much longer
Major brain structures	Pregnancy weeks 3–6
Large brain cell generation, differentiation, and migration to assigned areas	Pregnancy week 6–full term
Prolific large brain cell production	Pregnancy weeks 15–20 and 25–full term
Glial cell and small brain cell production (facilitates specialization of brain cells)	Pregnancy week 5–infant age 7 months
Heavy myelination of brain cells (provides efficiency and speed)	Pregnancy week 20–infant age 18 months
Continued, but slower, myelination of brain cells	Infant age 18 months through childhood
Cerebral cortex (attention, activity/behavioral control, learning)	Pregnancy week 9–full term
Hippocampus (memory; stress reactions)	Pregnancy weeks 5–8
Limbic system (emotion)	Pregnancy week 7–full term
Cerebellum (balance, equilibrium, and coordination)	Pregnancy week 24–infant age 24 months
Thalamus (information relay station; learning)	Pregnancy weeks 18–34
Feminization or masculinization of brain	Pregnancy weeks 9–25
Prolific synapse formation and maturation	Pregnancy week 6–infant age 24 months
Continued but slower synapse formation	Infant age 24 months through childhood

Upledger (1996); Spreen, Risser, and Edgall (1995); O'Rahilly and Muller (1996)

Week Eight

All organ systems are established by the end of week eight and will continue to develop and refine their function. The baby now looks like a tiny human. The female clitoris and the male scrotum are developing, as well as external ears, taste buds, and palate.

Inside the baby's brain, all neuroblasts (nerve cell origins) are present. The limbic system (governing emotions) has begun developing. After this week the embryo is called a fetus.

Important Facts

Developing brain cells that either fail to proliferate properly or to migrate to their assigned locations can result in fewer wrinkles, or convolutions, in the cerebral cortex of the brain. Since wrinkling the brain is Nature's way of packing more brain into a small area, fewer wrinkles means a smooth brain with reduced brain area.

During brain cell growth and migration, synthetic chemicals in the mother's environment can interfere with these normal processes. Brain cells can become misplaced or brain structures can develop microscopic faults causing disorders such as ADD or behavioral problems later in childhood.

Month Three

The third month ends the risk of most obvious birth defects. Any problem occurring from this point on usually manifests as failure to grow and develop or to refine function in an affected structure or system. These conditions can often be treated once the baby is born.

All basic organ systems are in place by the beginning of this month. Cells are migrating to their proper position, differentiating into specialized cells, and acquiring function. External genitalia continue to develop.

Myelination (the sheathing of brain cells) initially begins in the cranial nerves connected to the midbrain and the medulla oblongata. By the tenth week the connections between brain cells, the synapses, are present. The outer layer of the brain, the cerebral cortex which does all the thinking, sensing, problem solving, etc, begins to form grooves and valleys to give the brain more surface area. This packs more brain tissue into the small skull. The hippocampus, which governs emotional responses such as fear and anger, forms.

Sexual hormone activity begins. Sensitization of the brain to sexual hormones begins in month three and lasts through month six. During months three and four, if the baby is male, the brain learns to respond to male hormones that will be released in puberty. If the baby is female, a cycling hormone pattern is established that will be stimulated during puberty.

Sexual orientation is determined in this prenatal stage.

Month Four

The scrotum forms and the baby now has eyebrows and hair. The baby is inhaling and exhaling fluid through its mouth. All rudimentary senses are now developed and carrying out their functions. This is the beginning of motor function, and the fetus can turn and move its hands together.

Month Five

The female uterus separates from the vagina in month five, and the middle ear develops. This month also sees increased motor development resulting in more movement of the baby. The motor neurons are in intense development. The spinal cord begins to myelinate as glial cells cover and insulate it to provide efficiency and speed. Nerve cells, or neurons, which carry sensory information to the spinal cord from the body, and nerve fiber tracts, which carry instruction from the central nervous system (CNS) motor areas to the muscles, develop. If the fetus is a male, sensitization of the brain to male hormones continues, and the baby develops male sexual behaviors and acquires the programming that will determine its male appearance at puberty. If male hormones are disrupted by chemicals, or if the fetus is a female, feminine sexual patterns will govern.

Month Six

Skin glands and lymph follicles which help protect the fetus from toxic substances through life appear during the sixth month. Most of the CNS neurons are formed by the end of this month. The cerebral hemispheres cover the top and the side of the brain now. The cerebellum begins to develop and continues until the baby is about age two. According to Dr. John Upledger (1996), substances that affect cerebellum development may well contribute to disorders in balance, equilibrium, and motor coordination.

The cerebellum determines how and when a child walks, and how good balance and hand–eye coordination will be. The thalamus, which relays information to and from the thinking parts of the brain, begins its development now.

Month Seven

Month seven starts rapid bone growth, while the testes descend to the scrotum and the eyelids open. Wrinkles in the cerebral cortex (thinking, sensory, problem solving) become more prominent. The central lobe of the brain forms connecting the frontal and parietal lobes of the cerebral cortex and limbic system (emotional responses). Rapid growth, differentiation, and organization of brain structures continue.

You Should Know . . .

The brain works by sending information via chemical messengers (neurotransmitters) from one brain cell to the next. These same chemicals also have the ability to alter the developing brain's physical structure. Therefore, anything that alters the chemical balance, like neurotoxic chemicals, can change brain structure.

Month Eight

The baby's body and organs grow in size and refine their functions in the next-to-last month of pregnancy. The nervous system heavily increases the formation of synapses, the connections between brain cells. The baby is receiving more sensory information and demonstrates increased movement and organ function.

Month Nine

During the last month of fetal development, all bone ossification points are in place so skeletal structure can proceed. The brain continues rapid growth with phenomenal increases in the number of connections between nerve cells. The baby is fully active.

Birth to Two Years

Although previous theory held that no new neurons form after birth, now experts know that new glial cells and small neurons are created up until about seven months of age (Spreen, Risser, and Edgall 1995). The baby's brain forms millions of new connections (synapses) in response to demand. One nerve cell can have 100,000 different connections. And we know that it is the number of synapses, rather than the number of neurons, that create skills and intelligence (Upledger 1996).

Preterm Births

Hormonal signals produced by the fetus initiate labor. Since we know that various chemicals simulate or disrupt hormones and many teratogens are associated with preterm births, it appears that synthetic chemicals play a role in triggering early delivery. Emotional stress also increases production of these hormones and may also be implicated in early deliveries.

A total of ten billion synapses and one trillion glial cells are present at birth. The number of synapses in the visual cortex at birth number amount to around 2,500. This number increases during infancy to 18,000. The weight of the brain doubles in the first nine months of life due to production of glial cells, formations of dendrites (the "arms" of the neurons that form connections), and brain cell myelination. The cortical areas of the brain experience a major growth spurt between six and twelve months. After birth, the brain produces trillions more neural connections, then, after age ten, it eliminates those that are not used. This makes the brain extremely malleable during the first few years of life.

The highest rate of myelination occurs between birth and two years of age. Myelination wraps brain cells with a highly conductive material that speeds up psychomotor functions and increases the efficiency with which information travels down the neurons. Synapses, the tiny gaps that facilitate the transport of messages from one nerve to another, remain immature until anytime between six and twenty-four months of age. All brain areas in the cerebral cortex, including visual, somatosensory, motor, and prefrontal areas, probably develop at similar rates.

The language areas of the brain go through another growth spurt between twelve and eighteen months but only if the child's brain has been stimulated with language input. If there is fetal trauma to any language area of the brain, extra stimulation seems to help the brain compensate so that the healthy language areas increase their rate of development to compensate for the damaged areas.

Two Years to Eighteen Years

At age two, the baby's brain has twice as many synapses as an adult's. By age six, the brain is 90 percent of its adult size. The number of synapses increases significantly until about age seven and synapse growth then slows substantially. During this period, the brain develops many more connections than it can use. Because of this, child development experts have found that remedial education is much more effective in the preschool years (O'Rahilly and Muller 1996; Ramey, Bryant, and Suarez 1987; Hart and Risley 1995). Myelination of the nerve cells continues and nerve cell connections proliferate rapidly until around age ten when the process slows and those connections and neurons that haven't been used die off. Myelination of the nerve cells is nearly complete by early adulthood but continues to some extent throughout life (Upledger 1996).

Age Eighteen and Up

New synapses continue to form throughout life as new learning takes place. There is now evidence that new brain cells can continue to form even later in life, something that until recently was thought impossible.

Critical Periods of Development

Critical periods of development refer to "windows" or times when an organ or system is most susceptible to damage. This period usually occurs when the cells which comprise the organ are rapidly proliferating or dividing, moving to their assigned position, or taking up their assigned role in the body.

The first critical period occurs during the first two weeks after conception when the fertilized egg moves to the uterus for implantation. Damage to or interference with the embryo by chemicals or other factors simply prevents implantation and the mother experiences a miscarriage. An estimated 15 to 20 percent of all recognized pregnancies end in miscarriage while 40 percent of all pregnancies are lost before the seventh month of gestation (Welch 1993).

The next critical period occurs from day eighteen to day fifty-five when the fetal organs develop from genetic instructions and the cells of these organs differentiate or begin to follow their basic functional instructions. Protecting the fetus from environmental influences at this embryonic period helps prevent major structural defects and severe functional disorders in the baby.

A third critical period begins on about the fifty-sixth day once major organ structures have formed. During this time organs, cells, and systems grow rapidly, refining their areas of specialization. They become good at the jobs they are programmed to do. This period ends at different times for different organs and systems.

For the brain, this sensitive period continues until well after birth. The brain remains especially vulnerable for an extended time because brain tissue is still demonstrating rapid growth. Receptor cell development, control mechanisms that balance brain chemicals, and myelination of brain cells experience an incredible rate of growth until about age two. During this time, developmental disorders, subtle defects in the structure of brain structures, and disorders of function such as behavioral problems and other neurological deficits can originate.

Early Chemical Exposure and Cancer

The predisposition for cancer may be established very early in life. Immigrants who move to a new country as small children tend to develop the same types of cancer found in their mother country. Their children develop cancers typical of the new country (Hood 1990).

Animal and human research shows:

- Brain tumors in children are often related to the parents' exposures to chemicals. Leukemia has been associated with maternal smoking. In some cases, environmental exposure of one or both parents may result in tumor production in offspring they have not yet conceived. Cancer tendencies can be passed on to the next generation also.

- Any amount of a cancer-causing substance can be dangerous to a developing child. Because rapidly developing tissues are more susceptible to cancer-causing chemicals, newborns are more vulnerable than adults.

- Exposure to chemicals during fetal development may make the newborn more susceptible to cancer-causing substances encountered later in life.

- Some cancer-causing chemicals seem to affect tumor production more if exposure occurs very early in the pregnancy, while others seem to require transformation by the placenta later in the pregnancy to cause tumors.

Windows of Sensitivity

The current definition of critical periods creates a problem in that many experts define such periods very narrowly. As explained by most professionals, these are periods in which organs or systems are damaged in such a way that obvious birth defects are present at birth. This definition neglects the silent birth defects that can occur from damage after the basic organ systems have been created. (That is, defects that may be present but do not manifest until later in life.)

Ignoring developmental disorders becomes easy since the effects of damage often don't appear until the child must perform in school or behave appropriately in society. The developmental schema presented at the beginning of this chapter illustrate the critical periods for organ formation in each of several systems and the subsequent sensitive periods in which organs continue to form and establish their function. During these periods of functional development, any damage that occurs affects the organ more subtley, may be hard to detect in infancy, and will alter performance of a brain area rather than its basic structure (Isaacson and Jenson 1992).

The promising news about this type of damage is that if caught early enough, it can often be turned around.

Developmental War

A continual struggle wages inside the developing fetus as chemicals disrupt the baby's development while its brain and body fight to compensate for the toxic effects. While the developing brain can often repair minor damage, more extensive damage can create birth defects and developmental disorders. Past theory held that chemical exposure must occur above a certain level for any damage to occur, but current research suggests this may not always be true. That means that even small amounts of chemicals that don't create obvious birth defects may create subtle effects that don't appear until the child is older.

Most organ systems continue to develop at a slower rate for a few weeks or months after the critical period. For most organs, this represents "windows of sensitivity," which are less critical than the periods in which chemical damage creates birth defects. The exception to this rule is the brain which continues to develop and grow at an incredible pace throughout the pregnancy, after birth, and up to age two, and then to a lesser degree throughout life.

As the brain refines itself, any damage from chemicals becomes more subtle, changing from structural defects to changes in where cells migrate, how they divide and proliferate, how effective they are at performing their function, and how fast and smoothly they operate (Pratt, Goulding, and Abbott 1987). Even after birth the child's brain continues to add myelin sheaths to many nerve cells and make new connections until age ten, continuing to create new synapses as a response to learning throughout life. This continual development makes the brain susceptible to damage for a long time after birth. Because neurons continue to grow and form new connections in the growing baby, they remain sensitive to trauma. Fortunately, this continuing development also makes the brain plastic and renewable.

Vulnerable Periods

Behavioral or cognitive deficits can occur from low doses of teratogenic substances during fetal development after critical periods. This period of continued vulnerability begins at approximately twenty-five weeks of fetal age when rapid brain growth initiates. During this time, nerve cells mature and send out extensions, glial cells multiply at a fantastic rate, myelination begins, and in general the brain grows tremendously in size (Dobbing 1968; Spreen, Risser, and Edgall 1995).

The Renewable Brain and Windows of Opportunity

Developmental brain damage can often be corrected by early childhood stimulation. An American television news program recently featured a little girl who, at age three, had nearly half of her brain removed to stop severe seizure activity. The program showed her again at age ten. Her parents and various specialists had worked with her persistently over several years. She had recovered enough function to attend school and carry on a reasonably normal life with only minimal deficits.

Most children exposed to chemicals in utero or during childhood will not suffer damage even close to this level. And even when exposure is considerable, we can show you how to overcome developmental effects before they surface. If a baby's brain function has been damaged by chemical exposure in fetal life, to some extent those functions often can be reprogrammed.

Reprogramming is easiest if done in the few years following birth. As the child becomes older, correcting errors of function becomes more and more difficult. From birth to age two represents a crucial time of plasticity when the synapses can reorganize and recover from damage. In fact, it is the number of synapses that determines intelligence and skill levels rather than the number of neurons (Upledger 1996).

Brain cells recover from interference in different ways. Brain cells can compensate for damage to other brain cells by spreading out and sending thousands of nerve endings, called dendrites, which form synapses (connections) with other neurons. Synapses are formed by the juxtaposition of the dendrite of one neuron to the axon of another. The gap in between, across which neurotransmitters move, is called the synapse.

Brain cells can also connect to areas they normally would neglect. For example, if the part of the brain that governs speech were damaged, neurons from the surrounding areas could move in and form connections that would take over some of the lost verbal functions. Such remedial actions occur during the baby's fetal life and can be encouraged during early infancy.

Even children who are judged mentally handicapped at birth can be stimulated to do much more than would normally be expected of them. Parents and medical professionals often give up once a diagnosis of mental impairment has been made. However, children with mental disabilities can learn to function well if worked with from birth. In chapter 11 we discuss specific "windows of opportunity" in which specific functions can be influenced and present ways that children can be stimulated to overcome any possible damage incurred during fetal development.

Such windows do not slam shut at certain ages but later retraining requires more time and more effort to be successful.

The Role of Myelin

Your child's nerve cells continue to myelinate (i.e., to form sheaths around the axons—or nerve bodies) until about the age of twenty to twenty-five. A fat-rich substance, myelin coats and insulates the neurons to make them transmit messages faster and more efficiently. Myelinated neurons conduct messages faster than unmyelinated neurons. Such neurons are generally concerned with acute pain messages, movement, and speed and efficiency in information conduction.

Glial cells provide the building blocks for myelin. They also cover the brain's blood vessels to create the blood-brain barrier. Glial cells control the recovery of neurotransmitters, form scar tissue after neural injury, correct chemical balances in the brain, remove waste products and dead cells, and guide the neurons to correct positions in the developing brain. Glial production continues well into infancy along with the production of small neurons, rapid development and maturation of synapses, and development of the cerebellum, the brain structure that controls balance and coordination (Upledger, 1996; Spreen, Risser, and Edgall 1995).

Fact

Myelin, the conductive material that insulates and facilitates brain cells, consists mostly of fatty tissue. That makes it a magnet for fat soluble toxins which can interfere with myelin's action, formation, or function during development. Lesions that disrupt myelin in brain cells cause muscular weakness, poor motor control, visual problems, and any number of problems involving brain cell function.

Fatty tissue in animal brains is destroyed by significant exposure to chemicals like solvents. Some symptoms appear to be long-term and others surface much later. Researchers feel this indicates a "persisting loss of myelin membranes" (Kyrklund, Kjellstrand, and Haglid 1990).

Solvents cause glial cells to form long filaments, indicating brain damage. The worst damage in one study occurred in the sensory motor areas of the brain and the hypothalamus.

Like electrical insulators, myelin keeps nerves from short-circuiting and losing information. Disrupted myelination allows messages to leak out into surrounding brain cells, or to alter electrical impulses that carry information through the brain. Any condition or substance that affects myelination can cause all kinds of symptoms depending on the function of the particular nerves impacted.

The Placental Barrier

The placenta exists not as a protection against disease and toxins but as a fetal defense against the mother's immune system. Without a placenta, the fetus, as a foreign object within the mother, would trigger the mother's immune cells to attack and destroy it. The placenta filters out large molecules such as immune cells and allows smaller molecules such as oxygen, nutrients, and toxins to pass freely. In fact, almost anything that enters the mother's bloodstream moves through to the baby (Dowty, Storer, and Laseter 1976). This fact was first suspected in the 1950s and '60s when babies whose mothers took thalidomide during pregnancy were born with limb deformities.

Important!

Most chemicals cross the placenta from the mother to the baby (Cummings 1983). However, a brief whiff of a solvent is not going to damage your baby. Usually, it is the chronic daily exposure to multiple chemicals, or heavy exposures that can create a problem.

Drugs and chemicals differ in how well they cross the placenta. Some substances cross readily while others reach the fetus in lower concentrations than are present in the mother's bloodstream. The placenta may be able to partially block transport of some chemicals as long as they are in very low concentrations. That gives pregnant mothers added incentive to keep their chemical levels as low as possible.

The placenta may even metabolize chemicals into more toxic substances as they pass through to the fetus. During the latter part of pregnancy, the placenta becomes thinner, enabling substances to pass through even more effectively. The placenta can also hold chemicals in and cause them to accumulate on the fetal side, at times not allowing them to be excreted by the mother. This knowledge becomes especially important given the incredible number of chemicals the average pregnant woman encounters in her everyday life. It also places responsibility on the mother to reduce the amount, frequency, and number of toxic exposures she experiences. In that way, she can protect her growing baby who remains sensitive throughout the pregnancy and long after.

The Blood-Brain Barrier

The phrase "blood-brain barrier" conjures up the totally inaccurate image of a membrane covering the brain. In actuality, blood is provided to the brain via miles of tiny vessels, called capillaries, which supply brain tissue with oxygen and nutrients and remove waste products. However, since blood is lethal to nerve tissue, it is never allowed to touch the brain. Instead, the blood remains inside the capillaries while nutrients and oxygen move through tiny pores in the capillary walls to the brain tissue. Likewise, waste products move from the brain through the capillary walls back to the blood where they are eventually filtered out by the liver and kidneys. The blood brain-barrier consists of these capillary walls and insulating glial cells.

While this barrier prevents certain brain chemicals, like neurotransmitters, from leaving the brain, many toxic chemicals pass through freely. A chemical's passage through the barrier depends on fat solubility, electrical charge, and size of the molecule. Many toxic chemicals are fat soluble and of small molecular size thus facilitating their movement into brain tissue. A baby's blood-brain barrier remains poorly developed until around the time of birth, making it especially vulnerable to substances in the mother's bloodstream. Chemicals from the mother's blood moving across the placenta find the baby's brain an easy target.

Ova and Female Fertility

Exposure to chemicals at any stage of a woman's life can affect her pregnancy. In fact, chemicals that she contacts prior to her pregnancy can affect her grandchildren.

The cells that create eggs in the ovary first form as oocytes during fetal life. Female children are born with all the egg cells they will ever have. So you are born with the eggs that produce your daughter and your daughter will be born with the eggs that produce your grandchildren. Later, 300 to 500 of these egg cells will mature into ova, one or more of which will be made ready for release during ovulation each month.

During a woman's life there are countless opportunities for chemical exposures. Unfortunately, since no regenerative process exists in the female body to repair any damage to the oocyte, the damage can accumulate over a lifetime. Exposure to toxic chemicals and especially to mutagens (chemicals that alter the genetic structure of these DNA carriers) can cause permanent hereditary changes or developmental defects and disorders that may not manifest for decades and/or generations. Thus, your daughter may be affected by changes that occur to your egg cells before she is conceived, and those alterations may affect the children she produces. Protecting your own body against exposures can therefore help your progeny for generations to come (Riley and Vorhees 1986).

Sperm and Male Fertility

Your baby is also susceptible to chemicals that its father encounters. After a man reaches puberty, his sperm are continually renewed, requiring approximately seventy-four days to mature. Environmental toxins can affect sperm in several different ways depending on the time of exposure during that period.

In fact, exactly how sperm are affected by chemicals and other environmental factors without dying presents a serious question today. In the past, job-related environmental effects on male semen have been primarily held responsible for reducing or eliminating sperm production. Damaged sperm were assumed to die or to fail in propelling themselves adequately to unite with the egg. However, it is now thought that during early stages of sperm development, environmental exposure may cause sperm death, but damage at later stages may damage or deform the sperm without killing it but leading to abnormalities in the embryo. A substance that kills some sperm may mutate or damage others in the process. Also, damage that affects the testes may permanently alter a man's ability to produce healthy sperm (Welch 1993). Currently, male-mediated effects on pregnancy outcomes and developmental disorders are under active research by concerned medical scientists.

Recently, increased rates of spontaneous abortions have been recorded for women whose husbands were exposed to lead, inorganic mercury, organic solvents, anesthetic gases, and other toxic agents. As we have said previously, spontaneous abortion is usually related to a serious defect in the fetus. Those pregnancies that survive toxic exposures may still be affected although less seriously. For instance, children of males employed in electrical or petrochemical occupations show elevated rates of nervous system cancers. This certainly suggests the possibility of changes in the fetal immune and nervous systems originating from a problem in the sperm.

You Should Know . . .

Sperm that survive exposure to toxic chemicals may be damaged enough to produce birth defects, developmental disorders, or cancer in the child. A man who works with toxic chemicals and who wishes to father a child can reduce the risks of environmental influences by eliminating exposures for about three months before attempting conception.

Many male Gulf War veterans have fathered children with multiple deformities (Haley 1998). Although no final determination of chemical exposure or causality has been made, these cases certainly lend credence to the practice of caution with regard to exposed males intending to father children in the future.

Another interesting issue concerns the significant drop in the number of male babies born in industrialized societies. While male infants are known to be more susceptible to disease, this finding invites the question of whether male-producing sperm are being damaged, whether fewer males are surviving in the womb, and whether these possibilities are related to the increase in indiscriminate chemical use across the world. In fact, some researchers suggest that chemical contamination of semen, from the father's exposure to chemicals, may be affecting sperm or the fertilized egg (Hood 1990).

Because men produce sperm continuously, eliminating exposures may sometimes correct a case of infertility or defective sperm. Even in cases where there is no living sperm in the semen, a period of four or five years may allow for recovery. Laboratory tests can determine levels of active sperm and the body burden of a toxin that may be suppressing sperm production or interfering with sperm vitality or mobility. Environmental exposure may not be the only factor that contributes to infertility or to abnormal sperm. Other factors such as medical conditions may also be involved. (Case Studies, U.S. Dept. of Health and Human Services 1993)

Toxins Affecting Male Reproduction

(These data are drawn from human and animal studies.)

Boron	Reduced sperm count, testicular damage
Benzene	Decrease in sperm motility, testicular damage
Benzo(a)pyrene	Testicular damage
Cadmium	Reduced fertility, testicular damage
Carbon disulfide	Reduced sperm count, decreased sperm motility
Carbon monoxide	Testicular damage
Carbon tetrachloride	Testicular damage
Carbaryl	Abnormal sperm morphology, testicular damage

Chlordecone	Reduced sperm count and mobility, testicular damage
Chloroprene	Reduced sperm count, abnormal morphology, decreased libido
Dibromochloropropane	Reduced sperm count, azoospermia, hormonal changes
Dimethyl dichlorovinyl phosphate	Reduced sperm count
Epichlorohydrin	Testicular damage
Estrogens	Reduced sperm count
Ethylene oxide	Testicular damage
Ethylene dibromide (EDB)	Abnormal sperm mobility, testicular damage
Ethylene glycol ethers	Decreased sperm mobility, testicular damage
Heat	Decreased sperm count
Lead	Decreased sperm count/mobility, testicular damage, abnormal sperm
Manganese	Decreased libido, impotence, testicular damage
Polybrominated biphenyls	Testicular damage
Radiation, ionizing	Decreased sperm count, testicular damage

Adapted from Welch, L. S. 1993. Reproductive and Developmental Hazards. Case Studies in Environmental Medicine. September. U.S. Dept. of Health and Human Services, Agency for Toxic Substances and Disease Registry.

Development of your baby will, unless interrupted by unnatural influences, proceed persistently along a natural course until your baby arrives. As you can see, there is no bad time to start preparing for a healthy baby. You can even begin well before you plan a pregnancy.

 ## Simple Solutions
To Ensure a Healthy Pregnancy

Future mothers and pregnant women can't start too soon to reduce their body's toxic burden. Begin now by using safe, organic methods for gardening and home bug control.

- Avoid unnecessary and accidental chemical exposures. Don't take trash to the dump where toxic chemicals may be hiding, and avoid driving in a closed car with freshly cleaned clothing from the dry cleaner.
- Learn to replace stress with a calm, peaceful state. Let unimportant issues go. Get your life and relationships under control for a truly relaxed pregnancy.
- Start reading labels on the items you purchase.
- Visit your local health food store to look for safer products, and find a reliable source for organic foods.
- A future father can facilitate healthy sperm development by avoiding toxic chemicals for three months before attempting to father a child.
- Organize a healthy eating plan. Make a list of the foods you like in each of the following food groups: protein, mineral, and vitamin foods.
- Drive past fast-food restaurants and purchase fresh fruits, vegetables, and other healthy snacks instead.
- Switch to whole grain products as a simple way to improve your diet.
- Make having a healthy baby a true priority for the time it requires. Being a parent is the most important job you will ever have.

The Healthy Mother

Danielle plans to become pregnant next year. In her mid-thirties, this career woman and her husband want to do everything possible to ensure that their baby is healthy. Because she understands that a lifetime of chemicals may be stored in her body fat, Danielle is reducing her chemical body load by following a healthy diet, losing weight, exercising, and avoiding further chemical use.

At twenty pounds overweight, she wants to lose the extra pounds to avoid exposing her baby to stored chemicals during her pregnancy and breast-feeding. Since exercise helps to eliminate chemicals in the body, she also exercises regularly and eats foods high in antioxidants to assist the cleansing process.

Danielle has also made sure her immunizations are up-to-date. She intends to begin a program of moderate vitamin supplementation a few months before she stops using birth control pills. At the same time she and her husband want to start growing some of their own vegetables organically in their backyard.

Regardless of the stage of pregnancy you might be in, you will want to read the information in this chapter. If, at some point, you wish to have another baby, you will have learned how to reduce the chemicals stored in your body well before pregnancy takes place. This book will also tell you what to do about chemical load during pregnancy and breast-feeding.

Most women do not see their doctors or even realize they are pregnant until the fourth or fifth week of pregnancy or even later. By that time a significant amount of embryonic development has taken place. The fetus may have already been exposed to many negative environmental influences. So pre-conception is the best time to start preparing your body for your baby's optimal development.

Since the most critical period for the development of serious birth defects occurs during the first fifty-seven days of a pregnancy, it is important that women preparing for pregnancy and women who may become pregnant take certain precautions. According to the March of Dimes, only 26 percent of women planning a pregnancy see their doctors beforehand and more than half of all pregnancies are unplanned (Williams 1996).

Dr. Henry M. Lerner of Tufts University School of Medicine (1997) makes the following good point: "It must be remembered that even when the expectant parents do everything right, there is no guarantee of a perfect baby. Even under optimal conditions, miscarriage, congenital malformations, and premature labor can still occur. However, a healthy baby is the norm rather than the exception."

Evaluate Toxic Load and Chemical Use

We suggest that any woman who wants to become pregnant or who is already pregnant have blood tests to evaluate her toxic load. This is especially important for a woman who has worked on a job site where chemicals are used or one who has used pesticides and chemicals at home. Although you may not know what chemicals you have contacted that will affect your developing baby, reading this book will help you to recognize those substances.

If you discover through laboratory testing that your body carries a heavy toxic load, you may choose to postpone pregnancy until those levels are reduced. (See the appendix for information on laboratories that perform blood and urine tests for chemicals and drugs.)

If you are already pregnant, see chapter 9, "Breast-Feeding and Baby Food," where you will find help for providing the optimal conditions for the baby and for breast-feeding.

Dr. John Laseter of AccuChem in Richardson, Texas, an internationally recognized biochemist and advisor for this book, directs blood testing on mothers prior to conception, during pregnancy, and before breast-feeding. Blood and urine tests provide indicators of just how much chemical load a woman has, so that if she wishes to reduce that load prior to conception, she can do so in an informed manner. Testing can pinpoint very quickly what toxic chemicals your baby will be exposed to within your body. Tests called "detoxification enzyme panels" can alert you to deficiencies in your system for metabolizing chemicals.

Also, according to Dr. Laseter, a small amount of fluid can be expressed from the breast at any time and tested for chemicals. This gives a mother some idea of whether her breast milk tests safe for her baby. See the appendix for a list of resources where your doctor can send your blood or urine samples for chemical analysis.

Avoid Chemicals

Before and during pregnancy you will want to avoid adding to your body's chemical stores. Since many chemicals remain in the body for an indefinite length of time, keeping your chemical burden under control protects your baby. Avoiding chemicals may also mean you need to change some unhealthy habits. Smoking, drinking alcohol, ingesting large quantities of caffeine every day, or using recreational drugs become very crucial health issues during pregnancy since each of these behaviors can negatively affect a developing baby.

Many women become addicted long before they become pregnant. They may possess vague notions about the dangers to their babies and fail to recognize just how toxic these substances can be to a developing fetus.

If you are planning to conceive and you follow the directions in this chapter for detoxing, your body can do a fairly good job of cleaning itself within a couple of months. If you are already pregnant or breast-feeding, you will definitely want to follow these recommendations to protect your baby. Remember, it is never too late to take positive steps for your baby's health.

Smoking

Stop or reduce smoking. Many women stop or restrict their smoking during pregnancy. Appropriately so, since smoking increases the risk of birth defects, preterm births, miscarriages, and low birth weight. Babies exposed to nicotine in the womb average one-half pound less in weight and one-half inch shorter in length. They also tend to be harder to calm when crying. Studies show that Sudden Infant Death Syndrome (SIDS) is twice as frequent among babies whose mothers smoked during pregnancy, which suggests damage to respiratory centers in the brain (American College of Obstetricians and Gynecologists 1997).

Maternal smoking during pregnancy is strongly related to persistent and violent criminal behavior in grown male offspring and the more cigarettes mothers smoke, the more criminal behavior the offspring are likely to show. This study controlled for other causes of criminal behavior and concluded that central nervous system damage was responsible. Another similar study from a different ethnic group was in strong agreement (Brennan, Grekin, and Mednick 1999; Rantakaillo, et al. 1992).

Children whose mothers smoked during pregnancy score lower in reading and math, and they tend to grow more slowly (Fried 1992).

Cigarette smoke contains hundreds of chemicals, many of which can cause problems for a developing fetus. Carbon monoxide, which reaches higher levels in the fetus than in the mother, reduces the amount of oxygen available for the developing baby by as much as 20 percent. Nicotine causes fetal blood vessels to constrict, thus reducing fetal oxygen and nourishment. Cyanide in cigarettes can reduce the baby's ability to process vitamin B12, which developing babies need to manufacture protein and red blood cells. Even secondhand smoke has been associated with the above affects on newborns.

The earlier in her pregnancy that a woman quits smoking the better. After a woman quits, her blood oxygen level can go up as much as 8 percent within forty-eight hours. Many good treatments for smoking cessation are available. Women planning for pregnancy can stop smoking with the aid of nicotine patches, nicotine gum, or by using bupriopon (Zyban, Wellbutrin), a drug that must be prescribed by a doctor. These drugs, however, may not be safe during pregnancy and you should check with your doctor before using any chemical method to quit smoking.

Women who can't quit will want to cut back on their smoking as much as possible. Pregnant women should avoid smokers, ask household members who smoke to smoke outside, and, when in public, sit in nonsmoking areas.

Caffeine Use

Reduce caffeine use. Caffeine is a nervous system stimulant that increases heart rate, blood pressure, and metabolic rate. Caffeine causes a rise in epinephrine which reduces the amount of oxygen and nutrients available to your baby. In fact, your baby's blood levels of caffeine actually may reach higher levels than yours since the baby's undeveloped liver can't process the chemical as fast.

High doses of caffeine can also cause premature delivery, growth retardation, and birth defects in animals. Low chronic caffeine exposure, such as you might get from drinking several cups of coffee or soft drinks per day, has been shown to inhibit learning ability and to reduce the activity levels of the infants of laboratory animals. A significant correlation exists between human caffeine consumption and miscarriages (Srisuphan and Bracken 1986).

Since high levels of caffeine use can result in developmental disorders, women contemplating pregnancy will want to begin reducing caffeine consumption well before conception or as soon as possible during pregnancy. Reducing intake slowly will prevent the "caffeine headache" associated with abrupt decreases in caffeine intake. Start by cutting out one Coke or one cup of coffee per day. Reduce caffeine intake to no more than two cups of coffee, tea, or cola a day, and do it over a period of one to two weeks depending on how much caffeine you are currently ingesting. If a headache occurs, try drinking a few sips of the beverage rather than the entire cup or glass.

Alcohol

Avoid alcohol and street drugs. Alcohol and street drugs put babies at risk at every stage of pregnancy. To their credit, many women reduce or discontinue the use of street drugs during pregnancy. This does not hold true to the same extent with alcohol. Many mothers continue to consume alcohol heavily up to, during, and after pregnancy.

Approximately one in ten babies experience exposure to illegal drugs during gestation and an untold number have mothers who drank alcohol during their pregnancy. *Drugs and alcohol cross the placenta and even occasional use can harm the baby.*

Ideally, women who drink alcohol should stop drinking prior to conception. Alcohol consumption by a pregnant mother affects the fetus quickly and the baby's alcohol level corresponds to the mother's. The more the mother drinks the more she harms her baby. One study showed that the risk of miscarriage goes up 3 percent for every day a mother drinks (Klein, et al. 1981). Fetal Alcohol Syndrome (FAS) is the most common cause of mental retardation in children. FAS babies show a wide range of effects: small heads, defective hearts, abnormal facial features, poor muscle tone, bone and joint defects, hyperactivity, extreme nervousness, behavioral problems, and attentional deficits. They also have neurological defects, learning disabilities, and speech or language disorders. Even moderate drinking, occasional drinking, or binges can cause neurological disorders such as tremors and learning disabilities.

Alcohol combined with smoking can create more problems than one or the other alone. If a woman drinks and smokes a pack of cigarettes a day, her risk of miscarriage is four times greater than a woman who does neither (Stein and Kline 1983). If you need help to stop drinking, that help is available through Alcoholics Anonymous or specialized clinics and hospitals with addiction programs.

Marijuana

Marijuana accumulates in body fat and remains there for an extended period of time. Marijuana smokers can become "stoned" even when they are not smoking the drug due to the breakdown of fat cells and the release of stored THC, the active ingredient of marijuana, into the bloodstream. They have to become hungry enough so that their body starts breaking down their fat for energy.

THC can reach significant levels in the fetus, its effects being similar to those of steroids that affect the baby's hormonal balance. In fact, THC levels in the fetus often reach eight times that of the mother's. Some studies have found birth defects, low birth weight, and prematurity at higher risk in women who smoke marijuana (Zachirias 1983). Marijuana use results in sperm deformity and causes developmental disorders in animals (Stenchever, Kunysz, and Allen 1974; Samuels and Samuels 1996). Mothers who smoke marijuana more than five times a week may have newborns who suffer tremors, strong startle reactions, and poor visual response. Babies who ingest marijuana via breast milk show reduced psychomotor functioning (Fried 1980; Ashley and Little 1990).

Both women and men who have frequently smoked "pot" should consider "detoxing" for a period of two to three months prior to conception. This can easily be accomplished through exercise, abstaining from the drug, and implementing the detox diet described later in this chapter.

Cocaine and Crack Cocaine

Pregnant women who use cocaine increase their chance of early delivery by about 25 percent. Their babies may have delayed growth patterns, smaller heads, developmental disabilities, irritable temperaments, and neurological effects resulting in long-term physical, emotional, and behavioral problems. Also, babies born addicted to cocaine go through withdrawal after delivery (American College of Obstetricians and Gynecologists 1997; Holzman and Paneth 1994).

Heroin

Heroin use has increased significantly in the last decade, especially in individuals of childbearing age. Like most street drugs, heroin passes readily through the placenta to the baby. These babies are born addicted and, after birth, they experience sudden and painful withdrawal symptoms. Mothers who use heroin often miscarry or experience preterm labor. Their babies weigh less and experience behavioral problems, poor fine motor coordination, and poor concentration later in childhood. Maternal opiate use also seems to affect a baby's arousal systems causing a low frustration threshold and hyperactivity.

Women using heroin or other opiates are advised to discontinue use prior to conception. Methadone, routinely administered as a replacement for heroin under a doctor's supervision, can also have deleterious effects on a fetus since it also affects the central nervous system (CNS). If already pregnant, a mother can benefit her baby by discontinuing heroin use as soon as possible.

Amphetamines

As stimulants, amphetamines such as methamphetamine place the fetus in a dangerous position. These substances reduce blood supply to the baby and lessen the amount of nutrients available to the developing baby. This can have devastating effects on the baby after birth, causing agitation, sleep problems, and poor appetite. Reducing blood supply and nutrition to a developing brain can cause brain damage and developmental disorders (Morgane, et al. 1992).

PCP and LSD

Both PCP and LSD negatively affect the developing baby's brain. PCP use during pregnancy often results in undersized babies born with motor problems, irritability, hypersensitivity to sound, tremors, twitching, and bizarre eye movements. LSD use by the mother causes neurological dysfunction which tends to persist in spite of nurturing postnatal environments. These babies exhibit poor fine motor functioning, poor adaptive behavior, and poor language and social development even at the age of eighteen months old.

Glues and Solvents

The effects of significant solvent abuse on the fetus are very similar to those of Fetal Alcohol Syndrome, a fact that has led some researchers to suggest calling the two conditions Fetal Solvent Syndrome. Alcohol is, in fact, a solvent. Usually, however, solvents are not ingested as alcohol is and they are more likely to be abused by inhalation including glue and paint sniffing. (See chapter 6 for a full discussion of solvents and their effects.) Terminating the abuse of glues or solvents prior to conception prevents the serious neurological effects those substances can have on the developing child.

The U.S. Supreme Court recently held a woman who ingested illegal drugs during her pregnancy criminally guilty of harming her child. This opens the door to all sorts of possibilities where chemical teratogens are concerned. Dr. John Laseter, international chemical consultant, speculates that, in the future, because of this precedent, women who knowingly use toxic chemicals during pregnancy may one day be held responsible if their child is born with birth defects or serious developmental disorders.

The implications of this dilemma for women working with toxic chemicals on their jobs presents a real conflict. If the woman continues to work she endangers her child; if she quits she may not be able to feed herself and her family adequately.

Reduce Your Body's Chemical Load

Unless you have seriously avoided chemical use and exposure for the last few years, you may have a significant store of chemicals in your fat tissue. Prior to conceiving, you want to reduce that chemical load as much as possible. The most important reason to reduce that load is that chemicals stored in your body expose your baby during its fetal development. Fat stores are needed for energy but fat cells in your body often break down and release stored chemicals when you miss a meal, go too long without eating, or when you physically exert yourself. Reducing your chemical load is not difficult and there are several ways to accomplish the task. Follow these recommendations, and your body can do a fairly good job of detoxing itself within a couple of months.

The Detox Diet

A good detoxification diet should be low in fat to facilitate fat mobilization, high in fiber, and built around complex carbohydrates such as whole grains, vegetables, fruits, nuts, and seeds—with a minimum of meat and dairy products. Chemicals are often excreted through bowel eliminations so an increase of vegetable fiber is desirable. High quality protein from vegetable sources like legumes, tofu, tempeh, and unpolluted fish should replace red meat. Pears, strawberries, papaya, and apples help detoxify the body as do vegetable juices, especially those containing dark green leafy vegetables combined with carrot, beet, or garlic (Rapp 1996).

If possible, all foods should be organically grown, either from a supplier or your own garden. Avoiding refined sugar and eliminating alcohol, tobacco, and caffeine will help. White flour goods, fatty or fried foods should also be eliminated.

Once you are pregnant or breast-feeding, adding a little more fat to your diet is advisable. You do not want to break down large fat stores during pregnancy or breast-feeding since stored chemicals can be dumped into your blood and expose the baby. This is especially true for the woman who has had many chemical exposures, who uses chemicals regularly, or who has been unable to detox before pregnancy. Fat can be added to salads in the form of unrefined olive oil or canola oil. Fatty fish like salmon are a good choice as a fat source. To add calories, include such foods as natural peanut butter, nuts, seeds, and avocado.

Pure Water

Clean water intake facilitates detoxification and is an easy and effective way to clear the body of toxic substances. Water eliminates chemicals by increasing their excretion through bowels, saliva, perspiration, and urination. Drink several glasses a day and make sure your water is pollutant-free. (See chapter 4.) Drinking water should be at room temperature or cool to the touch since cold water tends to shock the body.

Exercise

Exercise provides an excellent way to eliminate stored chemicals from your body. Women preparing for pregnancy can eliminate stored toxins by stimulating their adrenal glands to produce greater quantities of adrenaline and noradrenaline, natural chemicals that speed up body processes. The easiest way to accomplish this is to exercise to the point of perspiration at least five days a week. Not only will your body dump the toxins from metabolized fat but the rate at which your body metabolizes toxins will increase.

Most women in their twenties and early thirties who are in reasonably good shape will find that they must exercise for twenty to thirty minutes before they begin to perspire. Carrying even a little extra weight changes this. A woman twenty pounds overweight and/or out of shape may begin to perspire within ten or fifteen minutes. Any woman who has a heart condition, a serious health problem, or who is considerably overweight should check with her doctor before beginning any exercise program.

Once you are pregnant, strenuous exercise is not advisable and you will want to substitute a program of moderate exercise that maintains optimum oxygen to the baby and stops short of releasing stored chemicals. Strenuous exercise during pregnancy can reduce the amount of blood flow and therefore lessen the amount of nutrients and oxygen that go to the fetus (Lerner 1997). It can also cause the breakdown of body fat and the release of stored chemicals (Essen 1977).

If you are pregnant, exercise is still important and can help reduce stress and prepare your body for labor. The positive effect of exercise is cumulative and small frequent amounts of exercise have similar effects to more intensive exercise programs. Exercising ten minutes, ten times a week keeps the body in good cardiovascular fitness. A release from the National Institutes of Health (1998) says that even small amounts of exercise during the day add up, rivaling a full exercise program.

So if you are pregnant, it may be more beneficial for you to exercise moderately for short periods. Try walking for ten minutes, take the stairs, and park further out at the shopping center. During lactation, mothers who are concerned about passing stored chemicals to the baby can implement this kind of exercise program to help reduce the release of stored chemicals into breast milk.

Saunas

Before conception, saunas can help the body sweat out stored chemicals. Some clinicians use saunas for individuals who have experienced heavy chemical exposure and toxic loads. This intensive approach should be attempted only under the supervision of a physician, so that key body functions can be monitored. However, taking hot baths at home can accomplish similar results.

If you are pregnant, avoid the sauna since overheating your body can harm the fetus. In fact, during early pregnancy you should take warm, rather than hot, baths and during an illness keep your fever down to avoid negative effects on the fetus from excessive heat.

Massage

There is some suggestion that massage may help speed up elimination of chemicals via skin and muscle tissue stimulation (Rapp 1996). Massage has the additional benefit of relaxing you and thus reducing stress hormones that affect your baby.

Weight Loss

Losing weight offers an effective method of mobilizing and eliminating stored chemicals before pregnancy. Mothers who are of normal weight or underweight will want to look at other methods for detoxing since optimal conditions for the baby require that the mother carry adequate weight prior to conception.

Once you are pregnant, you will want to avoid weight loss for two reasons. One, your baby will need all the nutrients it can get, and, two, you don't want your fatty tissue to break down and dump chemicals into your bloodstream. If you have a heavy load of stored chemicals or are routinely exposed to chemicals and you are going to breast-feed, you should also avoid losing a lot of weight after child-birth. Chemicals tend to collect in breast milk. You do have other options for resolving those issues; they are discussed in chapter 9.

Get Plenty of Natural Antioxidants

Before, during, and after pregnancy natural substances called antioxidants can help capture chemicals as they circulate in the blood-stream and move them out of the body via urination and perspira-tion. Additionally, since they modulate the effects of hormones, they may be able to offset the effects of endocrine disruptors. Vitamins C, E, and niacin promote the removal of chemicals from the blood-stream. These antioxidants can be found in many over-the-counter vitamin and mineral supplements but should not be taken in high doses during pregnancy. Normal minimum daily requirement (MDR) amounts should be adequate.

Of course, your best and healthiest source of antioxidants is found in fruits, vegetables, and whole grains. You don't need a doc-tor's advice to use these sources which are readily available, less expensive, and taste better.

Tons of research has been done to search out and evaluate natu-ral food factors that act as natural antioxidants in the body. And, yes, you can argue that supplements purchased in the store have higher concentrations of these substances than natural foods. But higher con-centrations may not be necessary if you combine the right foods and eat enough of them regularly.

Common Foods Loaded with Antioxidants

Eat at least five servings of fruits and vegetables on this list, two to three ounces of beans, and six to eleven servings of grains each day to get a good range of foods and an adequate amount of antioxidants.

- Broccoli, brussels sprouts, cauliflower, cabbage, bok choy, kale, chard, and turnips, all members of the Brassica group of vegetables, provide potent antioxidants.
- Potatoes, carrots, beets, and yams contain alpha lipoic acid known to be a potent antioxidant. Alpha lipoic acids also seem to enhance or increase the longevity of other antioxidants such as Vitamins C and E and glutathione.
- Glutathione is found in asparagus, tomatoes, potatoes, peaches, avocado, watermelon, and winter squash.
- The red pigment in tomatoes, watermelon, and strawberries contains carotenoids like lycopene. Cooking tomatoes increases the body's ability to absorb lycopene, so canned tomato products can be very healthy.
- Soy products contain genistein.
- Peppers have capsaicin.
- Green tea provides epigallocatechin-3-gallate. However, green tea should be avoided during pregnancy because it also inhibits blood vessel growth. Black teas contain catechins, but herbal teas do not appear to have adequate antioxidants.
- Red grapes, strawberries, and raspberries contain ellagic acid which can protect the body from cigarette smoke and air pollution. Cherries have dozens of antioxidents.
- Citrus fruits, especially oranges, have 60 different substances known to be antioxidants and cancer fighters including limonene, Vitamin C, and glucarase.
- Orange or yellow fruits contain high levels of beta carotene, a popular antioxidant.
- Rice, wheat bran, soybeans, and other legumes provide inositol hexaphosphate.
- Garlic, leeks, shallots, and red or yellow onions, uncooked, contain over 30 different allium compounds.
- Whole grain products provide Vitamin E.

We recommend that you purchase foods from organic sources if at all possible since chemical pesticides can increase the presence of free radicals in the body. Or you can grow your own produce without using chemicals.

Polyunsaturated Fats

The use of polyunsaturated fats such as vegetable oils can help replace the contents of fat cells and reduce stored toxins. Before, during, and after pregnancy you will benefit from consuming a greater percentage of unsaturated fats. Note that unsaturated fats are usually liquid at room temperature while saturated fats tend to solidify.

Unsaturated Fats	Saturated Fats
Canola oil	Butter
Peanut oil	Coconut oil
Sunflower oil	Palm oil
Olive oil	Lard
Corn oil	Bacon or pork fat
Fish oil	Flaxseed oil

Chemical Detoxification Programs

If you find that your body has a heavy chemical burden, if you have recently had a heavy chemical exposure, if you are chemically sensitive, or if you work with toxic chemicals, you may want to consult an environmental medicine specialist before embarking on a self-directed detoxification program. Mobilizing fat to release large amounts of stored chemicals could make you ill. Environmental medicine specialists provide comprehensive programs for detoxifying chemical body load under medical supervision.

Build Your Nutritional Status

Women who are nutritionally deficient prior to conception have a hard time catching up during pregnancy. In fact, there is evidence that mothers who are undernourished prior to conception deliver babies who weigh less, are smaller, and have smaller heads (Kirchengast and Hartman 1998).

Furthermore, mothers who have nutrient deficiencies tend to be more vulnerable to chemicals, as are their babies. Before conceiving you want to build your nutritional stores, and develop good dietary habits. Everything you do to improve your diet will benefit your baby who draws on your nutritional stores during pregnancy.

If you have been ill or emotionally upset, had difficulties with a previous pregnancy, or have delivered a baby within the last year you will want to increase your calorie intake substantially during the first stage of your pregnancy. The Montreal Diet Dispensary Method suggests an additional 200 calories and 20 grams of protein per day for each of these factors. So if you were ill, had difficulties with a previous pregnancy, and delivered a baby in the last year, you would add another 600 calories and 60 grams of protein to your diet per day.

Chemical Sensitivity

Studies suggest that children who are exposed in the womb to chemicals may become hypersensitive to chemicals after birth and may pass that sensitivity on to their children. Female laboratory animals who were exposed in the uterus to a developmental toxin became more sensitive to the chemical's toxic effects than their mothers. In addition, the following generation were even more sensitive than their mothers and grandmothers and showed different toxic effects (Tabacova, Nikiforov, and Balabaeva 1983).

Some environmental physicians are discussing new ways to detoxify patients prior to pregnancy. Since the best way for a woman to rid her body of excess chemicals is to breast-feed, some experts are considering giving certain hormones to women with heavy toxic burdens who wish to conceive. These hormones would cause the woman to produce milk which would then be extracted using a breast pump until her blood exhibited a satisfactory chemical load reduction.

Folic Acid Supplements

Medical experts strongly recommend that women who are attempting to conceive take 400 mcg of folic acid per day. Folic acid can help prevent neural tube defects, such as spina bifida, that tend to occur during the first months of pregnancy. Most women do not even know they are pregnant until after this crucial time period when defects may have already occurred. Ideally, all women of childbearing age should take folic acid on a daily basis as a precaution.

Recently, the U.S. government required that food manufacturers add folic acid to starch products like breads, pastas, and cereals. Although this may help prevent many instances of neural tube defects, taking additional supplements of folic acid at the recommended doses will protect babies even further, especially since diets vary and some women avoid starches to keep their weight under control. Most standard vitamin combinations contain recommended amounts of folic acid and provide an easy way to make sure you are getting what you need. Note that too much folic acid can create a problem for the fetus too. Talk to your doctor about how much folic acid you should be taking.

Iron Supplements

Iron facilitates the production of red blood cells in the fetus. Because of menstrual blood loss, breast-feeding, and low iron intake, many women of childbearing age have insufficient stores of iron. This is the one case where your developing baby will deprive you of a nutrient, so iron supplementation prior to pregnancy ensures that you will have good reserves on hand for your baby.

A supplement of 30 to 60 mg per day is recommended in the second and third trimesters. However, prior to the pregnancy most women will benefit from the amount usually found in an over-the-counter daily vitamin tablet (often 18 mg). Because Vitamin C aids in the absorption of iron, a supplement amount of 250 mg., also usually found in a daily vitamin supplement, should be taken. Your doctor can tell you if you are iron-deficient via a simple blood test.

Iodine Supplements

Iodine is crucial for your baby's brain development and thyroid functioning. A lack of iodine in the mother's diet can lead to mental retardation. Regular use of iodized salt products will provide you with enough iodine. Adequate amounts of iodine can also be found in most mineral supplements and seafoods.

Control Medical Conditions

In chapter 8 we discuss medical conditions and medications that can affect a developing fetus or infant. Anything you consume during pregnancy has the potential of affecting your baby. Sometimes, however, the need for maternal health outweighs fetal risk, sometimes not. Before conceiving, if you are using a medication on the FDA's X list (see chapter 8), inform your doctor immediately. If you are using any other medication, ask your doctor if the medication can be reduced, eliminated, or replaced by another less toxic drug, or if there are valid alternative ways to control your disorder. Do not attempt to discontinue any prescribed medication without first getting your doctor's advice, since, in some cases, doing so could actually put your baby at greater risk. A good source of information about the effects of a medication on the fetus is the *Physicians' Desk Reference* (1997), available in bookstores and libraries.

Remember that medications take time to clear from the body. Most medications will need at least one to two months to clear. If your doctor has advised you to terminate your medication prior to conceiving, you may want to continue your method of birth control for a few more months while your body cycles out any remaining traces of the medication. During this time you should consider regular exercise to further eliminate any traces of the substance from your body.

Prevent Disease

All immunizations should be current prior to conception since several common diseases can disrupt fetal development. The best possible situation is for immunizations to be administered at least three months prior to any attempt at conception. This is especially true for rubella and varicella vaccines. Rubella, or German measles, presents a serious threat to your baby if you contract the disease in early pregnancy. Exposure during the first four weeks results in 50 percent birth defects; during the second month 22 percent; during the third month 10 percent; the fourth and fifth month, 6 percent. The rubella vaccine itself can cause harm to the fetus and should never be given during pregnancy. If you have been exposed to rubella and you haven't been vaccinated, you should discuss this with your doctor and determine what to do (Samuels and Samuels, 1996).

Other immunizations can be given during pregnancy if necessary. Tetanus can be given when needed, especially after a deep puncture wound. Any woman who is pregnant or considering pregnancy and may have been exposed to hepatitis B should consider getting the vaccine series for hepatitis. Hospital and medical clinic workers, women exposed to blood products, and those who work with individuals having the disease are among those at risk. Check with your doctor regarding other immunizations appropriate during pregnancy.

Vaccines Contraindicated During Pregnancy

These vaccines must be given no less than three months prior to conception.
- Rubella
- Varicella
- Measles
- Mumps

Women who have a chance to alter their routines and prepare for pregnancy give fetal development an extra boost. However, once you are pregnant, you will still have hundreds of opportunities to increase the safety of that tiny, growing human you will soon hold in your arms.

More Simple Solutions
To Ensure a Healthy Pregnancy

- Change unhealthy habits. Stop smoking, using alcohol, and/or using recreational drugs. Avoid inhaling secondhand smoke.

- Reduce caffeine use to one or two cola drinks or a cup of coffee a day.

- Find out what your toxic load is. If it is too high, postpone your pregnancy until you can reduce your body chemicals to acceptable levels.

- Get lots of regular, but moderate, exercise.

- Eat nutritious food high in antioxidants.

- Follow a detoxification diet for several months before conception, if possible.

- Get rid of excess weight before becoming pregnant because chemicals stored in fat cells can be released and cross over to your baby.

- Drink eight glasses of pollutant-free water every day to help remove the toxins.

- Take folic acid supplements before conception and during early pregnancy. Ask your doctor if you require iron supplements.

- Discuss with your doctor any medications you may be taking for chronic conditions to see if they are contraindicated during pregnancy.

- Be sure that all of your immunizations are current before conceiving. Discuss with your doctor any need for immunizations during pregnancy.

- Before conception, use hot baths (but not hot enough to burn) to help excrete stored chemicals.

- Nurture these healthy habits throughout pregnancy and breast-feeding. Keep them afterwards, too, for your own health and to teach your children.

Food and Water

In 1979, authorities discovered two Woburn, Massachusetts municipal wells had been contaminated with trichloroethylene, a common dry-cleaning solution. The chemical levels measured thirty to eighty times higher than the Environmental Protection Agency's (EPA) maximum acceptable limits. The babies born to mothers who had used the water during their pregnancy suffered from sensory impairments, reflex abnormalities, nerve damage, increased rates of childhood leukemia, and birth defects.

Food Additives

Human beings have been using additives for centuries. Since ancient times honey, salt, and innumerable spices have been valued for their ability to make bland foods tastier and as preservatives to ensure food availability during times of need. The last fifty years or so, however, has seen a shift from the use of natural food additives to synthetic additives that promise to make our foods attractive and healthy for longer periods of time. In fact, in the United States alone, the EPA approves about 800 man-made food additives. Unfortunately, a good portion of these "safe" substances can create adverse health effects.

Artificial Flavorings

Food markets today sell hundreds of foods whose flavors have been enhanced or altered by the use of synthetic chemicals. From artificial sweeteners to the nine different chemicals used to simulate strawberry flavoring alone, much of our food is bombarded with unnatural substances—many of which we remain unaware. That's because in the United States and several other countries, manufacturers are not required to list individual chemical ingredients. Instead, they group multiple chemical flavorings together under the general heading of "artificial flavors." As you can imagine, this practice makes it difficult to know which harmful substances you and your baby may be consuming.

Monosodium Glutamate

Monosodium glutamate (MSG) is a flavoring added to many Chinese and Japanese foods, canned soups, dry soup mixes, lunch meats, fish, seafood, chips, condiments, sauces, and nondairy creamers. MSG is a sodium salt of glutamic acid, which is actually one of the vital amino acids in our bodies. In excess, however, MSG acts as a stimulant causing hyperactivity, the death of nerve cells which leads to brain damage, and "Chinese restaurant syndrome," which is characterized by headaches, skin flushing, nausea, vomiting, and heart palpitations. As with the labeling of many other additives, MSG is commonly hidden under some general categories such as natural flavorings, hydrolyzed vegetable protein (HVP), and autolyzed yeast.

Artificial Sweeteners

In the past two decades, sugar has been vilified as the cause of excess weight gain and hyperactivity in children. As a result, artificial sweeteners have been embraced as a way of satisfying children's desire for sweets without the unwanted effects of sugar. Although these sweeteners may indeed cut down on dental caries and total caloric intake, they can cause a multitude of other health problems.

Aspartame (Trade names NutraSweet and Equal)

Aspartame, a common sugar substitute, is made when two amino acids (aspartate and phenylaline) are bound together by methanol (wood alcohol). Approved in the United States in 1981 as a safe food additive, some scientific studies have shown it to be both a neurotoxin and a possible carcinogen (Shephard, Wakabayashi, and Nagao 1993; Pinto and Maher 1988; Olney, et al. 1996; Camfield, et al. 1992). Long-term studies on behavior and cognitive effects in humans are not yet available. What we do know about this chemical, however, suggests that it should be avoided, especially by pregnant women and the developing fetus.

Aspartame has been related to significant changes in brain chemistry in laboratory animals. Research suggests that aspartame is a mutagen and may cause brain cancer in animals. Some experts point out that after it was introduced into the consumer market, there was a sharp increase in brain tumor incidence and malignancy (Olney, et. al. 1996).

Aspartame breaks down into phenylalanine, aspartic acid, methanol, formaldehyde, and diketopiperazine (DKP). Some researchers describe these levels as insignificant and claim they leave the body quickly. Other researchers, however, say that high levels are reached when people drink diet drinks in large quantities (1 to 3 liters a day), and that some of these chemicals (such as formaldehyde) are stored in body tissue (Zorumski and Olney 1992; Stegink, et al. 1981).

Consumers report a wide range of health effects after the ingestion of aspartame from products like diet sodas, sugar-free gum, breakfast cereals, instant coffee and tea, pudding and pie fillings, and other diet foods. Some of the reported symptoms are headaches, migraines, dizziness, seizures, mood swings, depression, nausea, vomiting, and abdominal cramps (Millichap 1993).

Saccharin

Saccharin, found in products like Sweet 'n Low, is an artificial sweetener that has zero calories and is 300 times sweeter than sugar. It is, however, derived from petrochemicals, some of which are known carcinogens and suspected as developmental and neurological toxicants. Saccharin was removed from soft drinks long ago due to research that suggested it contributed to cancer. Although these studies involved huge amounts of saccharin and were not adequately replicated, we feel saccharin should be avoided by pregnant women and those wishing to become pregnant since there is no known threshold for cancer-causing substances that damage the fetus.

Artificial Colors

Because of their dependence on commercially produced food, consumers in developed countries have been caught in the competition between food manufacturers who have convinced us that good food must be beautiful. We search for the shiniest apple and the brightest orange. We even buy meat that has been dyed, not because it makes the meat tastier or healthier, but because it looks better in the display case.

Many of us do not even know that much of the food we buy has been cosmetically enhanced or that the "cosmetics" can have adverse health effects. In fact, most artificial colors are derived from petrochemicals and coal tars. Artificial colors are found in some breakfast cereals, juices, sports drinks, candy, frozen foods, sodas, ice cream, cookies, pizzas, soft drinks, salad dressings, waffles, and pancakes.

Artificial colors may accumulate in brain tissue and cause neurological disorders like ADD and hyperactivity (Boris and Mandel 1994). Many are known or suspected carcinogens. Waxes and oils commonly applied to produce, such as apples and tomatoes, can also be harmful since they, too, are derived from petrochemicals and mineral oils.

Carcinogenic Artificial Colors

Known carcinogens are as follows:
- Red Nos. 8, 9, 19, and 37
- Orange No. 17

Suspected carcinogens include the following:
- Red No. 3 (erythrosine)
- Red 40
- Citrus Red 2
- Yellow No. 5 (tartrazine, which is also a neurotoxin)
- Yellow No. 6
- Green No. 3
- Blue Nos. 1 and 2

Avoiding harmful artificial food colors is not difficult if you consistently read labels and/or shop where natural food products are available. Many natural food colors are used as alternatives to potentially dangerous artificial colors and some manufacturers are beginning to acknowledge the growing public concern by marketing these alternatives.

Artificial Preservatives

In any society it is important to be able to preserve food in order to avoid waste and to store reserves for future use. Unfortunately, many of the preserving agents currently used to prolong food life are known to produce negative health effects.

Natural Food Colors

- Annatto
- Beet juice
- Blueberry juice
- Grape juice
- Turmeric
- Beta-carotene caramel
- Carotene
- Carrot oil
- Grape extract
- Cochineal extract
- Carmine

Sulfiting Agents

Sulfiting agents (sulfur dioxide, sodium sulfite, sodium bisulfite, sodium meta-sulfite, potassium bisulfite, and potassium meta-bisulfite) are preservatives used to avoid browning and spoilage. Although not synthetic, these agents are known to cause allergic reactions, sometimes severe. A short list of the many foods they are routinely added to includes frozen vegetables, dried fruits, salad dressings, pickles, meat, salad bar lettuce, relishes, beer, wine, shrimp and seafood (Millichap 1993).

Nitrates

Nitrites and nitrates, which inhibit the growth of bacteria, are used as preserving agents on cured meats, beef jerky, luncheon meats, broccoli, collard greens, spinach, and root vegetables. These preserving agents are also used on fresh and canned products. Nitrates become extremely toxic when combined with naturally occurring amides and amines in the body. The combination produces nitrosamines, which are known to be some of the most dangerous carcinogens (Millichap 1993). Furthermore, pregnant women become more vulnerable to nitrates during the last two to three months of pregnancy because of changes in their blood. Nitrates bind with oxygen in the blood. Excess amounts of nitrates can limit the amount of oxygen available to brain tissue.

Vitamin C (ascorbic acid, ascorbate) can inhibit the formation of nitrosamines. Some manufacturers even add Vitamin C along with nitrates to their products. In fact, Vitamin C can also be used as a preserving agent instead of using nitrates.

Synthetic Antioxidants

Synthetic antioxidants prevent the spoilage of many lipid-containing (i.e. containing fat) products when exposed to oxygen.

Two of the most common synthetic antioxidants used as food preservatives are BHA (butylated hydroxyanisole) and BHT (butylated hydroxytoluene) both of which are derived from petrochemicals. Some food products that may contain BHA or BHT include instant potatoes, baking mixes, and many cereals eaten by children.

BHA is a recognized carcinogen and a suspected gastrointestinal and liver toxicant, neurotoxicant, and respiratory toxicant. When combined with nitrites in the body under acidic conditions such as digestion, BHA can form highly mutagenic products (Millichap 1993). Japan has banned BHA as a food additive. The United States, however, is waiting for more research to be published before acting to ban it.

BHT is a suspected gastrointestinal and liver toxicant, kidney toxicant, neurotoxicant, respiratory toxicant, and organ toxicant. BHT has been shown to cause internal and external hemorrhaging in lab animals, sometimes severe enough to cause death (Millichap 1993).

Simple Solutions For Food Preservation

Healthier food preservation techniques than the ones discussed above have been used for hundreds (sometimes thousands) of years and are still used by many manufacturers in response to the concerns of today's consumers. Many foods are advertised as preservative-free, including many baby foods; and they are as free from spoilage and botulism as are the foods that have been synthetically preserved. It's ironic that these are now the "alternative" ways to preserve food.

Natural food processing includes the following methods:

- Drying
- Canning
- Freezing
- Salting
- Pickling in vinegar

Natural food preservatives include the following:

- Vitamin E (tocopherol)
- Vitamin C (ascorbic acid, calcium ascorbate, sodium ascorbate)
- Calcium propionate
- Citric acid (calcium citrate, potassium citrate, sodium citrate)
- Erythorbic acid (sodium erythorbate)
- Sorbic acid (calcium sorbate, potassium sorbate, sodium sorbate)
- Benzoic acid (sodium benzoate)
- Salt (sodium chloride)

Other Food Contaminants

Most commercially grown food has been directly or indirectly contaminated with chemical pesticides, herbicides, insecticides, or fungicides (see chapter 7).

Pesticides

If you want to reduce your pesticide consumption, you should thoroughly wash, peel, and cook all pesticide-treated foods. In fact, as you will see in the section on baby food in chapter 9, one reason why processed baby foods demonstrate nondetectable (i.e., safe) levels of pesticide is because of the processing to which they are subjected.

To reduce your intake of pesticide residues on commercial food, there are several commonsense steps you can take at home.

Simple Solutions To Reduce Pesticide Exposure

- Trim fat from meat and poultry because many pesticides are fat-soluble and concentrate in fat. Discard fats and oils from broth and pan drippings.
- Wash fruits and vegetables with cold water and scrub them with a vegetable brush. Peel if possible.
- Cook your produce if possible since heat breaks down and destroys many toxic chemicals found on food.
- Don't eat fish from contaminated lakes, streams, or rivers. Consult with fish and game officials if your are unsure which waters may be contaminated.

- Cut away and discard any damaged or bruised parts on fresh produce since these areas may contain toxic chemicals that cannot be washed off.

Dioxins and PCBs

Dioxins (2, 3, 7, 8-tetrachlorodibenzene-p-dioxin) are toxic chemicals produced in the manufacture of chlorinated insecticides, herbicides, disinfectants, wood preservatives, and chlorine-bleached paper products. Subsequently, dioxins, recognized by the EPA as carcinogens, have been found in food (especially fish and seafood), drinking water, breast milk, milk cartons, food packaging, paper plates, coffee filters, toilet paper, tampons, paper towels, facial tissue, writing paper, and are present in significant amounts in food, water, air, and soil (Rapp 1996). Dioxins, known endocrine disruptors, remain in body fat for years.

PCBs, also known endocrine disruptors, are chemicals used in manufacture of electronic equipment, appliances, transformers, fluorescent light ballasts, plasticizers, adhesives, pesticides, inks, lubricants, and carbonless paper. Higher than acceptable PCB levels have shown up in breast milk samples collected all over the world (Wolf 1983). They cause increased susceptibility to disease in babies whose mothers ate food grown from fields located near streams contaminated with runoff from manufacturing plants using PCBs. Babies whose mothers ate fish from PCB-contaminated lakes had lower birth weight, smaller heads, motor immaturity, weaker reflexes, and greater startle responses. When tested later at seven months, the babies with higher levels of PCBs at birth scored lower on a test of infant intelligence. At four years old, these children scored lower on verbal and memory scales and were noticeably less cooperative (Jacobson, et al. 1990).

Simple Solutions
To Reduce Dioxin and PCB Exposure

- Don't eat fish from ponds, lakes, streams, or rivers located downstream from chemical plants or paper mills.

- Trim any fat from meat before cooking it.

- Do not use chlorine bleach and chlorinated insecticides, herbicides, disinfectants, and wood preservatives.

- Use unbleached paper products if possible or ask the manufacturer if chlorine bleach was used in production. Peroxide used to bleach paper products does not produce dioxins.
- Don't disassemble electrical appliances. If possible call the manufacturer to find out if PCBs were used.
- Heat can cause the release of dioxins and plasticizers into the foods you cook in plastic containers. If you microwave food, heat it in a glass container instead of on the plastic microwave plate.

Aluminum

Aluminum is a suspected cardiovascular and blood toxicant, neurotoxin, and respiratory toxicant. Accumulation of aluminum in the brain has been linked with Alzheimer's disease (Millichap 1993). We are exposed to aluminum on a daily basis from a variety of sources. Found in food cooked in aluminum pots and pans and pans with nonstick surfaces, aluminum also is found in many baking powders, baked goods containing aluminum phosphate, processed cheeses, and aluminum soda cans (Millichap 1993).

Simple Solutions
To Avoid Aluminum Exposure in Food

- Avoid cooking with aluminum pots and pans, even those with Teflon or Silverstone coating. Instead, use stainless steel, glass, or Corning Ware.
- Don't drink beverages from aluminum cans. Use glass bottles instead (they can be recycled).
- Make sure your table salt does not contain aluminum anti-caking substances.

Organic Foods

The organic foods industry has advanced phenomenally during the past decade, rising from near obscurity in most industrial countries to become a billion-dollar business. Gone are the "health nuts" faithfully pursing inaccessible products in out-of-the-way health food stores. They have been overtaken in ever-increasing numbers by concerned parents and grandparents aware of the many health hazards caused by the consumption of chemically treated food. In fact, one United

States study found that about one-half of American consumers want to consume organically grown foods (Loftus and Marcus 1998). Supermarkets are rushing to compete with health food stores to offer their customers organic food alternatives.

Despite the increasingly widespread popularity of organic foods, many people remain unaware of the potential and avoidable health risks associated with the chemical residues found on conventionally grown foods. One of our goals in writing this book is to expose and explain the negative effects of chemical use on the developing fetus and the growing child, and to inform the readers about the ways those dire consequences can be avoided. Obviously one of the best ways to avoid chemical consumption, as many people already know, is to buy foods that have not been chemically grown or processed. You'll find there are even some hidden benefits in organically grown foods.

Chemical-Free

Of course the most obvious benefit organic foods provide is that they are free or virtually free of chemical pesticides. Why only virtually? Some organically labeled foods contain barely detectable pesticide residues. However, these levels are still significantly lower than those found in conventionally fertilized and processed foods. These pesticides probably show up as a result of the polluted air and rainwater that none of us can escape. Remember, it is impossible to live in a chemical-free bubble. We can, however, take control and reduce our chemical exposures. Eating as much organically grown food as possible is an important step in attaining a chemically reduced lifestyle.

Quality

Consumer Reports (1998) conducted a study which found that organic food could not be distinguished from conventionally grown food on the basis of appearance. Some people, however, continue to assume that organic produce is worm-ridden and covered with mold. We concede that organic produce may not always be as attractive as conventionally grown and processed foods since it hasn't been dyed or coated with wax. However, despite what advertisers want us to believe, food doesn't have to look perfect in order to taste great.

Just as there is a discrepancy between fashion models and those of us born on the Earth, there will be variations between fresh produce that has been treated with chemical pesticides, waxes, and dyes and those that are allowed to grow naturally. This doesn't mean you should ever buy badly bruised, rotten, or foul-smelling food. Nature doesn't get it perfect every time, so you can expect varieties in the colors, sizes, and even the shapes of foods. Personally, we are slightly suspicious of produce (and models) that look too good to be true since, generally speaking, there has probably been some sort of chemical, or surgical, alteration performed on the product on the way to market.

Taste

As of yet, no scientific evidence proves that using chemicals on food lessens taste. However, many organic food experts, growers, and consumers contend that chemical-free food tastes better than food contaminated with chemicals. It seems almost elementary that foods treated with systemic pesticides, chemical waxes, and synthetic dyes might have a slight aftertaste, doesn't it? And, in fact, many chemically sensitive people can readily detect by smell and taste when chemicals have been used on food. Also keep in mind that individual foods may have been treated with multiple chemicals between the time they reach the grocery and the time they end up in your grocery cart.

Nutrients

Scientific research remains unclear as to whether organically grown foods are more nutritious than their conventional counterparts. However, one expert from the Tufts University School of Nutrition Science and Policy told *Consumer Reports* (1998, 14) that how a food is grown "probably does affect nutrition, but it does it in ways so complex you might be studying the problem forever."

One of the most important benefits of consuming organic food is the peace of mind and the sense of empowerment it provides. In reality, there are many factors, from politics to ignorance, involving the sale and use of chemicals on food that we just can't control overnight. But we can change the use of chemical food additives—if we insist that our grocers make organic food available.

Water

Every living creature depends upon water for survival. This need increases during pregnancy when the mother's body fluids must increase to provide sufficient fluids for the baby. It is imperative that you drink at least two quarts (about eight large glasses) of water a day to help maintain a healthy pregnancy. Although water alone probably won't account for your total daily fluid intake, it should be a significant contributor. Your water intake will continue to be an important factor in your baby's health if you decide to breast-feed. Therefore, the water you drink must be free from contaminants that can have a negative effect on your baby's development.

The Availability of Organic Foods

If you are worried that your total food needs can't be met with organic products, think again! Here is a sample of the organic foods that are available from many health food stores and supermarkets today:

Fresh produce	Canned goods	Pasta
Sauces	Drinks	Snacks
Cereals	Chemical-free meat	Eggs
Milk	Butter	Cheese
Sour cream	Yogurt	

We all know that a serious issue of world concern is the availability of clean water. In years past, this concern was mainly centered on various bacterial contaminants that cause sickness and death. Now people are becoming more and more concerned about the chemical pollutants from agricultural and industrial runoff that is contaminating our water supplies. However, there are steps you can take to protect yourself and your developing baby from water contaminants.

Water Contaminants

The first step you can take to protect yourself and your baby from harmful chemicals found in water is to learn to distrust what comes out of your faucet. Just because your water has gone through a municipal water treatment plant does not mean it is safe for your baby's optimal development. Indeed, because a treatment plant's job is to eliminate any bacteria that might infect us, chemicals such as chlorine and fluoride are added to our water.

If you suspect your tap water is seriously contaminated or you are just curious, call the EPA's Safe Drinking Water Hotline (800-426-4791) to get a copy of National Drinking Water Regulations. Then, obtain a copy of your local water department's water analysis and compare their chemical and bacterial levels with the legally allowable levels. However, you must understand that the readings are not always accurate because many treatment plants are required to test only once a month. Chemical and bacteria contaminants can vary from day to day. You must also take into account the long, mysterious route your water travels from treatment plant to your faucets, often picking up harmful contaminants from sources such as rusting, lead, or plastic pipes along the way (Rapp 1996).

The next step you must take to ensure that your water is contaminant-free is to test it. Various do-it-yourself testing kits are available or you can send samples of your water to independent testing laboratories. We list some resources at the back of this book, but you can always call your local or state health department for the telephone number of a laboratory in your area. If you suspect a serious problem, some water departments will even test your tap water. Once you have a good idea of the contaminants you are facing you will be better able to take the necessary steps to protect yourself. Keep in mind, however, that water contaminants vary so you need to retest every year if not more frequently. The most common water contaminants are discussed below along with easy solutions you can implement to reduce their presence.

Chlorine

One of the most pervasive chemicals in our environment, chlorine regularly comes to us in a deceptively innocent medium, our tap water. Used to kill bacteria and prevent disease in 98 percent of America's water supply, chlorine is considered safe by the EPA at levels of 100 ppb (parts per billion), a level which some experts claim is too high. We are exposed to chlorine when we drink chlorinated tap water and also when we bathe or swim in chlorinated water because the chemical may be absorbed through skin and inhaled as chloroform.

Once added to our drinking water, chlorine reacts with organic elements to form chemicals called trihalomethanes such as chloroform. To give you some idea of why this is a concern, chloroform is used to make solvents in the lacquer industry and as a coolant in air-conditioners. Chloroform evaporates into ambient air from chlorinated tap water used during showers and baths, in swimming pools and automatic dishwashers.

Chronic high level exposures to chloroform may affect the liver and kidneys with effects like jaundice or burning urination and may cause central nervous system effects like persistent depression and irritability. Reproductive effects in animals include decreased fetal weight, fetal resorptions, increase in abnormal sperm, and decreased rates of conception. Pregnant women should be particularly concerned about reducing their exposure to chlorine, chloroform, and other trihalomethanes since these substances cross the placental barrier. Additionally, the products of chloroform metabolism can accumulate in amniotic fluid.

Simple Solutions To Limit Chlorine/Chloroform Exposure

- Limit tub or shower time to a few minutes to reduce chemical absorption rates.
- Drink filtered or purified water and use it for cooking too.
- Use filters on water taps and special filtering shower heads in the bathtub or shower stall. Change filters frequently.
- Use a ventilating fan in the bathroom to reduce air concentrations of chloroform when showering or bathing.
- Implement safer ways of purifying swimming pool water.

If you are fortunate enough to own a swimming pool, it's not just the chemicals in the water you should be concerned about. Pool test kits that measure acidity and chlorine often contain harmful chemicals. Developing infants and pregnant or nursing mothers should avoid swimming pools and the toxic chemicals they contain. Other methods of reducing bacteria in pool water include ozonators which use ozone to kill bacteria. Still other methods are available but all require the use of at least small amounts of chlorine.

Fluoride

For the average person, the largest source of daily fluoride intake is from fluoridated tap water followed by toothpastes and mouthwashes that contain fluoride, often in extremely high concentrations. Fluoride is chemically similar to chlorine and causes many of the same health problems. Excessive and/or prolonged fluoride intake can cause cancer, central nervous system damage, and fluorosis (insufficient development of tooth enamel that leads to permanent tooth discoloration), brittle bones, and death (Rapp 1996).

It is a good idea to reduce fluoride intake during pregnancy if possible. In fact, recent studies have shown that fluoride does not decrease cavities (ICRF Newsletter 1995). Fluoride should never be given to children under the age of two. One good alternative to tooth-paste is baking soda, although health food stores carry fluoride-free toothpaste.

Lead

Lead exposure, which is still a serious problem today, can occur from a variety of sources and is extremely harmful to your baby's brain development. Water is a major contributor to an infant's lead consumption. Most commonly, lead reaches our water through lead pipe plumbing, which has been banned in the United States since the 1970s. In most cases, replacing your plumbing is not going to present a realistic option, especially when faced with the expenses of raising a family. If, after testing, you find that your water contains significant amounts of lead you can protect yourself in several ways. Simple lead testing kits can be obtained at your local hardware store.

Simple Solutions
To Reduce Exposure from
Lead-Contaminated Tap Water

- Drink and cook only with bottled water. Never cook with lead-contaminated water since boiling for five minutes can increase lead concentrations threefold.

- Water from the cold side of your faucet tends to have fewer chemicals since hot water leaches more chemicals from pipes. Also, before using water from your tap, let it run until there is a noticeable temperature difference (from warm to cool) so you are drawing water from the main water line rather than household plumbing. It is a good idea to do this every morning and anytime you haven't used your water for six hours.

- Do not store liquor in crystal decanters.

- Do not use cans or uncertified lead-free pottery or china to store liquids.

- Use a water filter that eliminates lead.

Nitrates

Nitrates, a component of most chemical fertilizers, have, in the last decade, become a significant health problem especially in rural areas. Accumulating in the soil, nitrates eventually wash down into groundwater supplies, often contaminating shallow and, sometimes, deep-water wells. Although municipal water utilities are required to test regularly for nitrates, the Environmental Working Group reports that as many as 2.2 million Americans drink from water sources that contain levels of nitrates occasionally exceeding recommended standards.

High nitrate levels cause particular problems in children. Babies under six months of age are especially susceptible to nitrates because they have bacteria in their systems that reduce nitrates to toxic nitrites. Nitrites bond to oxygen-transporting hemoglobin cells in the body preventing the baby from getting the oxygen it needs. "Blue baby syndrome" can cause breathing problems, heart attack, and even death from asphyxiation.

Pregnant women are also at risk from excessive nitrates, especially around the 30th week of pregnancy because of changes in the blood. While most adults metabolize small amounts of nitrates quickly, heavy exposures can lead to shortness of breath, cardiac problems, circulatory failure, and central nervous system effects ranging from dizziness and lethargy to convulsions in severe cases (Pope and Rall 1995).

Although the most common source of nitrates is drinking water, other sources include the following:

- Seepage from septic systems
- Sausages and other meat products preserved with nitrates
- Many vegetables such as fresh broccoli, collard greens, spinach, and root vegetables
- Industrial salts and industrial solvents
- Room deodorizer propellants
- Local anesthetics such as benzocaine
- Mothballs
- Sulfa drugs

Simple Solutions
To Reduce Exposure to Nitrates

- If you live in a rural area and use well water or water from a community well, get it tested at the County Health Department or at an approved laboratory. The EPA considers drinking water containing nitrates at over 10 ppm (parts per million) a risk to your health.

- If your water has significant nitrate pollution, use a safe bottled water when drinking or cooking and for mixing baby formula.
- Be conservative when using preserved meat products.
- Remember that boiling water concentrates, rather than removing, nitrates.
- Use a water filtration filter that reduces nitrate levels. Good choices are reverse osmosis systems and distillation systems.

MTBE (methyl tert-butyl ether)

In 1990, the U.S. Congress, as part of the Clean Air Act, mandated that oxygenates and additives designed to reduce air pollution be required in gasoline sold to smog-intensive areas of the United States. Now some governmental entities are issuing health advisories due to the hazardous infiltration of water supplies by the gasoline additive MTBE (methyl tert-butyl ether). MTBE, a volatile organic compound (VOC), is produced from methanol, a poisonous substance.

The intensity of people's symptoms appears to be directly related to the amount of MTBE in their blood. As reported, health effects of MTBE include respiratory problems and neurological symptoms such as insomnia, dizziness, anxiety, nausea, headache, ADD, spaciness, short-term memory problems, difficulty concentrating, and developmental effects seen in laboratory animals, such as late resorptions, dead fetuses, maternal toxicity, skeletal variations, and decreased viability (Joseph 1997).

Pregnant women and breast-feeding mothers should avoid any ingestion of or skin contact with MTBE-contaminated water. MTBE circulates through the body and directly enters into the fetal brain. For this reason, infants and toddlers must also avoid contamination.

Simple Solutions
To Limit MTBE Exposure

- Call your EPA office and find out if MTBE is being used in your area.
- Get a printout of the water analysis in your water district.
- Complain to your state and local senators and representatives by letter rather than petition (although it never hurts to sign a petition, too).

- Educate others about this problem. More information can be obtained at the following web page: http://www.oxybusters.com/mtbe_lay.htm
- Never pour gasoline on the ground or in water.
- If possible, use a brand of gasoline that states it is free of MTBE.
- Use filtered water if your water is polluted above 36 ppb.
- If your tap water is highly polluted, you may want to take sponge baths using filtered water during pregnancy and while you are breast-feeding.

Plasticizers

Plasticizers are chemicals added to plastics to permit varying degrees of flexibility. We are exposed to plasticizers through water typically when water has been stored in a plastic container, although plastic plumbing can also contribute to exposure. Like other chemicals, plasticizers can be stored in the body causing adverse health effects. To avoid plasticizer leaching into your water, you need to use only glass storage containers and to purchase bottled water and other liquids in glass. This may not always be realistic, however, since plastic liquid containers have largely replaced paper and glass. Today, even most baby bottles are made out of plastic.

If you must use plastic, a good rule to remember is that the softer, more flimsy containers will leach more chemicals such as vinyl chloride into your liquid. The harder, less flexible containers leach fewer chemicals. Also, the longer liquids are left standing in plastic, the greater the amount of vinyl chloride will wind up in the liquid. To avoid plasticizer leaching via plastic baby bottles, do not store liquids in them. Instead, fill them just before use and buy glass baby bottles when storing is a must.

Synthetic Pesticides

Synthetic pesticides, herbicides, fungicides, and fertilizers used on crops and lawns eventually make their way into our water supplies. Treatment plants do not usually filter these chemicals from potable water since their main concern is combating bacteria by adding more chemicals. Those who get their water from private wells should also be concerned about these contaminants, especially since many private wells are located in agricultural regions and statistically show higher pesticide levels.

If you are concerned that your tap water is contaminated, an analysis from your water department will show the pesticide content. We can almost assure you that there will be varying levels of pesticides, although hopefully at levels below EPA tolerances. Since it is our opinion that no amount of chemical exposure is acceptable, here are some ways you can avoid synthetic pesticides via water.

Simple Solutions For Avoiding Synthetic Pesticides in Your Water

- First, use a water filter. The merits of varying filters are explored in the section on water filters below, but always identify the problem you want to remedy before making your purchase.
- Second, if you decide that a filter is not for you, buy bottled water. If you go this route, remember to buy enough for cooking, too.

Metals

There are many harmful metals that contaminate our water supplies. Many metals accumulate in fetal brain tissue and cause neurological damage. Some of the most common metal contaminates of water are aluminum, arsenic, barium, cadmium, copper, iron, lead, mercury, nickel, selenium, silver, and zinc. Aluminum, for instance, is routinely used to help clean public water supplies. A water analysis will identify the metals in your water. Some water filters screen out metals.

Microbes

The existence of microbes such as viruses, bacteria, intestinal parasites, algae, mold, and fungi in the water supply are the main reason that public water is treated with chemicals. These organisms can be extremely dangerous and have caused innumerable deaths around the world. Even in highly developed urban areas it is not uncommon to turn on the news and discover that some water plant "goofed" and that citizens are being warned that their tap water may contain harmful bacteria. These organisms, of course, are not preferable to chemicals. However, heavy contamination because of toxic chemicals is beginning to present a comparable threat.

In many areas of the world, people combat microbes by boiling their water. This is not the most reliable weapon; sometimes, however, it is the only one available. And we know that boiling water can cause increased concentrations of many metals, lead in particular. Water must be boiled for a minimum of ten minutes to kill most harmful bacteria. If you obtain your drinking water from a private, untreated well you may need to control microbes with a water filter that eliminates microbes, or use bottled water for cooking and drinking.

Bottled Water

During the mid-eighties, the United States Senate conducted hearings on the status of water quality in the continental U.S. What they learned was that within ten years all the ground water in the country would be seriously polluted (Committee on Government Operations 1985). Meanwhile, water companies have been scrambling to meet demands for pure drinking water. As consumers, you need to know that, although much of it is filtered, as much as 25 percent of all bottled water is simply tap water drawn off another city's water supply and may contain as many contaminants as your own (Breecher and Linde 1992). However, if you know that your water has significant contamination, it may be to your advantage to use bottled tap water.

Because there are no real standards for bottled water, any water you buy can contain contaminants. Some self-regulation within the water industry does take place. The International Bottled Water Association (IBWA) makes unannounced inspections on their members to ensure that products at least meet tap water standards. If the water passes, it becomes NSF-certified (National Sanitation Foundation) and that term will appear on the bottle label. Labels on bottled water can also give you information about the cleaning process and what remains in the water.

If you find a bottled water you like, feel free to query the company regarding contaminant analysis of their product and their cleaning processes. Compare those analyses to ones you get from your city water department. There is really no other way to accurately determine product quality. The best possible purity standards for water are met when two cleaning methods are used. Carbon filtering and distillation produce the purest water. Also, bottled water should be packaged in glass, not plastic containers, since the plastic itself adds to contamination. In fact, the longer liquids remain in plastic containers, the higher the concentration of vinyl chloride (Benfenati, et al. 1991).

Remember to refrigerate bottled water after it is opened. This is important since bottled water usually hasn't been chemically treated for bacteria and, when exposed to air, it can become a bacteria breeding ground. Also beware of the bottled water machines in many supermarkets. The water in these machines is usually not treated for bacteria and putting it in your own nonsterile containers promotes bacterial growth. If bottled water is too expensive or not readily available, you might want to consider using a water filter to correct your water contamination problems.

Know Your Water

- Drinking water or bottled drinking water is usually water from a city water supply that has to meet tap water standards set by government entities.
- Distilled water has no minerals left, usually tastes flat, and can contain some volatile organic compounds.
- Purified water has been distilled or forced through reverse osmosis, and has lost minerals and retained some volatile organic compounds.
- Mineral water contains some minerals since it is undistilled.
- Natural water comes from wells or springs and still contains minerals.
- Spring water comes from naturally flowing springs and has not been modified by the addition or removal of minerals.

Water Filters

There are many types of commercial water filters with varying ranges of effectiveness and affordability that will help ensure you and your baby are drinking the cleanest water possible. Home water filters do come with risks, however, and must be installed according to the manufacturer's specifications. Many different filter brands must also be cleaned and maintained or they will become contaminated themselves. The most commonly used water filtration systems that you usually see on bottled water labels and that can be obtained commercially are listed on the next page.

Unfortunately, no system can filter all the contaminants discussed above, so it is important that you know what you are controlling for before you make your purchase. The National Sanitation

Foundation International (800-NSF-MARK), a nonprofit organization in the United States, tests water filtration systems to see if they perform according to manufacturers' claims. They can help you with the purchase of a reputable filter.

Sediment filters remove or reduce microbes, iron, dirt, sand, silt, clay, and other particulate matter. They don't eliminate minerals, nitrates, radon, salts, most metals, or high total dissolved solids. For optimum performance, install sediment filters on the main water line entering your home.

Activated carbon filters contain charcoal particles that trap unwanted chemicals. They remove chlorine, PCBs, radon, tannic acids, many VOCc (including chloroform and THMs (trihalogenated methanes), and many pesticides. A few filter out lead and nitrates. They do not, however, remove most metals, salts, high total dissolved solids, or bacteria.

One drawback to activated carbon filters is that, since they remove chlorine and not bacteria, metallic silver which can adversely affect health is usually added to the filters to prevent bacterial contamination. They also need a great deal of maintenance time since they aren't effective when the filters are saturated which can lead to additional bacterial buildup. Activated carbon filters should be installed beneath your sink or at point of use on cold water lines.

Reverse osmosis units work by sending water through a membrane that separates out pollutants. They remove metals (such as aluminum, arsenic, cadmium, chromium, copper, iron, lead, manganese, mercury, silver, zinc), minerals, dirt, sand, silt, clay, and parasite cysts. They will not remove VOCs, bacteria, chloroform, chlorine, radon, or pesticides. This filtration system has many negative aspects, one being the waste of four gallons of water for every drinkable gallon. The units can also be expensive and, like distilled water, the elimination of minerals can be a health drawback. Install these filters beneath your sink or at point of use on cold water lines.

There are also filters for faucets, shower heads, and liquid containers. Most of these filters don't really work that well and have a history of bacterial contamination.

As you can see, every filter has its strengths and weaknesses with none being good for everything. This may necessitate your using a combination of the above methods to get the cleanest water.

Eating the cleanest food and drinking the purest water available are crucial steps in protecting your baby from the effects of chemicals. Because of consumer awareness and demand, it is easier than ever to obtain organic products. But you don't want to stop there. Next you will want to take a long, hard look at the environment in which you spend most of your time, your home.

The Healthy Home

For the last decade scientists have known that the most toxic places in our lives are our homes. A study done in the late 1980s clearly showed that breathing air inside your house is much more toxic than breathing the air in traffic-clogged downtown New Jersey (Pellazzari, et al. 1985). What causes such high pollution in homes? The answer, of course, is found in the chemicals we use to construct our homes and the items we use to furnish them.

Indoor Air

Commercial products used in home building and home improvement are significant sources of indoor air pollution. This is obvious considering the variety of chemicals used in almost every facet of construction and home decorating. Paints, varnishes, stains, strippers, thinners, adhesives, wood treatments, and insulation all emit toxic VOCs (volatile organic compounds) that pollute our homes. Even pressed wood, molding, and wood veneers contain harmful chemicals. Fortunately there are numerous ways to reduce your exposure to those substances that affect the development of your baby.

Volatile Organic Compounds

The most common sources of indoor air pollution generally can be classified as *volatile organic compounds* (VOCs), chemicals that evaporate at room temperature. Volatile organic compounds become trapped inside our homes when we use certain household products and can reach levels up to 1,000 times higher than VOCs found in air outside.

Breathing contaminated air allows VOCs to enter the body. They also enter the body through skin absorption and, once there, readily cross over into brain tissue where they can cause neurological effects such as headaches, nausea, mental confusion, impaired memory, visual disorders, fatigue, and depression. In addition, many VOCs are developmental toxicants, mutagens, and carcinogens (Environmental Defense Fund 1998).

Common Volatile Organic Compounds (VOCs) in the Home

- Trichloroethane in spray cans, insulation, and spot removers
- Methylene chloride in cleaning fluids, spray cans, wood treatments, and adhesives
- Tetrachloroethylene found in dry-cleaning solutions
- Benzene in gasoline
- Formaldehyde from plywood, fabrics, and insulation
- Para-dichlorobenzene (P-DCB) from mothballs and air fresheners
- Toluene found in solvents, cleaning fluids, and wood finishing products
- Xylene found in paints and finishing products
- Acetone found in nail polish removers and other solvents
- Butanone in various household products
- Styrene in foam, carpets, and adhesives
- Carbon tetrachloride in dry-cleaning solutions and paint removers
- Chloroform in chlorinated water
- Perchloroethylene in cleaning solvents

In the following material we discuss some of the most common and most recognizable VOCs that contaminate our homes to give you some idea how harmful indoor air can be to you and your baby. This list is far from complete. Notice that the names of many of these chemicals end in *ene, one, ane, ide,* or *yde.* When you are purchasing household products, these endings should give you a clue to identifying other toxic substances. Some product labels also list these chemicals as *halogenated hydrocarbons*. While you may not be able to completely rid your home of these toxic substances, the good news is that you can certainly control them to the point that the risk to your health is reduced significantly. In the following material you will find tips for reducing VOCs in your own home.

Solvents

Note that this is an admittedly general category. Solvents are petroleum derivatives used in many chemical solutions. In home construction, they are found in products like paints, paint thinners and removers, and glues and adhesives. Unlike many of the chemicals we have previously discussed in this book, it is not always easy to find safe alternatives to many of the products listed above. You can, however, find safer products. In the appendix you will find a list of alternative product sources, and many hardware stores are beginning to carry less toxic paints.

Pregnant women or nursing mothers and small children will want to avoid any chemicals used for home construction and decoration, even if the products involved are considered safer than their conventional counterparts. For instance, many of the paints advertised as nontoxic or safe still contain multiple chemicals. Although one of the many joys of pregnancy is preparing a pleasant room for the baby, pregnant mothers should not handle or inhale paint or any other chemical used in redecorating (a whiff or so won't hurt). If you can, leave your house while work is being done on the baby's room, and be sure to close the room off, leaving the windows open for ventilation, when you return. Complete remodeling projects before your baby arrives to give the chemicals a chance to break down. Listed below are just a few of the many solvents you may encounter during home construction.

Methylene chloride is a common indoor air pollutant produced from methane gas and used in cleaning fluids, spray cans, wood treatments, adhesives, paint strippers, and aerosol propellants.

Acetone (dimethyl ketone, 2-propanone, beta-ketopropane) is used in the production of paint thinners and removers, plastic, and fibers and can also be found in tobacco smoke and vehicle exhaust. It is a suspected cardiovascular and blood toxicant, gastrointestinal and liver toxicant, kidney toxicant, neurotoxicant, respiratory toxicant, and skin/sense organ toxicant. Acetone exposure also causes birth defects, nerve damage and reproduction problems in animals (Mast et al. 1989).

Toluene is a petroleum-derived solvent used in paints, paint thinners, fingernail polish, lacquers, glues, solvents, adhesives, cleaning solutions, and rubber. It is also found in tobacco smoke. Toluene is a recognized developmental toxicant and a suspected immunotoxicant, neurotoxicant, and reproductive toxicant. High levels of toluene exposure can result in brain and speech damage and decreased mental ability. Pregnant women exposed to high levels of toluene are at risk to have babies with neurological problems, retarded growth, and developmental problems.

Formaldehyde may be the most dangerous chemical in our homes due not only to its toxicity but also to the enormous variety of products in which it is found. Probably one of the most ubiquitous problems we face in keeping our homes with lower levels of chemicals is that of formaldehyde *outgassing*. ("Outgassing" is the term used to describe the release of chemicals into the air.)

Used in glue, foam, plastics, preservatives, and bonding agents, formaldehyde can be measured in significant quantities in homes that have the following items: carpeting and carpet pads, unsealed plywood and particleboard, furniture, roofs, cabinetry, paneling, urea-formaldehyde insulation, permanently pressed clothing, and even wet-strength paper towels.

A general rule with formaldehyde outgassing is that it decreases over time. So a brand-new house with pressed wood products and carpeting will have much higher formaldehyde levels than the same house one year after its construction since formaldehyde outgassing will have decreased significantly in that time. However, just because formaldehyde levels may have decreased during that one year doesn't mean the levels are safe. In fact, formaldehyde outgassing in some products, such as carpet padding and carpet backing, can continue for years.

Significant formaldehyde exposure can increase the incidence of: bladder infections (acute and/or chronic cystitis), ear infections (especially in children), headaches, fatigue, memory loss, skin irritation, respiratory infections, flu-like symptoms, asthma, allergies, and other immune disorders. It is also a known carcinogen and neurotoxicant and a suspected developmental toxicant. There is also some concern that formaldehyde may be associated with Sudden Infant Death Syndrome (SIDS) (Breecher and Linde 1992; Harland 1993; Rapp 1996).

You can call your state health department to find out how to get formaldehyde levels tested in your home or for information on doing the testing yourself.

Simple Solutions
To Reduce Formaldehyde Outgassing

- Seal cracks around electrical outlets, baseboards, and ceilings.
- Seal (with two coats of polyurethane) or remove furniture and cabinets made from pressed wood.
- Avoid the use of urea-formaldehyde insulation.
- Increase ventilation and the use of air filters, exhaust fans, and plants if your home has significant formaldehyde levels, or if you live in a mobile home—most of which have been constructed with multiple products made with formaldehyde.
- If you must use plywood in your home, use exterior grade rather than interior grade since it emits less formaldehyde.
- When building a new home, ask your contractor to use formaldehyde-free or low formaldehyde-releasing products. Buy only solid wood or metal for furniture and cabinets.
- Control heat and humidity since those factors increase outgassing.

Lead

Most people know that ingested lead is a dangerous substance. What most people don't know, however, is how many potential lead sources we regularly come into contact with. Lead is found not only in leaded paint (mostly banned since the 1970s), but it is also in many pesticides that contaminate our food supply, cans used for food storage, some pottery and china, hobby, craft, and artist paints, and lead solder used on water pipes. Tobacco smoke also contains lead.

According to experts, *no* amount of lead is needed in the human body (Millichap 1993). Therefore, it seems strange that governments provide us with "acceptable" body lead levels. Children exposed to chronically low lead levels suffer from central nervous system damage, learning difficulties, and behavioral problems.

You must be aware that lead crosses the placenta and that this can result in spontaneous abortion and miscarriage. Lead exposure presents one of the most serious developmental hazards we face. High lead levels in a pregnant mother can retard growth hormone secretion, interfering with fetal and childhood growth, and cause chromosome anomalies, decreased sperm count, brain damage, learning problems, dyslexia, and deficiencies in fine motor skills, coordination, and reaction time (Millichap 1993).

Symptoms of lead poisoning vary and may include abdominal cramps, anemia, constipation, dizziness, headache, irritability, kidney failure, listlessness, memory lapses, nausea, and sleep problems.

Simple Solutions
To Avoid Exposure to Lead

- Avoid lead paint. Have your house tested if it was painted before lead paint was banned in the 1970s. Never try to remove the paint yourself. The inhalation of even minute paint chips should be avoided at all costs.
- Don't use pottery or cans to store food and beverages.
- Don't use china dishes for heating or microwaving food unless they have been certified lead-free.
- Beware of imported, highly decorated, glossy, multicolored ceramic dishes or mugs.
- Don't store liquor in crystal decanters.
- Get your soil tested if you live near toxic waste dumps or factories. Numerous children have sustained increased lead levels just from playing in contaminated dirt in their yards.

Carpeting

Carpeting deserves a general discussion due to common misconceptions surrounding it and its potential health effects. At one time, the prevailing opinion among experts was that carpeting was harmful because it contains formaldehyde. We know now that carpets contains *many* toxic chemicals. In fact, the chemical 4-PC is found in the backing of about 95 percent of all synthetic carpeting.

The chemical 4-PC comes from a combination of styrene and butadiene that forms the latex adhesive for carpet fibers. 4-PC gives off an unpleasant odor often associated with new carpets. For many people, breathing this substance can cause serious health problems. In 1987 the EPA installed new carpeting in its Washington offices, creating a health crisis that affected more than 100 employees. After evacuating the building several times, they finally removed the carpet (Rapp 1996).

Some of the other toxic chemicals found in carpeting include acetone, toluene, decane, hexane, benzene, phenol, and xylene.

Remember that these are solvents and can cause permanent neurological effects, among other problems. The EPA has found a total of sixty-four neurotoxic chemicals in the carpets they have tested (Rapp 1996).

Chemicals found in carpeting have been found to interfere with children's learning ability. These chemicals can cause neurological symptoms such as nausea, vomiting, dizziness, headaches, sleepiness, lethargy, and fatigue. Some carpets like Nature's Carpet in Vancouver, British Columbia and Foreign Accents in Albuquerque, New Mexico show a very low chemical content. Both products have been tested by Anderson Laboratories in West Hartford, Vermont. If you wish to install new carpet in your home, you can have a sample tested at a variety of labs. (See the appendix.)

Simple Solutions
For Chemicals in Carpets

- Tile floors are good choices if you avoid grouts and caulks that contain chemical solvents.

- Wood floors are a nice option if you avoid toxic glues.

- Vinyl composition tile tests well in chemical evaluations as does linoleum.

- All cotton and wool rugs can be used for warmth and decoration. Cement floors can be patterned with multiple designs and colors for an inexpensive and, if safe dyes are used, low toxicity floor.

- Floating floors seem to be the latest home fashion rage. These floors, however, often contain toxic glue and usually rest on synthetic foam padding that contains multiple toxic chemicals that will outgas for years. Less toxic padding is more expensive but safer.

- If you have carpet in your home and intend to keep it, make sure you have good ventilation and that you reduce chemicals in other ways.

- Sprinkling baking soda on your carpet and working it in before vacuuming can help clean the carpet and will absorb some chemicals.

Fuel Burning Heat Sources

Older homes are more likely to use fuel burning sources of energy such as gas, kerosene, propane, wood, and coal. Although they tend to be cheaper than electric energy, fuel-burning heat sources can pollute indoor air in ways that may have serious health consequences (Zhang and Smith 1996).

Benzene, for example, is a product of gas heat although it can also be found in tobacco smoke, automobile exhaust, and industrial emissions. It is a recognized carcinogen, developmental toxicant, reproductive toxicant, and a suspected endocrine toxicant, immunotoxicant, and neurotoxicant. Animals exposed to inhaled benzene during pregnancy had offspring with low birth weights, delayed bone formation, and bone marrow damage (WHO 1993).

Carbon monoxide is also a dangerous product of any fuel-burning heat source. It is a recognized developmental toxicant and a suspected neurotoxicant and reproductive toxicant. If you have gas heat of any kind and/or a fireplace, you should buy a carbon monoxide detector. It looks like a smoke detector and works similarly, and can be found at hardware stores. Install a carbon monoxide detector near sleeping areas, and consider a second detector located near the furnace to give advance warning of this odorless, colorless, and lethal by-product of combustion.

To avoid any carbon monoxide exposure, do not idle your car in your garage since carbon monoxide fumes can enter your house. Fuel-burning heat sources are not easy to avoid since converting to electric can be extremely costly. You can, however, decrease inhalation of toxic by-products.

Simple Solutions
To Decrease Exposure to Fuel-Burning Heat Sources

- Ventilate areas around fuel-burning heat sources adequately. Make sure your chimney and appliance outlets are unblocked and open. These outlets should be checked frequently.

- Install a vent-a-hood over your gas stove and oven.

- Use air cleaners and plants.

- If possible, close off any fuel-burning appliance but make sure it is ventilated. For example, enclose your gas clothes dryer in a laundry closet or room and never use slatted doors on your gas water-heater closet.

- Don't use fans around fuel-burning heat sources since they can draw chemicals away from vents and into rooms.

Synthetic Fabrics

Most people would never think that the fabrics used in their homes can contribute to indoor air pollution. They do, however, and the problem usually occurs when synthetic fabrics and fabric treatments are used. Most of the fabric-covered commercial furniture contains polyester. This is also true for most cushioning materials. Polyester contains many chemicals including formaldehyde. Just as formaldehyde outgasses in adhesives and carpets, it also outgasses in fabrics.

Avoid synthetic fabrics whenever possible. In many cases, this is easier than you think; in some cases, however, more effort may be required. For instance, many furniture stores carry natural fabrics, cushions and pillow forms, and batting. These items can also be found at fabric stores. All-natural futons are nice since many have removable covers that can be washed and changed for a new look.

 Simple Solutions
To Reduce Exposures to Chemicals
in Fabrics

It may be impractical to replace your furniture with natural alternatives, especially when faced with the expense of a new baby. You can, however, reduce chemical exposure via synthetic fabrics in the following ways:

- Use air cleaners and plants in rooms that contain many synthetic fabrics.
- Keep your home well-ventilated.
- Replace bedding with natural fabrics. This is a must because so much of the time spent at home is spent in the bedroom.
- Cover furniture with natural fabric slipcovers to help reduce air emissions.

Stain Repellants

Another problem with many fabrics used for furniture, bedding, and draperies is that they are often chemically coated to repel water, fire, and stains. You will want to avoid chemical repellents as much as possible. Before buying new furniture, be sure to ask the salesperson if a repellent has been used. If you are concerned about stains, use alternative methods like having everyone take off their shoes before coming inside and don't allow children to eat or drink near stainable furniture. Keeping furniture covered with washable slipcovers also helps.

Dry Cleaning

Dry cleaning items such as rugs, draperies, and bedspreads contributes to indoor air pollution since chemical solvents are used in dry-cleaning solutions. One solvent, tetrachloroethylene, is a recognized carcinogen and a suspected developmental toxicant and reproductive toxicant. Many dry-cleaning solvents are neurotoxic.

A toddler was recently found dead after sleeping in a closed room where freshly dry-cleaned drapes had been hung (Garnier, et al. 1996). That gives you an idea of how toxic cleaning products can be to a baby's brain. Any dry-cleaned item should be allowed to outgass (free of plastic coverings) outdoors for 12 to 24 hours before wearing it or bringing it inside. Although this may be inconvenient, doing so will help avoid any negative health effects for you and your developing baby.

Plastics

Modern homes are full of plastics. Plastics contain chemicals called *plasticizers*, many of which are derived from petrochemicals. As with other chemicals of this nature, plasticizers outgas and pollute indoor air. Many plasticizers are known endocrine disruptors (Colborn, Dumanoski, and Myers 1996).

In many homes, major plastic sources are the toys and other products children use because plastic is inexpensive and durable. Therefore, many children have toy boxes, table and chair sets, toddler beds, desks, play tents and houses, push toys, walkers, high chairs, infant swings, tricycles, playpens, and innumerable other toys and furniture items made out of plastic. This can make for a lot of chemical outgassing, much of it in the room in which the child sleeps.

Avoiding exposure to harmful plasticizers can be as simple as getting rid of what you have and refusing to buy more. Unfortunately, plastic is so pervasive in our society, avoiding it in every instance is probably unrealistic.

Simple Solutions
To Decrease Exposure to Plastic

- A general rule with plastic is that if it smells, you will inhale it. You should begin to notice that the flimsier a plastic is, the more it smells due to the use of more chemicals.

- Try to keep large plastic toys such as play houses and bikes outside. Remove plastic toy boxes and table and chair sets from your child's sleeping area.

- Use air cleaners and plants to help remove harmful airborne chemicals.

- If you use a microwave oven, use glass containers rather than plastic. Coffee pots should also be made of glass.

Radon

Radon, which is an odorless gas and the product of uranium decay, seeps into homes (estimated at 8–10 million in the United States) from underlying bedrock. The second most prevalent cause of lung cancer, heavy radon exposure is tantamount to having hundreds of X rays in a single year. Approximately one out of every 100 people exposed to significant radon levels, i.e., 2 pCi/L (picocuries per liter of air) will develop lung cancer. Infants and children, because of their immature immune systems, and smokers, because of the synergistic effects of cigarette smoke and radon, are particularly susceptible.

Radon can be a problem in your home no matter where it's located. That is, your home may be affected while your next-door neighbor's will be radon-free. So everyone should test their homes for radon levels.

Testing for radon first involves screening with a radon detection device that is available at local hardware stores or directly by phone from manufacturing companies. Ordering by phone ensures that the detector has not been sitting on a shelf for an extended period. The most effective detectors (charcoal-absorption detectors and diffusion barrier charcoal-absorption detectors) should be used according to the instructions included with the instrument. The device is then submitted to a laboratory that sends results back within two weeks. The EPA recommends taking action if the measurements show as much as 4pCi/L in your home. However, note that prolonged exposure to low levels can have the same effect as abbreviated exposure to high levels.

To read more about radon, several booklets on the subject are available from the Environmental Protection Agency, the Centers for Disease Control, and the U.S. Department of Health and Human Services.

Simple Solutions
To Reduce Radon Levels

- Increase ventilation in your home (a temporary measure).
- Reduce the time spent in areas of your home with high radon concentrations, such as the basement or ground floor.
- If you have a crawl space under the house, keep it vented all-year round.
- Stop smoking and ask others not to smoke in your home.
- Whenever possible, open windows and turn on fans to increase ventilation.

To Permanently Prevent Radon from Entering Your Home

- Install a radon gas suction system.
- Increase air pressure within the home.
- Seal off radon entry routes.

Electromagnetic (EMR) and Microwave Radiation

We are constantly bombarded with electromagnetic (EMR) emissions from sources like cell phones, radars, radio and TV transmitters, telephone relay towers, computer screens, and automatic garage door openers. The possible health effects from EMR exposure has caused much debate among researchers, governments, and health regulatory agencies.

Studies have shown that people who work around high levels of electromagnetic radiation tend to get more breast cancer, whether they are male or female, and tend to have a higher risk of brain cancer (Szmigielski 1996). Children and adults who develop leukemia are more likely to live near high voltage electric lines that emit EMR (Wertheimer and Leeper 1979; 1982). Some experts, however, contend that much of this research is flawed, that some studies use abnormally high levels of EMR, and that the studies have not been replicated. In short, not enough research has been done to date. Since it is highly unlikely that EMR has *no* effect on us, reducing exposure makes sense, especially for the developing baby.

Simple Solutions To Reduce EMR and Microwave Exposure

- Stand at least three feet away from an operating microwave or electric oven, air conditioner, television, audio system, or laser printer.
- Keep as far away as you can from operating computers. This includes the back of others' computers that may be next to your work area.
- Use your cell phone only when a regular phone is not available.
- Wear an ear-piece microphone or hands-free car kit when using your mobile phone.
- Try to use your standard mobile phone outside your car since this requires lower transmission levels.
- Avoid wearing your phone and use a phone shield.
- Don't leave a cell phone close to your bed at night. Maintain a distance of at least three feet.
- Use an electric blanket only to warm your bed. Turn it off before retiring.
- Don't place refrigerators and other appliances against a wall where a bed is on the other side.
- If you can, avoid living near or letting your children play near high voltage electric lines.

Household Cleaners

Household cleaners are significant sources of indoor air pollution. There are hundreds of products available to clean anything from toilets to windows to floors, many of which contain harmful chemicals. There is a good reason why the labels on most chemical cleaning agents warn us to use the products in well-ventilated areas. A few common and recognizable substances used to clean and beautify our houses are discussed below.

Ammonia

Ammonia, a chemical used by itself or added to many antibacterial cleaning agents, is a known carcinogen and a suspected neurotoxicant.

Chlorine

Added to our water supplies to kill bacteria and used as a cleaning agent for the same reason, chlorine is a suspected neurotoxicant and releases chloroform into the air. For these reasons, infants and pregnant women or nursing mothers should stay away from running dishwashers. You can purchase chlorine-free dishwasher detergent but since chlorine is in the water your dishwasher uses, chlorine inhalation is still possible.

Petroleum

Many dish soaps, laundry detergents, and floor waxes contain petrochemicals, synthetic dyes and fragrances, and even formaldehyde, all of which leave behind harmful residues on clothing, dishes, and other surfaces. As mentioned several times previously, most petroleum-derived chemicals are either known or suspected carcinogens and developmental and neurological toxicants.

Boron (boric acid, boron oxide, salts of boron, borax)

Boron is actually a natural substance used in many soaps and cleaners. In many cases it has been considered a safe alternative to conventional chemical cleaners. In fact, boron is a suspected endocrine toxicant, neurotoxicant, cardiovascular and blood toxicant, and gastrointestinal and liver toxicant. Animal studies reveal that when boron is ingested, it can result in birth defects and low sperm count (Environmental Defense Fund 1998). As a result, boron can by no means be considered safe, and although using it for cleaning does not mean you ingest it, the substance will end up in waterways and in the environment. If you are using a conservative approach, sodium bicarbonate is probably a much better choice.

Sodium Bicarbonate

Sodium bicarbonate or baking soda is another natural cleaning agent that is considered safe. When ingested in large quantities, however, sodium bicarbonate is a suspected intestinal and liver toxicant, kidney toxicant, and respiratory toxicant. Up to this point there is no indication that baking soda affects the developing fetus. And, like boron, it is unlikely that significant ingestion will occur when baking soda is used as a cleaning agent. For that reason, baking soda can be an effective alternative to a variety of chemical cleaning agents and deodorizers.

Water

In this age of fast and easy-to-use chemical cleaners, water, which is actually a great cleaning agent, tends to be overlooked. One TV news magazine show recently conducted a test to determine if chemical cleaners were more effective than water. People who unknowingly used water to clean windows and surfaces could not distinguish its effectiveness from that of a chemical agent. Furthermore, most tap water already contains chlorine that will get rid of bacteria. Admittedly, using water as a household cleaner may require more time and more scrubbing. However, the health risks you will avoid by using water (not to mention the money you will save) will be well worth the extra elbow grease.

Vinegar

Most people never consider vinegar as a cleaning agent. A natural substance, it is actually very efficient since it can be used safely on everything from clothing to windows to floors to dissolve dirt and kill bacteria. We keep vinegar-filled spray bottles on hand to clean bathroom and kitchen surfaces, walls and doors, and spots on our rugs.

 Simple Solutions For Safe and Natural Household Cleaners

There are some natural cleaners you can use instead of harmful chemical solutions to clean and beautify your home. We obtained these alternatives from experience and from varying sources. The most helpful source was *The Safe Shopper's Bible* (Steinman and Epstein 1995), which also contains the names of safer chemical cleaning products for those of you who don't feel comfortable giving up chemicals for some cleaning jobs.

- **Baking soda** works as a deodorizer, scrubbing agent, spot remover (as a paste and with a scrub brush), oven cleaner (as a paste), laundry detergent and fabric softener (we use one cup per load), carpet cleaner (sprinkled on carpet overnight before vacuuming), anti-bacterial, and anti-fungal cleaning agent.
- **Vinegar** can be used as an all-purpose surface cleaner and spot remover on windows and mirrors. (Dilute one cup vinegar in one gallon of water.) It can also be used as an oven cleaner, laundry detergent, softener, anti-static, anti-bacterial, anti-fungal, and deodorant. (It can be used straight or combine one cup vinegar with one cup of water.)
- **Olive oil** makes good furniture polish and furniture finish for natural wood. (Use one teaspoon olive oil with one cup of vinegar.). To freshen the smell, add one teaspoon of lemon juice.
- **Lemon juice** is a mild bleaching agent, wood floor cleaner (one cup lemon juice to two gallons warm water), toilet bowl cleaner (one cup lemon juice left in bowl several hours before scrubbing), immediate stain remover (rub lightly), and deodorant (place lemon peels in bowl).
- **Cornstarch** is a good scrubbing agent and linoleum floor cleaner (six tablespoons cornstarch to one cup water).
- **Water** gives you an all-purpose cleaner that is especially effective on glass and mirrors and as a furniture polish (use a damp rag).
- **Club soda** does a good job as a spot remover.
- **Sunlight** is an anti-bacterial, anti-fungal bleaching agent.
- **Hydrogen peroxide** is also an anti-bacterial, anti-fungal bleaching agent.

Using Plants to Control Chemicals

One great way to clean the air in your home is to place a few house plants in every room. A NASA scientist found that common household plants can cleanse indoor air of chemicals such as formaldehyde, trichloroethylene, and the benzene released from gas cooking and heating (Wolverton 1997).

Plants synthesize and break down toxic chemicals from both air and water. Their ability to absorb and metabolize a particular chemical increases after continued exposure, so plants actually learn to be more effective at their job. Because most indoor plants like as much indirect sunlight as possible, increasing light levels helps plants work better at cleaning the air inside your home.

Plants and Air Quality

Plants do more than just absorb chemicals. In fact, plants control air quality in the following ways:

- Plants freshen air by absorbing carbon dioxide and releasing oxygen.
- Microorganisms in the soil around the plants also absorb pollutants.
- Plants conserve negative ions, which increase feelings of well-being.
- Plants help to remove odors and some release natural fragrances.
- Plants control the humidity in a room by releasing water vapor.

To help diminish the effects of chemicals in your home, use one 10- to 12-inch potted plant for every 100 square feet of space. For a 10 by 12–foot room that would mean a single plant; for a larger area, such as a 15 by 20–foot living area, three plants would be required. In rooms that you suspect might have more pollutants, such as a kitchen with a gas stove, add even more plants.

Remember to use caution when buying indoor plants. Some plants are highly poisonous when ingested by small children and/or animals. Check with your garden center or library to identify dangerous plants before bringing them home.

Toxin-Eating Plants

Although most plants help to reduce pollution in one way or another, there are some common plants that are known to purify air quite efficiently. (The chemicals in parentheses indicate the substances that are affected.) Notice that these chemicals are the volatile organic chemicals (VOCs) discussed in chapter 4 (Rapp 1996; Harland 1993).

- Spider or airplane plants (formaldehyde, carbon dioxide)
- English, golden, and green pothos ivy (benzene, formaldehyde, trichloroethylene)
- Peace-lily (benzene, trichloroethylene)

- Philodendron (carbon dioxide, formaldehyde)
- Bamboo palm (formaldehyde)
- Mother-in-law's tongue (formaldehyde)
- Gerbera daisy (benzene, formaldehyde, trichloroethylene)
- Ficus tree (benzene, formaldehyde)
- Chrysanthemum (benzene, formaldehyde, trichloroethylene)
- Mass cane (formaldehyde)
- Warneck's dracaena (benzene, formaldehyde, trichloroethylene)
- Fig trees (formaldehyde)
- Aloe vera
- Snake plant
- Goosefoot plant
- Ivy arum
- Dwarf banana
- Chinese evergreens
- Peperomia genus

Some women spend most of their day in the home. They work in their homes as homemakers, artists, craftspersons, and run their own businesses, or they are raising small children and prefer to stay home rather than putting their children in day care. These women have considerable control over their environments and can make significant changes in their homes to accommodate a healthy pregnancy. Other women must spend a good deal of time making their living in an environment over which they have much less control, the workplace. The next chapter addresses the issues of health and toxicity in the workplace.

The Healthy
Workplace

"Katie," said the single mother of her pretty brown-eyed child, "never stops talking except to sleep or put food in her mouth." At five years old, Katie seemed unusually hyperactive and confrontational. Her mother had requested professional evaluation. Katie rated moderately high on evaluations for hyperactivity, Attention Deficit Disorder (ADD), and confrontational behavior. We were able to make suggestions regarding behavioral and environmental changes to help her develop some controls for her behavior problems.

Katie's young mother had worked in a dry-cleaning establishment during most of her otherwise normal pregnancy. "I had no choice but to work there. There was no one else to pay the bills, but I was worried about the chemicals the whole time. Sometimes they made me feel sick and dizzy."

At the facility where she had worked, the dry cleaning was handled on site and she had worked close to the area where the clothing to be cleaned was saturated in a solution made of solvents. Perchloroethylene and tetrachloroethylene, solvents used in dry-cleaning facilities, have been linked with developmental, neurological, and motor defects in animals. Since Katie's mother intended to have more children, she needed to learn about job safeguards and options for her next pregnancy.

Because a woman's employment and reproductive ages overlap to a major degree, over one million children are born each year to pregnant working women. The percentage of women in the U.S. alone who are sixteen or older and working has increased from 38.1

percent in 1970 to 46.4 percent of the working population in 1993. Naturally, the highest birth rates for women occur between the ages of fifteen and forty-four years.

If you work a forty-hour week throughout your pregnancy, by the time your baby arrives you will have spent approximately one-quarter of your pregnancy in the workplace. That makes your workplace environment a crucial factor in your baby's healthy development. If you work in an environment that involves a significant level of chemical exposure and/or is physically or emotionally stressful, you need to know how to balance those work risks for your baby's well-being.

Work-Related Developmental Disorders

Only about 5 percent of the chemical agents used in industry have been assessed in terms of their reproductive effects. Most studies look for obvious birth defects such as cleft lip and spina bifida rather than evaluating the more subtle developmental effects such as learning disabilities, ADD, and behavioral problems. Most of the available research on the developing baby, rather than testing for chemical effects, compares toxic levels of physical and emotional job stress to pregnancy outcomes. In fact, the chemical exposure standards that have been set by governmental agencies usually are not based on reproductive outcomes but on the appearance in adults of symptoms such as neurological dysfunction, cancer, or dermatitis.

Many studies conducted in the workplace often lack clear results because few industries restrict themselves to the use of a single chemical. Therefore, assessing a causative factor can be very difficult. However, as you read in chapter 1, *combinations* of several chemicals are ultimately much more toxic than a single substance.

Most work-related developmental disorders go unreported and may not even be recognized as job-related. There are several reasons for this. First, most developmental disorders remain undetectable at birth and rarely become evident until a child is around three to six years of age. At that time, social demands reveal the child's ability to perform school tasks, learn certain materials at an expected rate, and exert control over her/his behavior.

Second, by the time a problem is noticed, the mother may have changed jobs, be working part-time to better meet the demands of parenthood, or quit her job to stay home with her baby. For those reasons it is often difficult for industries to monitor the effects of their chemical use in producing developmental disorders. Therefore, any statistics gathered regarding work-related disorders will automatically downplay developmental effects to a major degree. In fact, skin disorders are the most likely problem to be connected to chemical exposures since they are the easiest to recognize and trace. Job-related skin disorders rate high on the list of chemical effects while developmental effects often go barely noted (Rosenstock and Cullen 1994; LaDou 1997; Levy and Wegman 1995).

Additionally, an employee may be disinclined to formally investigate the workplace simply because of potential repercussions that might make her unable to afford the medical and psychological care that her child needs (i.e., she might get fired for wanting to investigate).

Or she may not make the connection between job factors and her child's disorder because she believes that if a true danger existed, her employer, physician, or a governmental agency would warn her. If she did suspect a relationship between her child's behavior and her prenatal chemical exposure, it would be difficult to prove given the long period between the exposure and the emergence of the problem. She might feel, justifiably, that no one would take her seriously. However, we recently heard about one woman who was holding her employer responsible for her child's developmental defects. During her pregnancy, she had worked with a chemical used to produce computer parts, and she suspected a connection when her child showed neurological impairment at an early age.

The issue of toxic stress and chemical exposure during pregnancy and subsequent developmental disorders is now a global problem. Data on developmental effects from lead, mercury, and X rays has lead to controls for those factors in the more highly developed industrialized countries. However, many of the less developed industrialized nations do not maintain any controls and, statistically, can expect an even higher incidence of developmental defects in their children.

Job Factors That Increase Risk for the Developing Baby

In many countries an increasing number of women are now employed in jobs that were traditionally held by males. Many of these occupations include potentially dangerous reproductive hazards that were not an issue before women entered the workforce. This means that women often do not receive appropriate health information

and/or cautions specific to their gender and the possibility of pregnancy. It can also be a problem when equipment is made only for
men and is not available in women's sizes. Since most personal protective equipment is manufactured in sizes for men, women must
often purchase the smallest sizes of men's gloves, respirators, and
helmets, which consequently do not fit as well as they should (Quinn,
Woskie, and Rosenburg 1995).

 ## Simple Solutions
To Reduce Chemical Exposure
On the Job

Mothers-to-be who wish to protect their developing babies can
take on the responsibility by following five simple steps.

- First, evaluate your job-related chemical risk by identifying
  any hazardous agents to which you may be exposed. Just because your employer says a material is not hazardous doesn't
  mean you should take his or her word for it. Most likely,
  your employer does not know how the chemicals used will
  affect a developing child.

- Second, do some research on any chemical you have come in
  contact with and always be overly cautious. In the appendix,
  you will find Internet resources for toxic materials so you can
  assess whether there have been any reproductive or neuropsychological hazards associated with a particular substance.

- Third, remember, a substance that produces any type of birth
  defect, spontaneous abortion, preterm delivery, or any kind
  of reproductive problems in animals is also suspect for producing developmental disorders during the last two trimesters of pregnancy. And just because you can't find it listed in
  toxic materials resources doesn't mean it is safe. Again, 95
  percent of the chemicals we use regularly haven't even been
  tested for developmental effects. At present, only a few chemical agents have governmental work standards based on reproductive effects, including dibromochloropropane (DPCP), a
  pesticide, lead, ethylene oxide, an etherlike gas, and ionizing
  radiation produced by X rays, radon, and gamma rays.

- Fourth, most chemical agents found in occupational situations are not even covered by standards. In short, although
  we feel there is already enough hard data to draw conclu-
  sions about the potential dangers of many toxic materials,
  governments must have even more data to battle business in-

terests and place heavy restrictions on industry. That puts the responsibility for your baby's well being on *your* ability to find out about the chemicals you use at work.

Remember that chemical effects on your pregnancy most likely depend on the amount, timing, and length of exposure. Any efforts you can make to reduce your exposure will likely benefit you and your child. Which brings us to the last step you need to take in safeguarding your pregnancy:

- Fifth, take control and do whatever you need to do to restrict your exposure to chemicals on the job.

Neurotoxins on the Job

More than one-hundred chemicals and metals are known to cause central nervous system (CNS) depression and many of these neurotoxins can produce dysfunction in the peripheral nerves (outside the brain) as well. Many other chemicals can produce symptoms of psychosis.

Neurotoxic Occupational Substances

The following substances have neurological effects including neuropathy, tremor, sensory impairment, seizure, muscular impairment, paralysis, emotional or psychotic symptoms, or memory problems.

Seeing neurological effects in adults suggests that a chemical crosses the blood-brain barrier to the sensitive nerve tissue or that it may indirectly lead to neurological effects by depriving the CNS tissue of oxygen or other nutrients.

Since we know most chemicals cross over from the mother to the fetus, pregnant or breast-feeding mothers should avoid exposure to these neurotoxins, as should infants.

Alcohols	Ethylene oxide	PBBs
Carbamate pesticides	Metals	PCBs
Carbon disulfide	Some acrylics	Pyrethrins
Carbon monoxide	Organic metals	Solvents
Dioxins	Organophosphate pesticides	Organochlorine insecticides

Levy and Wegman (1995); Rosenstock and Cullen (1994); LaDou (1997)

You are always safer avoiding chemicals during your pregnancy and following an organic and environmentally safe approach to your workplace situation, just as you would in your own home.

Petrochemicals and Solvents on the Job

Solvents, commonly used as dissolving, thinning, or cleaning agents, are probably the most common substances used in the workplace. Although not all solvents have an odor, you can suspect the presence of a solvent anytime you smell a "gassy" fume because solvents evaporate and become a gas upon exposure to air. You are more likely to experience exposure to solvent *mixtures* than to a single solvent since these chemicals are often used in combination for greater effectiveness. Long-term exposure to many solvents can affect a developing fetus, and cause permanent neurobehavioral damage in the baby and the adult. For instance, methyl ethyl ketone, a common cleaning solvent, attacks the fetal brain and damages the cerebral cortex, consequences that can interfere with intelligence, reasoning, and judgment.

Neurasthenic symptoms, such as fatigue, depression, and anxiety, often occur in workers who have had chronic exposure to solvents. Adults heavily exposed to trichloroethylene vapor, a cleaning solvent, have suffered impaired psychomotor performance, loss of facial sensation, and facial weakness requiring up to two years for recovery. Acute exposure to mixed solvents causes impaired psychological function, inability to concentrate, dizziness, and poor balance. Many of these symptoms persist even after the chemical has been removed, suggesting long-term changes in nerve tissue. Experts suspect long-term damage may be caused by degeneration of nerves outside the spinal cord and a resulting impairment in the ability of the nerve to transmit information.

Solvents also cross into breast milk and expose the nursing infant at a time when brain cells are developing their outer sheaths. Some solvents are known to be destructive to this sheath, called *myelin*. In addition, many solvents are known or suspected to be endocrine disruptors, which can interrupt the sexual development of the growing fetus. Solvent use poses a threat to fetal competence and should be avoided by any pregnant or breast-feeding women.

When you are on your job, avoid areas where gaseous odors exist or reduce your exposure to the lowest possible level. Remember, solvents and petroleum-based products enter the body through the inhalation of fumes and through the oil glands in the skin. If the use of these chemicals can't be avoided, then be sure to use protective equipment such as solvent-resistant gloves, and arm and face protection along with a respiratory apparatus. When solvents accidentally contact your skin, be sure to wash immediately with soap and water.

Remember, *solvent mixtures* are frequently used in industry and can be much more toxic than isolated solvents. Most solvents and solvent mixtures will have one of the substances listed in the table below as a part of their name: for instance, trichlorotrifluoro<u>ethane</u> or iso-propyl<u>benzene</u>. Also notice that many of these names end in *ene, ane, one, ide, ine,* or *ol*.

Some Common Solvents

• Acetate	• Kerosene
• Acetone	• Ketone
• Alcohol	• Methane
• Benzene	• Methanol
• Butane	• Methyl chloride
• Chloroform	• Methylene
• Cumene	• Mineral spirits
• Durene	• Naphtha
• Ethanes	• Nitrites
• Ethers	• Phenols
• Ethyl chloride	• Propane
• Ethylene	• Styrene
• Freons	• TCE
• Gasoline	• Toluene
• Hexane	• Xylene
• Isopropanol	• Carbon tetrachloride

Levy and Wegman (1995); Rosenstock and Cullen (1994); LaDou (1997)

Pesticides and Fertilizers

Although many workplaces are principally concerned with the production and/or use of chemical pesticides, almost all industries, office buildings, and even restaurants use chemicals to kill insects. During your pregnancy you will want to avoid all chemical insecticides, herbicides, and fungicides. As you will learn in chapter 7, many insecticides currently in use were derived from nerve gases developed in World War II and can wreak hormonal havoc on you

and, especially, on your baby. Organic insecticide substitutes work better than chemicals, have a lasting effect, keep our water supply clean, and allow beneficial insects to thrive and protect plant life. Chemical pesticides and organic substitutes are listed in chapter 7.

Lead, Mercury, and Other Heavy Metals

Years of research have related lead, a well-recognized reproductive offender, to developmental damage. Longitudinal studies reveal that developing infants exposed to low levels of lead (10 to 20 micron/dL) show neurobehavioral deficits in early life. Many other metals cause developmental problems as well. In fact, with extended or frequent exposure, metals tend to accumulate in the brain tissue of mother and fetus (Hartman 1995).

If you work around lead, your employer should be monitoring its levels in the air and your physician or plant hospital should be monitoring its presence in your blood. Pregnant women have cause to be concerned if they work with lead, cadmium, mercury, and other metals and, if at all possible, should remove themselves from exposure. If they absolutely cannot be moved to another job, they should use respiratory equipment if inhalation is a possibility and any other protective equipment available.

Occupational Metals with Neurotoxic or Developmental Effects

Some metals in trace amounts are necessary in the human diet. However, significant exposure can be toxic and some have known or suspected developmental effects. Lead, mercury, cadmium, and arsenic are the best documented as developmental toxins (Hartman 1995).

Lead	Bismuth	Silicon
Mercury	Copper	Tellurium
Cadmium	Gold (organic)	Thallium
Aluminum	Manganese	Tin and organotins
Antimony	Nickel	Vanadium
Arsenic	Platinum	Barium
Selenium	Boron	

Organic metal compounds, like methylated mercury which is mercury combined with an organic material, are much more likely to cause developmental defects than the inorganic metals, like inorganic mercury. Also combining metals leads to a more toxic exposure due to synergistic effects. For instance, exposure to aluminum and lead in combination can affect children's visual motor abilities.

Antineoplastic Agents (Anticancer Drugs)

Chemotherapeutic drugs have been positively associated with nervous system impairment in children whose mothers used the drugs during pregnancy. If you are handling any cytotoxic (deadly to cells) drug, use great care; employ gloves, protective clothing, and laminar hoods to prepare the drugs; and use proper waste disposal techniques. If you can, ask another employee to perform this duty. Some experts recommend air level and biological monitoring. Urine and blood level tests may help the nurses and pharmacists who work with these drugs to assess their exposure.

Ethylene oxide (ether). Ethylene oxide is an ether-like gas used to sterilize medical instruments and in many manufacturing and chemical processes. It is one of the twenty-five most common chemicals produced in the United States. Ethylene oxide has been associated with spontaneous abortion and is one of the few substances that OSHA regulates and controls (Paul 1995).

Caution!

Pregnant and breast-feeding mothers may be well advised to work in areas away from the following substances:

Anticancer drugs	Solvents
Heavy metals	Ethylene oxide
Anesthetic gases	PCBs
PBBs	Pesticides
Radiation	

Always reduce your exposure to ethylene oxide to the lowest possible level. Self-contained breathing apparatus or airline respirators are the only devices that are effective with ethylene oxide. Medical surveillance procedures should include measurement of white blood cell count, hematocrit, hemoglobin counts, and neutraphil percentages. (Neutraphil percentages refers to the percentage of bacteria eating white blood cells in the blood.) If possible, work in another area away from ethylene oxide emissions.

Anesthetic Gases

Both men and women have exhibited reproductive effects from breathing waste anesthetic gases. Anesthetic gases also have been related to growth retardation in developing babies. Female operating room and recovery room personnel should transfer to other work areas at least one month before attempting to conceive due to the risks of both spontaneous abortion and learning disabilities associated with these chemicals. Males working in these hospital areas should understand that these gases can damage their sperm and put their offspring at risk. Of course, breast-feeding mothers will want to continue avoiding these areas.

If you work around anesthetic gas before you are pregnant, your employer should have installed air monitoring devices in the areas where the gases are used. Your employer should know and conform to the standards for control of nitrous oxide, halothane, ethane, and so forth. Surgery sites have low but significant levels of these gases.

Polychlorinated Biphenyls (PCBs)

PCBs, found in electrical equipment and transformers, increase the odds of a fetus having developmental defects, such as central nervous system impairment, growth retardation, and birth defects. Always reduce your exposure to PCBs to the lowest level possible whether you are pregnant or not. PCBs are stored readily in fat tissue and can stay with you for a long time.

PCB-resistant clothing, protective gloves, and approved respirators are available and advisable. Baseline skin examinations and liver function tests should be performed on workers prior to exposure so that later tests can be accurately compared with recent exposures. If you have been exposed to PCBs during your pregnancy, your physician should monitor your serum levels and/or fat PCB levels. The safest route, of course, is to work in an area away from any possible exposure before and during pregnancy, and during breast-feeding.

Occupational Agents with Teratogenic Effects and Occupational Locations

Anesthetic gases — Medical, hospital, laboratory, veterinary clinics

Anti-cancer drugs — Medical, drug companies, laboratories

Arsenic — Agriculture, smelting, pesticide manufacture, electroplating, microelectronic, pharmaceutical

Cadmium — Pigments, metal alloy, electroplating

Carbamate pesticides — Pest control, agriculture

Carbon disulfide — Agriculture, manufacture of rayon, cellophane, rubber

Carbon monoxide — Combustion of carbon-based materials; autos, firefighters, toll booth operators, furnace operators

Organochlorine Pesticides — Found in agriculture all over the world (including many areas where illegal), imported merchandise and foods

Dioxins — Chemical plants, transformers

Ethylene oxide/ glycol ethers — Explosives, munitions, pharmaceuticals, sterilization

Ionizing radiation — Aircraft, nuclear submarines, atomic energy reactors, petroleum/oil industry, assaying, medical, dental, radiology, fluoroscopy, gamma rays, scientific labs, television repair, mining; manufacture of cathode ray tubes, electron microscopes, gas mantles, vacuum tubes, fire alarms, liquid level gauges, luminous paints

Lead — Mining, lead battery manufacture, painters, welders, steel, munitions, glass manufacture, artists, potters, printing, electronics, trucking and transportation, auto body repair

Mercury — Furnaces, flues, retorts, metal recovery, dental, laboratory, fungicides, agriculture, electroplating, textiles, scientific instruments

PCBs	Electrical transformers and equipment
Organophosphate pesticides	Agriculture, worksites sprayed for insects, pesticide manufacturing
RF frequencies (high levels)	Medical, microwave equipment, law enforcement, air traffic control, telecommunications, RF heater and sealers
Solvents	Steel, textile, petroleum, painters, dry cleaning, artists, agriculture, electronics, lab workers, pathologists, rubber and plastics industry, steel industry, printers, semiconductors, shoe and book manufacturing, fuels for auto and aviation
Toluene	Printers, painters, artists, solvent mixtures in industry

Levy and Wegman (1995); Rosenstock and Cullen (1994); LaDou (1997)

Radiation Effects

Ionizing radiation. Ionizing radiation, the most widely recognized teratogen, gained notoriety when mental retardation and reduced intelligence functioning occurred in high percentages among Japanese children exposed to atomic radiation between the eighth and fifteenth week of fetal development. During critical stages even tiny amounts of radiation can cause malformations in animals.

In most cases, your employer will be required to notify you if you face potential exposure to radiation in your work. You should always monitor any ionizing radiation exposure especially if you are of reproductive age and could possibly be pregnant. The current limits are advised to be less than 0.5 sivert (50 rems) total for an entire pregnancy, and devices for measuring individual exposure usually are provided for technicians.

However, since these figures are not based on adequate postnatal developmental data, we suggest that you avoid or severely limit exposure to the lowest possible level. In any exposure situation, always use protective shielding and increase your distance from the source as much as possible because radiation fades with distance. When medical X rays of pregnant women are required, lead shields should be provided for the abdominal area. In many countries, medical facilities are required to provide lead-shielded walls for X ray technicians.

Video display terminals. Due to the increase in computer use in the last decade, video display terminals (VDT) have become increasingly necessary for the conduct of business in almost every industry. VDTs provide a primary source of exposure to extremely low frequency (ELF) magnetic fields, and women of reproductive age are heavily represented as VDT users. Clusters of birth defects and pregnancy losses in association with VDT use have caused some concern (Shaw and Croen 1993). As a result, animal studies are currently being conducted to determine whether this type of radiation affects fetal development. Although the evidence for negative effects remains vague at present, from the current pool of animal studies, we must conclude that a possible hazard for developmental problems exists with VDT exposure. As with other potential teratogens, the study of outcomes tends to focus on spontaneous abortions and obvious birth defects rather than on more subtle developmental disorders and so we urge caution.

Simple Solutions
For Video Display Terminal (VDT)
Hazards

Low-cost and simple solutions for VDT hazards are available.

- If you operate a VDT for several hours a day, you should place yourself at a minimum of an arm's length distance from the terminal. This can be achieved with desks that offer pull-out keyboards.

- If you work in a room where computer desks are in rows, you will want to maintain an even greater distance from the backs and sides of other terminals, given the greater level of ELF emissions from those parts of a VDT. Experts also warn that protective equipment probably does not reduce an ELF field but may just alter it.

The *ergonomic* aspect of VDT operation is another concern. Many health professionals agree that long hours in front of a computer can be a considerable source of psychological and musculoskeletal stress.

- If you are working with computers for most of the day, you should limit your time in front of the VDT by taking more frequent work breaks, alternating computer work with other duties, and paying attention to your fatigue level.

- Avoid sitting in a darkened area or cubicle where the major source of light is the VDT. Use good lighting to reduce the contrast between the VDT and the background area.

• Take a ten-minute break every hour.

Radio frequency waves (RF). RF exposures are different from ELF exposures because at high levels they produce heat which increases your body temperature. The effect is as if your baby is having a high temperature in utero. Microwaves are a type of radio frequency wave.

Thermal RF exposures are known to cause changes in metabolism, cell growth, cell division, and immune response. If the exposure to microwaves is enough to increase body temperature, the results can be physical burns, hypertension, and neuropsychological symptoms (Ducatmen and Haes 1994).

Animal studies show that nonthermal RF effects cause changes in bone marrow and temporarily modify the blood-brain barrier. Eastern European literature attests to the ability of microwaves to cause changes in the electroencephalograms of exposed individuals (Ducatmen and Haes 1994; International Labour Office 1986).

Female police officers using radar devices can receive up to 20,000 times the typical background RF exposures. Although this is still considered to be within current regulatory standards, it should be a matter of concern for the pregnant officer since no research has been conducted to measure safety for a developing baby at this level of exposure. Anywhere high intensity RF is used, the source should be shielded so that workers, especially pregnant women, will be protected. Some researchers recommend that men working with high intensity RF may wish to use protective equipment to shield their eyes and testicles (Rosenstock and Cullen, 1994).

Biological Agents

Since women may experience increased risk of exposure to viruses at work, vaccinations or booster vaccines should be administered to women of reproductive age. Some vaccines, such as the Rubella vaccine, should be taken as much as three months prior to pregnancy. See chapter 3 for information on vaccines before and during pregnancy.

Emotional Stress

Women make up a large proportion of the world's workforce. However, one factor appears to be consistent across countries and cultures and that is the significant degree of physical and psychological stress women face due to their diversity of roles. In addition to holding a job, many women must also raise food crops, keep the home, and assume major responsibility for child rearing.

Even though women frequently work as many hours outside of the home as their husbands do, they usually have the larger share of the domestic duties. Statistically, the working mother gets less sleep, gets sick more often, and has less leisure time than her husband. This same woman spends an average of forty-seven hours a week on housework while her husband spends ten. For the pregnant woman who already has children, this can create high-risk stress. The steroid hormones released in response to the stress are known to cross the placental barrier.

The nature of work itself has changed in the last few years with many companies laying off workers and expecting one person to do the work of many. This computes into compulsory overtime, work speedups, and less attention and caution regarding health and safety. Thus, a job that would have caused only moderate stress in the past now may fit a high stress category.

Additionally, women must often tolerate stressful situations specific to their gender. Studies of women at work indicate that as high as 60 percent have experienced some kind of sexual harassment on the job (Spangler 1992).

Having some degree of control over a stressful work situation seems to reduce the stress involved. For instance, workers who were given a "dummy" switch to control unpredictable high intensity noise suffered fewer adverse effects, even though none of them actually ever used the switch. Apparently, just feeling in control of the situation helped them to reduce their stress levels. In any situation where you feel out of control, you will want to list your options and take charge by taking action to reduce your stress in the most practical way.

Physical Stress

As opportunities in the workforce grow for women, they are being offered jobs that require physically demanding tasks. Studies have shown that pregnant women who perform strenuous work such as prolonged standing, physically stressful postures, heavy lifting/carrying, and long hours or work weeks are at risk for preterm delivery (Kipen and Stellman 1985; National Institute for Occupational Safety and Health Research Report 1977; Welsh 1986). This seems more likely to occur if the woman also has predisposing medical or obstetric risk factors such as previous preterm births or an incompetent cervix.

Highly Stressful Work Conditions

Shift work	Improper lighting
Night work	Excessive noise
Overtime	Inadequate work conditions
Pressured assembly line work	Depressing surroundings
Piecework	Unsanitary conditions
More than one job	Threat of physical or toxic danger
Lack of control of work hours	Potential for abuse from clients
Job insecurity	Objectives/responsibilities not known
Tedious work	Conflicting demands on worker
Problem solving not allowed	Competition/rivalry
Time pressure/deadlines	Commuting
Transfers, demotions, promotions	Unemployment
Job-related Post-Traumatic Stress Disorder	Sexual harassment

Levy and Wegman (1995); Rosenstock and Cullen (1994)

Heavy physical labor has been associated with preterm delivery (due to decrease in uterine/placental blood flow) and low birth weight in many studies (Kipen and Stellman 1985; Punnett 1995; National Institute for Occupational Safety and Health 1977). Low birth weight can present a serious concern for infants, since a factor that can retard development may be fully capable of creating other, more subtle, damage as well. Heavy lifting seems often to lead to spontaneous abortion, uterine contractions, and premature delivery, as well as to low birth weight.

Long work hours have also been associated with premature delivery, and when a mother stands for most of the workday her baby is predisposed to low birth weight. Variable shift work has been related to first-trimester miscarriages, preterm deliveries, and reduced birth weight (Punnett 1995; Marbury 1992).

Other, more specific, effects also occur with physical stress, fatigue, and emotional strain. Animal studies suggest that placental blood flow is decreased during these situations due to concentration of blood in large muscles. This seems to be the case especially where standing still in one place for a long time (called static exertion) occurs on a chronic basis. Placenta and uterine circulation is reduced and, since fetal nutrition depends upon adequate blood flow, prolonged static exertion could result in nutritional deprivation.

Physical exertion also results in breathing faster and taking in more air, thus increasing the potential for higher doses of inhaled chemicals and possibly wider distribution of chemicals in maternal and fetal tissues. Oxygen deprivation to the fetus, due to reduced placental circulation, occurring early in the pregnancy could even affect fetal enzymes and could compromise the effectiveness of the placenta in supporting the fetus adequately. Fetal oxygenation does not seem to suffer with mild exercise, which positively affects fetal growth in healthy women, and in the last six weeks of pregnancy seems to increase fetal weight. Exercise usually lasts for shorter periods than the chronic physical exertion involved in the workplace and tends to result in increased circulation once the exercise is finished.

If you expect to perform strenuous work on your job, be sure to use lifting aids and to increase the frequency and length of your rest breaks. You will also want to consider light duty options.

Jobs That Look Safe But Aren't

Some workplaces give clear messages that they are not safe places for a pregnant mother. Jobs in industry where the chemical odors permeate the air warn you of toxic conditions. Other hazardous job sites are not so obvious (Levy and Wegman 1995).

Simple Solutions
To Office Exposures

Office machines and supplies give off significant levels of solvents, however innocuous they may appear. The following list should enable you to make your office a safer place.

- For optimal safety in avoiding harmful chemical combinations in an office setting, copiers and duplicators can be vented and kept in a room separate from workers.

- Substitutes should be used for liquid eraser products and carbonless paper. In place of toxic markers, use nontoxic markers made for children.

- Hand-dispensed correcting tape can reduce your exposure to solvents. Pregnant mothers should leave the copying room while the machine is working or ask another worker to perform those tasks.

Toxic Substances Found in Ordinary Office Equipment

Photocopiers: Ozone, nitropyrenes, ultraviolet light

Duplicating machines: Ethanol, methanol, ammonia

Liquid eraser solutions: Solvent mixtures

Marking pens: Solvent mixtures

Carbonless paper: Formaldehyde

Household Work

The recognition of homemaking as an occupation places the proper value and importance on a workplace that is not subject to the usual governmental and regulatory controls. In fact, over one million women, most of reproductive age, are formally employed as household workers. Nearly one-third of married women in the U.S. are full-time homemakers, and the vast majority of working women perform household chores as an unpaid second job once they have left their primary place of employment. Refer to chapters 4, 5, and 7 for extensive information and cautions regarding toxic materials, household cleaners, and other risks found in the home.

 Simple Solutions To Exposures in the Electronics Industry

Electronics and semiconductor manufacturing involves the use of many toxic substances and processes including organic solvent mixtures, heavy metals, etching acids, and electroplating/soldering. Many of these are developmental toxins and should be avoided during pregnancy or lactation.

- On an electronics production site, all toxic chemicals and processes should be documented by your employer.

- Ventilation systems should be operational and completely effective. Always use all available protective equipment.

- Wherever available, nonhazardous processes should replace hazardous ones

Simple Solutions
To Exposures in the Medical Field

- Medical workers face a wide range of toxic situations. The transportation of all waste materials, blood, and secretions must be handled as though those materials are infectious.
- Exposure to anesthetic gases can be reduced with scavenger systems.
- Complete evacuation of ethylene oxide from sterilizer units before opening, maintenance of equipment, and the use of catalytic converters and aeration cabinets minimizes the hazards of ethylene oxide exposure.
- Patients can emit radiation following therapeutic implants and diagnostic tests, so pregnant medical personnel must maintain shielding and distance after such procedures as well as avoiding materials and waste from irradiated patients.
- Chemotherapeutic drug administration requires the use of biological safety cabinets when preparing drugs, careful labeling of drugs, and the strict use of gloves and gowns to protect the skin from exposure.
- Since inadvertent needle sticks present a real threat to nurses, doctors, and medical technicians, the use of the new "stick-proof" needles is highly recommended.

Simple Solutions
To Exposures in Arts and Crafts Work

Many supplies used in art work contain toluene, xylene, hexane, lead, methylene chloride, tri- and tetrachloroethylene, phenols, formaldehyde, and other highly neurotoxic solvents and toxic compounds. Most supplies consist of solvent mixtures. Electroplating and soldering, used in jewelry making, release toxic fumes. Glues used in large quantities have been known to cause severe deterioration of brain tissue in workers (Mikkelsen, et al. 1988; Bernsen, et al. 1992). In fact, most products used for art or craft projects contain at least some neurotoxic chemicals, most commonly adhesives, paints, sealants, and varnishes.

Pregnant women who must use toxic products during pregnancy, because they must make a living, should use adequate protective equipment. However, it may be difficult to find protection that does not contain plastics, and thus plasticizers, which often contain endocrine disruptors themselves. There are, however, some ceramic masks that are available through medical suppliers.

- Use water-based supplies, if at all possible.
- Wear protective charcoal masks when working with toxic materials indoors. Paper face masks protect only against large dust particles such as wood particles.
- Work outside or in an area with a ventilator fan to draw fumes outside.
- Cover your skin to avoid touching oil-based substances.
- Store art supplies in glass containers in an airtight cabinet or chest to reduce fumes.
- Allow projects to dry outside or in a garage area away from your living area.

Controlling Occupational Effects on Your Pregnancy

Many options are available for mothers-to-be who wish to avoid job-related chemical exposures and toxic stress during pregnancy. Some of the options discussed below may not be realistic for everyone because of the wide diversity of working conditions and family situations. The right solution or approach for you may be a combination of these or something else that works well for you and your child.

Stay home. Allowing your infant to develop in a clean and non-stressful environment during pregnancy may be just as important as staying home with your baby once he/she is born. This assumes, of course, that you maintain a reduced chemical and stress environment in your home. If quitting your job means you are going to lose your electricity, your home, or your partner, you would be better advised to choose another option. Staying home during your pregnancy will benefit your infant only if you are able to do so without exponentially increasing your emotional stress level.

Research has not demonstrated that working, in itself, has any specific harmful effects either on pregnancy or fetal development. However, if your job exposes you to high-risk factors, such as toxic chemicals, physical exertion, or extreme emotional stress, staying home may be the best decision you can make for yourself and your child.

Although some contemporary studies suggest that better pregnancy outcomes occur in women who are employed compared to those who are unemployed, those studies focus entirely on successful delivery of a baby with no obvious abnormalities. These studies fail to account for subtle developmental effects that may appear in the child as he/she grows.

Modify your work schedule. At age seven, Michael J. tested very high on hyperactivity on an ADHD evaluation. His mother said he was "just climbing the walls" and that the school was calling her daily about his uncontrollable behavior. Questions about the family history and lifestyle, however, revealed only a single possible source of Michael's dysfunction. During pregnancy his mother had held down three jobs simultaneously!

In the sixth month of her pregnancy she noticed that the baby had stopped moving and that she could no longer hear his heartbeat with her stethoscope. Her physician put her to bed for the rest of her pregnancy. The doctor determined that the baby was alive but felt that the mother's excessive stress level was causing problems for the developing infant. After Michael was born, his mother noticed he was different from other babies. He was colicky, required several formula changes, and early on, showed signs of behavioral problems and evidence of learning disabilities once he began attending school.

If you are working a second job or if you work long or odd hours you may want to switch to the day shift and restrict your working activities to a forty-hour week. Rotating shifts and night work have been related to a variety of stress related disorders, including sleep disturbances, nervous dysfunctions, and gastrointestinal problems (Seward 1997; Akerstedt 1990). Pregnant women will benefit from working a normal work week at a day job.

Reduce your time at work. In some instances going part-time may allow your body to eliminate its chemical and stress load. This may not be enough if you have been exposed to chemicals every day or for many hours at a time. If this is the case, you need a significant amount of time between your work shifts. Work every other day or at least make sure you spend your time away from work in a relatively nontoxic environment. Having to maintain a job where you are continuously exposed to toxic chemicals means that it is crucial to give your body a chance to metabolize and excrete excess chemicals between exposures.

Ask your employer to make adjustments. Ask your company to avoid or replace hazardous materials with safer agents. Doing so may or may not be possible but it never hurts to ask. Or ask fellow workers to help you avoid toxins during your pregnancy and lactation.

Many offices and industrial settings routinely spray with pesticides to control insects. Offer your supervisor alternatives to chemical pesticides and provide literature to help guide their use. See chapter 7 for pesticide alternatives.

Taking extra precautions in your work area may not be enough and, in some cases, you may need to ask your employer to move you to a different job. The goal, of course, is to reduce your exposure to chemicals and/or to limit your stress. The best time for a transfer is prior to conception and, if that is not possible, since many pregnancies are not planned, then as soon as possible after the pregnancy is discovered. You may need to present a doctor's note when requesting the transfer.

Change jobs. Find employment that offers healthier conditions during your pregnancy. You may need to consider a job with less pressure and low chemical exposure so you can reduce your stress level and protect your baby adequately. For example, there are many jobs that will have less impact on your baby than one where your boss yells at you, where you have your hands in cleaning solvents much of the time, or in a dentist's office where you breathe anesthetic gas frequently.

Wash frequently and use protective equipment. Many toxic chemicals are absorbed through the skin and frequent washing will limit your exposure somewhat. You should always use protective equipment like gloves and other skin coverings to prevent skin contact with toxic chemicals. Note that protective equipment should be used only with other alternatives and should never represent the primary method of preventing exposure in a high-risk chemical environment. Protective equipment provides only a cursory method of preventing contamination from toxic substances. In other words, your employer should also use monitoring devices, air contamination controls, blood-level monitoring, and contaminate-control equipment wherever and whenever needed.

Protective equipment can also be extremely uncomfortable, especially when your body is already feeling heavy and awkward. It probably should present only a temporary and short-term solution until you can be moved away from hazardous conditions.

Get counseling. If your job is stressful, visits to a counselor or psychologist can help you learn to minimize and manage your stress. Share your concerns regarding health risks to your baby and discuss your options. Chapter 8 discusses helpful approaches to controlling stress.

In the event that the options described above fail to fit your situation, you will want to work even harder to reduce chemicals and stress while you are away from the job. Although you spend one-quarter of your time in the workplace, the remaining three-fourths of your time that is spent away from work represents time that can be used to give your body and baby a break.

Pest Control

It's summer again and the bugs are really bad this year. The lawn has mysterious bald spots, the insect-generated holes in the petunias seem twice as big as they did yesterday, and, clearly, something has to be done. Dad knows what to do. Loading up his two-gallon sprayer with Diazinon, he plods out to the yard and "nukes" the tiny beasties that devour grass roots and flower leaves. Within an hour he covers front and back with the pesticide. Thoroughly satisfied with himself, he treks back across his newly sprayed, insect-free yard to store the equipment and goes inside to reward himself with a beer.

A well-kept sedan turns into the drive. Mom taps the horn and Dad jumps up to help her with the groceries. Mom gets out and puts Baby, who is crawling now, down inside the front door. Mom helps Dad carry the stuffed sacks through the yard and into the house, walking across the carpet to the kitchen several times. Baby crawls after them stopping to retrieve an occasional toy from the floor, then places the toy and her hands into her open mouth. Baby sucks her thumb thoughtfully and watches Mom and Dad put away the groceries. Baby begs for a cookie, eats it, then licks her hands to get at the crumbs. Baby is happy.

The bugs are gone. Mom and Dad are happy.

In November, 1996, the EPA reported that suburban infants are ingesting frightening quantities of highly toxic pesticides from home flooring and carpeting. Apparently, parents spray their yards with herbicides and insecticides at "acceptable levels," then track the dangerous substances inside, where their babies crawl across the floor, and then, as infants do, place their hands in their mouths. In fact, the chemicals persist longer inside than outside since the natural elements that break down pesticides, rain and sun, are not present inside the home. Thus an incalculable number of babies ingest multiple daily doses of substances known to cause cancer, immune disorders, learning disabilities, behavioral disorders, and developmental defects. All at the time when the brain, immune, and detoxification systems are engaged in rapid, active development. All for a beautiful lawn.

Although most people in the world do not have lawns, most of us regularly walk through recently treated areas such as parks, farm fields, playgrounds, stores, and other public and community spaces. Shoes that are worn to traverse these areas should not be worn inside where babies or pregnant women can be exposed.

Hormone Disruptors

Many synthetic chemicals, especially pesticides, act as hormone impostors in the body. A tiny exposure to one of these chemicals can trigger a full hormonal response. Hormones play a crucial part in the development and function of a baby's brain, reproductive organs, and sexual behavior. Since hormones regulate most body processes, a hormone impostor can create endless havoc if encountered during a baby's delicate building stages. Most of us have these chemicals in amounts several hundred to several thousands times higher than the normal hormones levels in our bodies should be.

Pesticides

Ancient civilizations recognized the value of pest and disease protection. Homer wrote of burning sulfur as a fumigant and Pliny the Elder described the insecticidal benefits of arsenic. By the sixteenth century, the Chinese were using arsenic and later nicotine as insecticides. By the nineteenth century, the French were using mixtures made from Bordeaux wine as herbicides.

Although many of the chemical pesticides known to us today were first synthesized in the late 1800s and early 1900s, their use in agriculture was not generally widespread until after World War II. Organophosphate pesticides were first used as nerve gases by the Germans during the 1930s (Rom 1998). The infamous organochlorine, DDT, was used as an insecticide in Switzerland in 1939 and in Italy during World War II to prevent the spread of typhus. In fact, DDT is credited with that war being the first one in history to lose more casualties to wounds than to disease. Rachel Carson's book, *Silent Spring* (1962), revealed both the dangers of chemical pesticides and the fact that these chemicals remain in our bodies and environment for long periods of time. The enormous popularity of that book resulted in the ban of DDT and other organochlorines in the United States.

Ironically, organochlorines are now being widely replaced by organophosphates that, although they do not persist in the environment, are significantly more toxic than organochlorines. The 1970s and 1980s saw the introduction of systemic pesticides. These are chemicals that contaminate not only the *surface* of food products, but are absorbed throughout the entire plant.

Organochlorines

Organochlorines, or chlorinated hydrocarbons, are generally considered the most harmful pesticides since they linger for long periods in the body and the environment. Some last for as long as twenty years. These chemicals have repeatedly been linked to cancer, central nervous system damage, and reproductive disorders. The use of most organochlorines has been banned in many industrialized nations, including the United States, since the early 1970s. Yet they consistently continue to show up in soil, water, fatty tissue, and breast milk. Despite the ban of many of these chemicals, such as DDT, they are still manufactured in industrialized countries, including the United States, and are exported freely to unregulated countries. Unfortunately, they routinely come right back in the form of imported foods. Several commonly used organochlorines are discussed below.

DDT has been used since the 1940s. It accumulates in our fat tissue and we are exposed to it mostly through the consumption of meat and dairy products. DDT crosses the placental barrier and is readily excreted in breast milk. In areas where many of the most harmful organochlorines have been controlled and restricted, breast milk shows decreasing amounts of chemicals such as DDT, compared to areas where harmful organochlorine use is unrestricted (Dogheim, et al. 1996).

Nevertheless, it is important to note that the amount of DDT that many breast-fed babies are ingesting and storing in their own fatty tissues may still negatively affect their development.

Hexachlorobenzene (HCB) is an organochlorine fungicide most commonly used on seeds. In 1956, HCB-treated seed wheat meant for planting was sold as food to Turkish villages. Until the seed was taken off the market three years later, HCB consumption resulted in outbreaks of acquired porphyis cutanea tarda, a disease that produces skin lesions, disfigurement, and liver dysfunction, and which led to the death of about 10 percent of the 3,000 people who contracted the disease. Most of the dead were infants who had been exposed to HCB-contaminated breast milk. The HCB poisonings also caused other health problems, mostly affecting breast-fed infants. In some villages, no children under the age of two were left alive (Rom 1998).

The Persistent Toxic Chemical

Many synthetic pesticides stay around for a long time. They have long half-lives. Simply put, half-life means the time required for one-half of a substance to deteriorate. Chemical half-lives can range from seconds to years. If a chemical has a half-life of six days, as some pesticides do, then in six days, half of it will be gone. In another six days, half of the remainder will be gone. And so on.

Because some highly toxic chemicals such as DDT, which has a half-life of twenty years, were overused in the '40s and '50s, even after eighty years a sixteenth of the total amount can still be around and active in the environment. Therefore, your baby is exposed not just to chemicals in the world today, but to yesterday's chemicals as well.

Pentachlorophenol (PCP), one of the most commonly used pesticides in the U.S., is an all-purpose organochlorine that has been used as a pesticide, fungicide, herbicide, an antimildew agent and, most significantly, as a wood preservative on lumber used for houses, furniture, playground equipment, telephone poles, and picnic tables. Nine newborns who were accidentally exposed to PCP in a hospital nursery in 1969 suffered from profuse sweating, rapid heartbeat and respiration, respiratory distress, liver enlargement, and changes in blood acid pH. Two newborns died (Rom 1998). Animal experiments show PCP to be "feto-toxic" especially when exposure occurs during the first trimester. PCP appears on the list of hormone disruptors and so is suspect for more subtle developmental disorders (Rom 1998).

Organophosphates

Organophosphates were widely introduced as nerve gas weapons of war (like Sarin) by the Germans in the late 1930s. Soon after, their insecticidal potential was discovered and their agricultural use spread worldwide.

These chemicals are known to cause central nervous system damage, impairment of normal muscle function, and interference with the brain's information processing. Apparently, organophosphate compounds tie up enzymes that release brain chemicals. Exposure to these chemicals has been known to result in delayed neurological symptoms, impaired movement, and abnormal brain wave patterns. Organophosphates alter the balance of brain chemicals and disrupt normal brain function. Exposure can occur by skin and eye absorption, inhalation, and ingestion. These chemicals store in body tissue for relatively short periods of from six to twenty-four hours but while they are in the blood stream, they can pass through the placenta or filter into breast milk. Well-known organophosphate examples are discussed below.

Parathion is an organophosphate pesticide that has caused more deaths than any other in its category. It is a known endocrine disruptor and a suspected developmental, reproductive, and neurological toxin.

Malathion, a commonly used mosquito poison, is routinely used in many malaria control programs and has caused many poisonings and even death. The World Health Organization changed its recommendations for this chemical but many countries do not enforce or even restrict use on most pesticides (Rom 1998). Malathion is also a general consumer insecticide and its widespread use suggests that most people feel it is safe. It isn't. The Environmental Defense Fund suspects malathion to be an endocrine disruptor and a neurological toxin.

Diazinon has become one of the best-known and widely used organophosphates since the large-scale ban on organochlorines took effect in many countries. The toxic effects of this chemical actually increase during storage. Many advocates of chemical use report that diazinon is safe. However, the Environmental Defense Fund and many experts think diazinon may be a developmental toxin, endocrine disruptor, and neurotoxin. The huge numbers of wildlife that have been poisoned by diazinon leave no doubt about its dangers (Colborn, Dumanoski, and Myers 1996).

Carbamates

Carbamates are synthetic chemicals used as pesticides, fungicides, and herbicides. Carbamate insecticides work by inhibiting enzymes that produce necessary brain chemicals. Carbaryl (Sevin) is the most widely used carbamate. In addition to its use as an insecticide, it is also used in the manufacture of clothing, medicines, and plastics. In adults, exposure is known to negatively affect the central nervous system, respiration, and memory function. It is also a suspected endocrine disruptor that can affect fetal development.

Combined Pesticides

Many pesticides are used in combination to make them more powerful and to cover a wider range of insects. Combining pesticides can make them a hundred times more toxic in the human body. For instance, if malathion is used with EPN, the EPN blocks the breakdown of the malathion and leaves it in the body for a lengthy period of time. Estimates place the level of toxicity at 50 times normal. Many of the pesticide products we researched contained more than one toxic chemical.

Some Neurotoxic or Hormone Disrupting Pesticides

Organochlorines

DDT	PCP	HCB	Aldrin
Lindane	Endrin	Heptachlor	Chlordane
Toxaphene	Endosulfan	Agent Orange	Chlordecone
Kepone	Telone	Mirex	TDE
Ethylan	Dienoclor	Dicofol	—

Organophosphates

Diazinon	Malathion	Ronnel	Parathion
Dimecron	Sarin	EPN	Mevinphos (Phosdrin)
Chlorpyrifos (Dursban)	—	—	—

Carbamates

Aldicarb	Sevin	Baygon	Maneb
Zineb	Adoxycarb	Allyxycarb	Aminocarb

Inert Ingredients

Substances added to pesticides often can be more harmful than the actual pesticide. These ingredients are not intended to actually kill the pest; they are added to increase concentration volume and/or as propellants and solvents (Rapp 1996).

Synergists are chemicals added to pesticide formulations to increase their potency. Some common synergists include known toxins such as asbestos, DDT, formaldehyde, and chlorine that are more poisonous than the active ingredient to which they are added. Inert ingredients are particularly frightening because often they are not regulated and are protected by "trade secret" laws. This is especially dangerous because, along with the active chemicals in pesticides, inert ingredient residues are contaminating our bodies and food supplies.

Systemic Pesticides

Systemic pesticides are absorbed by produce and can't be washed off or removed by peeling, an added incentive to buy organically grown produce. Examples include:

aldicarb	—
chlorpropham	demeton
dimethoate	methomyl
methamidophos	mevinphos
D CPA	—

Tolerances and Regulations

Government agencies within many countries, such as the EPA in the United States, regulate the use of chemical pesticides, herbicides, insecticides, and fungicides. Usually these regulations are based on health effects, but very rarely is a substance regulated because of its developmental effects on infants or the fetus.

The amount of pesticide residues found on food intended for commercial consumption is also regulated. These regulated levels are called tolerances and they are the maximum residue amounts for a particular pesticide permitted on food. Residues are the chemicals remaining on a food from the use of pesticides during the growing or processing of that food. Residue contamination of food can occur from soil, water, direct spraying or dusting, wind, storage treatments, or waxes and dyes used to prepare the foods for market.

The World Health Organization (WHO 1990) offers recommendations on the use of various pesticides but lacks the authority to enforce its own guidelines. Many developing countries have no regulatory agencies, and chemicals are used indiscriminately without regard to the amount of pesticide used or the timing of the applications. WHO reports that in these areas "pesticides are often applied hours or days before harvest [which allows] no chance for a good amount of the pesticide to break down." They say that it is not uncommon for market food in these areas to be directly treated with pesticides to control flies. Grain is also often treated to control rodents since, in Third World countries particularly, loss of stored food is a tremendous problem. According to WHO, these practices have lead to mass poisonings (WHO 1990).

What Government Agencies Ignore When Restricting Pesticides

- Infants and children are much more susceptible to pesticides than adults because their bodies are rapidly developing. Levels set for adults are totally inappropriate for babies and children.
- Few pesticides are regulated based on effects on fetal development.
- A food may have been treated or exposed to more than one pesticide, fungicide, herbicide, and dyes and waxes.
- By eating all day, we may ingest more than the "acceptable" tolerance for one pesticide.
- We are exposed to additional chemicals from water, home pesticides, and artificial additives and preservatives.

Bug Repellents

Diethyl toluamide, or DEET, is the active ingredient in most bug repellents. DEET can cause serious health consequences in children and developing babies. Children have experienced headaches, seizures, and unconsciousness due to significant exposures. One woman who used DEET and other chemicals throughout her pregnancy had a baby who exhibited severe neurological symptoms. However, in areas where malaria presents a serious health problem, often no other solutions than DEET are currently available.

Simple Solutions
For Nontoxic Bug Repellents

There are many ways to discourage bugs without dousing your skin with toxic chemicals:

- Use herbal bug repellants, many of which contain citronella. Citronella, however, has not been adequately tested for health effects. In addition, some herbal repellents contain penny royal which can harm a developing fetus. Peppermint is a great tick repellent. Make peppermint tea and then spray the tea directly on the skin.

- Cover arms and legs with lightweight, light-colored cotton clothing to absorb perspiration and to protect from both bugs and sunlight.

- Bathe with unscented soap before going out and use unscented body products. Bugs are attracted to body odors and flowery scents.

- Wash clothing with baking soda and avoid fabric softeners (bugs are attracted to the chemical fragrances in fabric softeners).

- Put food away immediately after you finish eating to avoid drawing insects.

How Are We Being Contaminated?

Air. Pesticides sprayed or dusted on crops are carried through air to contaminate soil, water, and human habitations. Many studies have shown the prevalence of pesticides even in urban smog (Pellizzari, et al. 1985). Indoor pesticide pollution, from sources like flea, roach, or rodent bombs or foggers, can be an even larger health threat. Enclosed areas, like houses or office buildings, are more dangerous when contaminated with chemicals because the pesticides persist longer in the absence of wind, sun, and rain. Therefore, these harmful substances accumulate on food, furniture, countertops, floors, etc., and flow through the air we breathe.

Studies show that ventilation does not always make a significant difference on pesticide residues in indoor air or on surfaces during the first few days after use. So don't use a flea bomb and think you can open your windows afterwards for a few hours and safely allow your kids inside.

Soil. Pesticide contamination of soil can occur in many ways. Air can contribute to soil contamination even in areas where pesticides have not been used. Pesticide residues from treated plants can also run off into soil. And soil can be deliberately treated against bacteria, weeds, or insect eggs. Chemically contaminated soil affects our food and water supply and our children when they play outside. Pesticides used in agriculture, home gardens, and public landscapes can easily leach through soil and into the ground water.

Water. Like soil, water can become contaminated in many ways. As explained previously, pesticide residues can contaminate water via air and soil. Chemicals covering pesticide equipment are routinely washed down drains or into the soil. There are actually areas of the world where pesticides are added to ponds or rivers to kill fish for food.

Food. Pesticides contaminate our food when they are directly sprayed or dusted on crops. Food can also absorb chemicals during the growing process from polluted soil, rain, and water. Fresh produce is often treated with chemical dyes and waxes to make it more attractive to consumers and to increase shelf life. Chemical flavorings, colors, and preservatives routinely contaminate prepared food. Meat and dairy products often contain harmful hormones that were injected into the animal to increase production. Most meat products also contain pesticides since any chemical the animal ingests via treated hay or grain is stored in its body fat and organs.

U.S. Food Quality Protection Act of 1996

Some tolerance levels for toxic chemicals will be lowered and infants and children's special needs will be considered when new tolerance levels are set. However, the EPA has three years to complete this task for the most hazardous chemicals and ten years for the toxic chemicals it already monitors.

Agricultural Pesticide Use

Pesticide use creates resistant insects leading to crop losses all around the world. According to WHO (1990), North America, Europe, and

Japan lose about 10 to 30 percent of their crops while the losses in developing countries can reach as high as 40 percent or more, due to the additional havoc caused by poor storage conditions.

Integrated Pest Management (IPM)

This approach to pest management with its emphasis on natural controls and limited pesticide use has proven effective and lowered costs all over the world. In fact, the United Nations Environment Program and the World Health Organization have developed the same system, calling it Integrated Vector Control, for introduction to public health programs.

The problem with integrative approaches is that the use of even small amounts of chemical pesticides negates a successful organic program. If you have built up a soil alive with healthy microbes and earthworms and your beneficial insects are balanced, then spraying with pesticides or using chemicals fertilizers can undo all the progress you have made. A really well-developed healthy soil makes the use of chemicals unnecessary since bugs and disease are not attracted to healthy well-fed plants. Integrative pest management makes sense as one changes over to an organic program, but once beneficials and healthy soil are established, only organic techniques should be used.

Pregnant and breast-feeding women face the same dangers in an integrated program as they do using chemical pesticides because integrated programs use pesticides too, but not as injudiciously. Many pesticides are known or suspected hormone disruptors and affect a baby's development. Even occasional use or small amounts of pesticides can make changes in a developing baby's endocrine system.

Alternatives to Pesticide Use

So far in this chapter we have discussed the dangerous, and scary, aspects surrounding the use of harmful chemicals as pesticides on our food and in our homes. The reassuring news is that there are safe, effective, and easy natural alternatives to this worldwide problem, alternatives that can be enacted on a large-scale, agricultural basis or on a smaller scale, around your home.

In general, this approach is called organics and it involves much more than just the absence of chemicals. Organics involves a deep understanding of how nature works to promote life, and this understanding in turn works for you to produce healthy food. Here are a few basic principles that will enable you to return to organics.

Sustaining Soil Without Chemicals

Besides water and sun, soil is the most important life-giving substance on Earth. The soil that grows our food teems with life. That is, unless we have killed its living entities with chemicals.

The use of chemical fertilizers and pesticides reduces soil to a dead substance that cannot support life on its own. Chemical fertilizers are full of salts deadly to the microbes that are necessary for breaking down soil nutrients so that plants can use them. Pesticides not only destroy the life in soil, they also kill the beneficial creatures that help protect plants from disease and insect invasion.

When pesticides, herbicides, and chemical fertilizers were first introduced, the results were impressive. It looked as if insect pests finally could be controlled. Plant diseases were annihilated. And crop yields out-performed even the wildest speculations. For a while. Farmers stopped combining different types of plants, failed to rotate crops, and no longer added manures to the soil because they believed the chemicals would do all the work for them. They felt that if a chemical worked, Great! If it didn't, just add more chemicals, combine chemicals, or develop new chemicals. Unfortunately, these practices caused a loss in soil fertility and, therefore, a loss in its life-giving potential. The soil died and became dirt. Then production rates began to go down.

In many areas of the world, the soil has become infertile due to poor farming practices and chemical use. The breaks in the State of Oklahoma constitute miles and miles of desolate, rutted ground speckled with an occasional struggling weed here and there. It is a vast wasteland of economically unreclaimable soil. No effort was made to maintain the life of the soil and all the trees that protected the soil from the wind were removed. The soil died, broke down, and the wind blew it away.

Up to six billion tons of soil are lost to erosion every year on the North American continent. This tremendous loss is most often related to a loss of fertility and soil structure. This kind of disaster doesn't happen where organic techniques are used. In Chinese farming, all organic wastes are returned to the soil as compost.

The Chinese have farmed the same land intensively for 4,000 years with no loss of fertility. And they have certainly not used Weed and Feed or malathion. They have no money for chemicals and definitely no need for them. They build soil fertility naturally by recycling all their living materials. (Of course, China still has a tremendous problem with chemical pollutants in their air and water.)

The Famous Haughley Experiment

In the 1950s two neighbors in Suffolk, England, Lady Eve Balfour and Miss Alice Debenham, combined their farms and divided them into three parts. The first section was farmed using crop rotation and compost for fertilizer. The mixed section used both compost and chemical fertilizers. The third section used only chemical fertilizers and pesticides. The results showed that long-term, organic fields yield consistent crop production, while chemically treated fields initially increase only to drop off due to insect infestation, weeds, and soil depletion. Recent studies of chemical vs. organic farms conclude that crop yields are comparable initially but chemical use causes eventual loss of productivity (Carr, et al. 1978). So much for the myth that the world's peoples will starve without chemical pesticides and fertilizers!

Trace Elements

Trace elements are naturally present in healthy, organic-rich soils and compost. Poor growing practices such as chemical fertilizer use and intensive cropping, along with erosion, lead to the depletion of trace minerals in the soil. The minerals are replaced effectively only through the application of organic-rich fertilizers. A balanced, organic fertilizer, such as a compost made from a variety of vegetative and manure materials, provides proper amounts of trace minerals.

Healthy Plants

Healthy plants that have proper nutrition and soil conditions actually can protect themselves from pests. Many plants produce toxins that kill insects when ingested, make repellents that discourage insects from attack, or exude steroid-like hormones which interfere with insect growth and development. Other plants grow fuzz or exude a bad smell. Some plants produce repellents or toxins continually, others only when under attack. One natural plant substance, systemin, causes plants to produce an enzyme inhibitor. This inhibitor gives bugs a bad case of indigestion by interfering with their ability to digest plant tissue. They take a bite or two, the plant releases systemin, triggering the inhibitor, and the insect decides to find a better lunch somewhere else. We, of course, salute the 30,000 young tomato plants that gave their lives for this particular study.

The healthier a plant, the more likely its defenses will work properly. A weak, sickly, or undernourished plant, perhaps low on trace minerals, cannot defend itself from pest attacks. This is similar to immune system failure in humans caused by malnutrition. Plants are best nourished by a healthy soil, one that has a balanced combination of microorganisms, macroorganisms, trace minerals, nutrients, humus, moisture, and oxygen. Chemicals upset this balance. They solve one problem only by creating another.

Bugs and diseases thrive on weak plants that produce excess carbohydrates, while healthy plants, being higher in protein and minerals, appeal more to humans and mammals. If plants are either too high or too low in nutrients they suffer from insect damage. Accordingly, a soil balanced in nutrients, such as healthy organic soil, protects plants the best.

Chemical fertilizers place too much nitrogen in the soil which then attracts aphids and spider mites. High nitrogen levels cause increased levels of amino acids, which attract aphids and many other insects that love amino acids. An imbalance of phosphorus, frequently seen in chemically managed soil, encourages the egg production of spider mites, while too little phosphorus leads to white fly infestations. Magnesium imbalances, also a result of chemical use, cause mites, and too much potassium blocks the availability of magnesium to plants.

Building up the life of the soil is the single most important task of the gardener or farmer. Healthy soil, the top organicists tell us, contains so much humus it looks like moist chocolate cake. If you dig down in the forest floor you will find this kind of rich organic material, the perfect self-sustaining growing medium, full of living creatures like earthworms, microbes, and insects.

 ## Simple Solutions For Sustaining Soil

- Feed the soil rather than the plant, then the soil feeds the plant.

- Return all living materials to the soil after composting.

- Use adapted plant species for your area. (These are native plants and plants that are known to do well in a particular area. Use them because they grow, because they prevent erosion, and because they do not need chemicals.)

- Avoid the use of chemical products.
- Use pesticide alternatives and organically formulated products.
- Protect plants from stresses like thirst and temperature extremes.
- Use natural mineral sources like lava sand to enrich soil.
- Keep the soil aerated.
- Cover bare soil with mulch materials.

Some Nontoxic Compost and Mulch Materials

Manure	Leaves
Untreated aged sawdust or chips	Household wastes
Fish wastes	Berry wastes
Food wastes from stores	Fruit residues
Shredded black and white newspaper	Dairy whey from cheese production
Cocoa hulls	Spent hops from brewery
Nut hulls (not black walnut)	Sugar cane waste
Cotton gin trash	Lava sand
Organic mushroom compost	Seaweed or kelp
Municipal sludge	Partially completed compost
Straw	Potato pulp and peel
Pine needles	Pecan hulls
Chips from tree trimmings	

Recycling

Compost can be used as a natural fertilizer or a mulch. Be sure to allow compost to break down into a fine, dark material before working it into the soil. Compost breakdown takes place faster when it is shielded from sunlight, so for the best results, keep it shaded or covered. Add leftovers and any spoiled food to your compost pile. You can also buy bags of composted material fertilizer at your local garden center. Composting not only recycles organic materials but it breaks down pesticides so they don't filter into soil and water.

Although organic products may be hard to find in some parts of the world, the natural supplies needed for chemical-free living and gardening are readily available everywhere. Just look around for anything that was once alive. Since a major goal of organics is recycling, the best materials for composting consist of wastes ordinarily thrown away or burned.

 ## Simple Solutions For Pest Prevention

When you have identified a pest problem in your home, yard, or farm, before figuring out how you are going to kill the little monsters, first determine whether or not there is an underlying problem that needs addressing. You could unknowingly be providing your pest with great accommodations. The following suggestions for preventing pest problems have been taken, in part, from the EPA's *Citizen's Guide to Pest Control and Pesticide Safety* (1995).

- Remove standing water inside and out. Pests need water too, and some, like mosquitoes, need water to propagate. Remove trays under container plants, repair leaky pipes and roofs, direct drainage pipes well away from house, and put up pet water bowls at night.

- Remove food sources inside and out. Clean floors, cabinets, countertops, and under the refrigerator. Store food in airtight containers and pest-proof garbage storage; don't leave pet food out.

- Remove or prevent pest access by sealing cracks around windows and doors, and place screening in windows, doors, and drainage vents. Discard paper articles. Keep bath tub and sink plugged. Clean up trash, rotting wood, and leaves around your house. For extreme pest problems, don't plant vegetation or use mulch near the house. Bathe pets and clean their sleeping areas regularly. Vacuum regularly to remove insect eggs.

- Keep plants healthy because healthy plants reduce pest problems.

The most beneficial aspect of organic programs is that they offer many natural ways to control insects. Beneficial creatures are one way Mother Nature limits destructive pests. The promotion of these natural predators in your yard or farm is an effective way to control the destruction of crops by unwanted bugs. It can be fun, too.

There are many natural, biological pest controls, too many in fact, to list all of them here. Well-known examples are the beneficial predators, whose local populations are routinely decimated by chemical pesticides, allowing for the infestation of harmful, chemical-resistant pests.

Natural Predators

Toads	Birds	Lizards
Bats	Ants	Praying mantises
Wasps	Spiders	Fireflies
Dragonflies	Centipedes	Snakes
Ladybugs	Biological pesticides	

Simple Solutions
For Homemade Insecticides and Plant Treatments

- Mistletoe. Spread the broken pieces on fire ant beds.

- Manure tea. Soak manure in water for 24 hours, strain and pour on the fire ant bed. Natural bacteria destroys molds and fungus.

- Boiling water. Pour a panful of boiling water into a fire ant mound until it collapses. Sneak up quietly so they won't have time to move their queen.

- Orange and other citrus peels. Store them in freezer, grind them up in the spring, and work them into the soil to repel and kill insects.

- Natural apple cider vinegar or 20 percent vinegar. Use full strength as an herbicide to spray on undesirable plants in sunlight.

- Garlic pepper spray. Systemic repellent and insecticide. Blend two garlic bulbs, two tablespoons cayenne pepper with one gallon water. Add one cup of concentrate to three cups of water for a spray. To avoid killing beneficials, leave out pepper.

- Molasses, apple cider vinegar, seaweed for a foliar feeding. One tablespoon each in one gallon water. Spray it on the leaves of your plants.
- Baking soda. Added to dry detergent kills roaches and ants.
- Diatomaceous earth. Dust on fire ant mounds. Dust leaves for flea beetles and corn ear worm.
- Rhubarb leaves. Boil in water 30 minutes; spray on bugs.
- Tomato leaves. Crush two cups in three quarts of water, add two tablespoons of cornstarch and refrigerate. Has solanine which inhibits black spot fungus.
- Tobacco leaves. Just crumble and add to soil to repel insects.
- Cayenne pepper. Use as a dust to keep pests and dogs off plants.
- Coriander or anise oil. Use one tablespoon in two quarts of water to repel insects.
- Tabasco sauce. Paint trunks of trees, etc., to deter rodents.
- Flour. Dust liberally for pillbugs.
- Charcoal. Sprinkle around house's foundation each season for carpenter ants.
- 00 sand ("double ott") or diatomaceous earth. Spread around home's foundation or under piers, making a barrier against termites.
- Earthworms. Till the soil and fertilize it with their castings.
- Banana peels. Chop and work into soil; provides phosphorus and potash.
- Eggshells crushed and sprinkled around seedlings. To add lime, nitrogen, and phosphorus to soil.
- Legumes, like beans, peas, rye grass. Plant as cover crops to pull nitrogen from the air into the soil.

Are Organic Pesticides Safe?

Organic pesticides are toxic materials produced from natural sources. The most common include citrus oil, pyrethrum, sabadilla, ryania, and rotenone. Each will kill bugs, even beneficial insects, so their use should be a last resort. Maintaining healthy soil is the best way to prevent plant-devouring insects, which prefer sick or poorly nourished plants.

Citrus oil. Made from the peels of oranges, lemons, limes, and other citrus fruits, citrus oil is effective against most insects although it must contact the insect to be effective. To date, citrus oil seems to be the safest form of natural pest control in terms of developmental toxicity and health concerns. It degrades quickly so it doesn't pollute. The active ingredient D-limonene can be found in many organic pest controls.

Pyrethrum. The most common organic insecticide, pyrethrum, is a neurotoxin. Produced from the *Chrysanthemum cinerarieafolium*, pyrethrum attacks insects' nervous systems, paralyzing and killing them. Insects may recover from low doses, however, and to increase killing power, synergists such as piperonyl butoxide and, sometimes, toxic pesticides may be added. *Pyrethrins* are active compounds derived from pyrethrum, while *pyrethroids* are synthetic chemical replications of pyrethrins. Pyrethroids tend to be more effective but less toxic to humans and animals.

Pyrethrins break down quickly under light and heat so they are most effective used indoors. When pesticides are taken into the body, they are broken down or "metabolized" into other substances called *metabolites*. These metabolites can be more toxic or less toxic than the original substance. Pyrethrins break down too quickly to be stored in human fat cells. The metabolites of pyrethrins show less toxicity.

Pyrethrins are absorbed more efficiently through the lungs than through the skin or gastrointestinal tract, so you should avoid breathing them. The most common toxic symptom is allergic reactions. Ingesting large amounts can result in central nervous system toxicity and even death. Additionally, these substances kill fish and bees, and can make birds sick.

Pyrethrins are hormone disruptors. Pregnant or breast-feeding women and infants and children should avoid them. Organic alternatives should be used instead.

Sabadilla. Unlike most other botanicals, sabadilla increases its toxic power during storage. Made from the seeds of a lily, it poisons on contact and is possibly a stomach poison. The active components of sabadilla degrade quickly in the environment leaving little residue. Sabadilla can cause irritation of the upper respiratory tract and skin in mammals. Ingestion of large amounts results in cardiac arrythmias and death. The substance will kill bees and, used as an insecticide, is most effective against the true bugs. (Note that spiders, bees, and squash bugs are not true bugs.)

Ryania. Ryania is a combination of numerous alkaloids extracted from a tropical plant, *Ryania speciosa*. It act on the stomach, and the insect may experience a slow death. Ryania appears to be less toxic to mammals than the other botanicals; however, it persists in the environment for longer periods and is mildly toxic to birds and fish. Ingestion in substantial amounts causes vomiting, weakness, and CNS depression leading to respiratory failure. There is little evidence that it accumulates in human tissue; however, very little research has been done on this plant.

Rotenone. Rotenone comes from some South American legumes. It can be fatal to mammals when inhaled in large amounts. It is more toxic when inhaled than when ingested and absorbs poorly through skin. Rotenone is moderately toxic to humans and nontoxic to bees, but kills fish readily. Toxic effects include skin irritation, sore throat, congestion, and vomiting while long-term exposure affects liver and kidneys. Metabolites tend to be less toxic than the original compound. Under normal environmental conditions, rotenone breaks down within days with no persistence in either water or soil.

Botanical pesticides are toxic and, with the possible exception of citrus oil, should be avoided by pregnant women and infants. Because they are either known or suspected hormone disruptors, pregnant and breast-feeding women should try organic alternatives. If you must use one of these substances, ask another person to apply them outside and then wait several days to touch those plants.

Simple Solutions
For Reducing Exposure When Others
Use Pesticides

- Make sure your food or herb garden does not receive runoff from neighbors' yards where pesticides are used.

- Ask neighbors who use chemicals to notify you so you and your children can avoid their yards. Stay indoors and keep windows and exterior doors closed. Ask these neighbors to remove their shoes before entering your house.

- Many communities across the United States have implemented mandatory "right-to-know" ordinances that require public notice (usually through posting) of lawn treatments and other small-scale outdoor pesticide use to protect residents.

- Workplaces, day care buildings, schools, apartment complexes, community centers, and hospitals—anyplace you or your child spend time—educate the people there about organic approaches. Educate people you and your child come into contact with on a regular basis about the dangers of pesticides. The workplace, the day care center, schools, community centers, churches, and local parks are excellent places to spread the word.

- Air out buildings after pesticides are used indoors. After indoor pesticide use, the air will usually be contaminated with low levels of residue. The residues break down more slowly indoors. Avoid those places for three to four days after pesticides have been used.

- Some chemical pesticides have no smell, so smelling doesn't always act as a warning.

- If you suspect that the air in your building is contaminated you can call your local health department or the EPA's pesticide hotline at 1-800-858-7378 for advice on what steps to take (Environmental Protection Agency 1995).

What to Do If Exposed to Pesticides

If you receive a significant pesticide exposure, for instance, if you are sprayed directly, here are some things you can do.

- Don't panic, there are plenty of ways to help protect your baby.

- Remove the source of the exposure as soon as possible.

- Wash all exposed parts of the body with soap and water.

- Ask someone else to wash any surfaces the pesticide contacted.

- Drink lots and lots of water for a few days.

- Eat a high-fiber diet with lots of antioxidant rich foods for several days to promote removal of the substances through the bowels.

- Decrease your fat intake moderately for several days to avoid storing the material and to reduce availability to the baby in breast milk or across the placenta. Do not totally remove fats from your diet since that may cause your own fat cells to break down and release stored chemicals.

- Take low (minimum daily requirement) doses of the antioxidants Vitamins C and E for several days to capture and move pesticides out of your body.

- Be especially careful about additional chemical exposures.

- Call your doctor if the exposure was heavy or if you accidentally ingested pesticides.

- If you are breast-feeding, see the recommendations in chapter 9.

That pesticides are toxic chemicals is an easy concept for most people to accept. After all, why wouldn't a substance that kills another living creature injure a human being? And in this case, a very vulnerable human, a developing baby? Other substances may be harder to picture as toxins. For instance, we tend to see medications as helpful, curative substances that save lives and make us feel better. Although that's true for the most part, our medicine cabinets can be a source of some powerfully dangerous developmental toxins. Chapter 8 discusses medications that may be harmful to your health and your baby's.

Stress, Medicines, and Health Conditions

More information is available today about the effects of medical chemicals on the development of the embryo and the developing child than ever before. Considering that fact, it is positively amazing that doctors are prescribing more and more medications for pregnant women and that more women are taking more over-the-counter drugs. The average pregnant woman takes at least three different medications during her pregnancy, none of which have been adequately tested for developmental effects.

A mother's medical condition can be dangerous in itself to a developing fetus. So it is true that in many cases where the mother has a serious health condition, doing without the medication may put the fetus at higher risk than exposing it to a drug. Women with serious health problems and medical disorders must not make these decisions on their own and should consult both their prescribing doctor and especially their obstetrician. Overall, most professionals agree that when women have serious medical concerns, a healthy mother is the best guarantee for a healthy baby.

However, it is often hard to tell whether a mother's medical condition or the medicine she must take will affect the developing baby. A general rule for pregnant and lactating women is to avoid taking any drug unless the doctor says it is absolutely necessary. Even then, the doctor may not be able to advise a woman accurately because, for most drugs, there have been no clinical trials involving pregnant women. The available information for medications comes from tests on animals and the effects that have surfaced after they have been used by pregnant women.

Important Notice for Pregnant Women

Mothers-to-be, don't become worried or upset if you discover you have a medical condition or if your doctor labels your pregnancy "high-risk." This does not necessarily mean that your baby is at great risk, just that you want to monitor your health and the progress of your pregnancy more closely (Samuels and Samuels 1996).

In fact, even though experts are learning more and more about the negative effects of medications on the fetus, the use of medications during pregnancy seems to be increasing. Most pregnant women remain uninformed about the effects of medication on their unborn baby. For some reason, most people consider medications safer than environmental chemicals. However, medications *are* chemicals; they are just chemicals that also have a benefit at a predetermined level. In addition, the increased amounts of chemicals in our daily environment may have the effect of increasing the negative effects of a medication.

Many substances while not necessarily harmful in themselves may potentiate (increase the strength of) the toxicity or teratogenicity of another drug. Doctors have appropriate concerns regarding combinations of drugs and chemicals during pregnancy. According to Dr. Henry M. Lerner of Tufts University School of Medicine (1997), "Almost all medications cross the placental barrier."

Many medications have been shown to harm the fetus only at a specific period in the pregnancy. In fact, some medications are rated in one category of harmfulness in the first trimester and in another category in the last trimester. Some experts warn that a substance that causes birth defects at one stage may cause developmental disorders in a later stage.

FDA Categories for Fetal Risk

Two decades ago, the FDA created several categories to reflect the risk to a fetus of a specific drug. Drugs are assigned a risk category based on animal studies or on reports of fetal damage in women who used the drug during pregnancy. To find the pregnancy risk category of a drug you are taking, ask your doctor or pharmacist to look it up for you, or find it for yourself in the *Physicians Desk Reference*, which is available in any library and most bookstores. Guides for nonprescription drugs usually will list the risk category also.

Note that these categories are only useful to get a *general* impression of a drug. Some experts have found that the FDA categories actually have poor correlation with real fetal risk (Fried 1980).

FDA Drug Categories for Fetal Risk

The FDA (Federal Drug Administration) has evaluated studies on the effects of certain drugs on pregnant women or animals. As a result of those studies, they have classified many drugs according to the following categories.

FDA Category A

Controlled studies in humans have shown no fetal risks. Relatively few drugs occupy this category; they are mostly multivitamins and prenatal vitamins.

FDA Category B

Animal studies have shown no fetal risks, but no adequate human studies have been conducted. Many commonly used drugs are in this category including the penicillin-based drugs.

FDA Category C

There are no adequate studies either in animals or humans that indicate fetal risk. Many (perhaps most) drugs occupy this category.

FDA Category D

There is clear evidence of fetal risk but the benefits are considered to outweigh the risks. These medications should be used only when absolutely necessary.

FDA Category X

The proven fetal risks outweigh any benefit.

Food and Drug Administration Drug Bulletin (1979)

Medications Whose Risks Outweigh Benefits—They Disrupt Fetal Development

These drugs have been determined by the FDA to have fetal dangers outweighing any possible benefit to the mother. There are numerous other drugs not included on this list that manufacturers voluntarily list as Category X, thus alerting consumers that serious dangers exist for the fetus. For instance, Halcion, Dalmane, and Restoril have been categorized as Category X. For any drug you take during pregnancy, ask your doctor or your pharmacist about the drug's category. If you discover that the drug is rated X, discuss this with your physician immediately. Each of these drugs may be found in the Guide to Common Chemicals and Developmental Effects in chapter 12.

Category X Drugs

Accutane	Halcion	Pravachol
Androderm	Halotestin	Premarin with Methyltestosterone
Android and Android capsules	Humegon	Premarin Vaginal Cream
Aquasol A Parenteral	Humorsol	Premarin intravenous
Aquasol A capsules	Lescol	Premarin tablets
Augestin	Levlen/Tri-Levlen	Premphase
Bellergal-S	Lo/Ovral	Prempro
Brevicon	Lupron Depot	Profasi
Cafergot	Lupron	Proscar
Casodex	Lupron Depot-Ped	ProSom
Climara	Lupron Depot 3.75 mg.	Quadrinal
Clomid	Menest	Restoril
Coumadin	Megace Sispension	Sansert
Cytotec	Methotrexate/ Rheumatrex	Stilphostrol

D.H.E. 45	Metrodin	Supprelin
Danocrine capsules	Mevacor	Synarel Nasal
Delatestryl	Micronor	Synarel
Demulen	Mithracin	Tegison
Depo-Provera Contraceptive	Nor-Q	Testoderm
Desogen	Nordette-21	Testred
Didrex	Norplant	Tri-Norinyl
Diethylstilbestrol	Ogen/Ogen tablets	Triphasil-21
Doral	Oreton	Virazole
Efudex	Ortho Dienestrol cream	Vivelle
Ergomar	Ortho-Cept	Wigraine
Estrace	Ortho-cyclen/Ortho-Tri-Cyclen	Winstrol
Estraderm	Ortho-Est	Zocor
Estratab	Ovcon	Zoladex 3-month
Estratest	Oxandrin	Zoladex
Floropryl Ophthalmic	Pergonal	All hormones
Floroplex	PMB	Radioactive iodine

During pregnancy and breast-feeding, it is important to go to a doctor who knows you and about your pregnancy. A doctor who doesn't know you are pregnant or breast-feeding may prescribe a medication that could harm your baby.

Simple Solutions For Informed Decision-Making About Prenatal Medications

Because you are concerned about the possible effects of medication on your developing baby, and because so little is known regarding the developmental effects of many medications, you may wish to discuss the following possible approaches with your doctor (Cunningham, et al. 1997):

- Reduce the amount of your medication during your pregnancy.
- Substitute a safer medication.
- Eliminate other medications that can potentiate toxic effects.
- Use a single medication for your disorder rather than multiple medicines.
- Stop or reduce the medication during critical periods.
- Take the medication for the shortest possible duration.
- Eliminate the medication until after delivery if possible.

Don't think that because you have a disorder that must be medicated during pregnancy, that your baby will automatically suffer developmental problems. Taking medications during pregnancy only increases the possibility of risk that your baby will have problems, usually by only a few percentage points. (In rare cases, the risk can increase by as much as 30 percent.) In fact, the issue of why medications affect some babies in the womb and appear to leave most babies unscathed presents an important question that is addressed in the following section.

Why Most Babies Are Unharmed by High Risk Medications

Most of the time, babies who have been exposed to medications in the womb are born healthy and undamaged. Even with a medication that causes a 30 percent rate of birth defects, the other 70 percent of babies born to mothers who have been medicated seem okay. Why is this? Here are some possibilities.

- Medications interact with other substances and maternal conditions including the following: nutritional state, stress level, chemical load, inadequate ability to metabolize toxins, genetic predisposition, and the presence of chemicals and other medications that may interact with the medication synergistically to increase effects on the fetus. Therefore, the healthier and more chemically reduced lifestyle the mother has, the more she reduces the baby's risk.
- The medication may not have been given at a critical developmental time. Or dosage may be low enough that the mother excretes it quickly, or the dosage may be low enough to avoid having a developmental effect on the baby.
- Fetal development overcomes the damage because it is minor.

- Stimulation of the newborn by the parents enables the baby's brain to repair the damage.

- The damage doesn't show up until later in life when the child goes to school. For example, diethylstilbestrol, which was used to delay delivery, was found to cause a high rate of cancer and sexual dysfunction when the children were older (Briggs, Freeman, and Yaffe 1994).

Reducing Medication Risk During Pregnancy

There are many options you and your doctor can consider to further reduce the risks of taking medication during pregnancy. In some cases, although this may be somewhat unusual, your doctor can choose to totally eliminate or significantly reduce a medication until your baby has been delivered. For instance, she/he may advise you to terminate or lower the dose of an antidepressant medication during your pregnancy if doing so will not endanger you or make you miserable for nine months. Or if you are currently taking two separate medications for the same disorder, you may be given the option of eliminating one of those. In addition, during your pregnancy, your doctor may choose to discontinue other less necessary medications you are taking which might add to the baby's risk. The goal is to eliminate all the chemicals you are taking that are not absolutely necessary for your health.

Your doctor may have the option of changing your medication to one known to be less threatening to a developing baby. Most classes of medication have some medications known to be safer during pregnancy. Although the safer medication may not be the optimal one for managing your disorder, it may offer a compromise that maintains your health and your baby's. In addition, a medication that you must take may have to be postponed until after a period of specified risk to your baby. Some medications have negative effects on development during a certain stage of your baby's growth. If taking the medication can wait until that developmental stage has passed or if taking it can be completed prior to that stage, your baby will benefit. Your doctor also will want to limit any short-term medications to the shortest period possible to avoid exposing your baby unnecessarily.

Women who use prescription drugs during pregnancy show 30 percent more birth defects than women who avoid drugs totally. The drugs that appear to be the most troublesome are tranquilizers, antidepressants, and narcotic pain relievers, all of which affect the central nervous system (CNS).

Developmental disorders that show up later in childhood remain hard to tie to a source. The medications listed in this chapter represent a handful of all the medications on the market (PDR 1997; American Pharmaceutical Assoc. 1993; Briggs, Freeman, and Yaffe 1994; Cunningham, et al. 1997).

Our goal in addressing certain medications in this text is to demonstrate that often there are safer substances for the pregnant woman whose doctor advises her to take medicine during pregnancy. If you are taking a medication, spend the time to investigate that substance so you will understand the risks involved, the alternatives, and the necessity of its administration in your case.

More Medications Known or Suspected to Affect the Developing Fetus

Aspirin	Flagyl	Lithium	Valium
Streptomycin	Aminopterin	Methotrexate	Dilantin
Amphetamines	Anesthetic Gases	Tetracycline	Thyroid drugs
Sulfonamides	Demerol	Coumarins	Hormones
High dose Vitamin A	Warfarin	Podophyllin	Penicillamine
Valproic acid	ACE inhibitors	Carbamazepine	Morphine
Cyclophosphamide	Methimazole	Griseofulvin	Barbiturates
Thalidomide	Diethylstilbestrol	Busulfan	Trimethadione

Samuels and Samuels (1996); Cunningham, et. al. (1997)

Medical Disorders That Can Influence Fetal Development

A compromised immune system due to physical disorders can enable toxic chemicals to remain in your body longer, thus increasing the risk to your baby. Mothers with disorders that affect immune or liver functioning will want to be especially careful. Physical problems that compromise the immune system include but are not limited to the following:

- High stress levels

- Malnutrition or poor nutrition

- Liver disease
- Enzyme deficiencies
- Kidney disease
- Autoimmune disorders
- Significant obesity
- Infections

Infections and Viruses

Infections in the pregnant mother present significant risk to the developing baby. High or persistent fever is neurotoxic and the baby may suffer while the mother is ill or taking in fewer nutrients. There are multiple antimicrobials that can cure an infection without harming your baby, as judged by years of use in pregnant women without any observable effects surfacing. Typically, most of these medications have not been adequately tested in pregnant women. Many experts have written books on drugs and their effects on the fetus. Most of these sources use research that relies not on controlled experiments but on patients' and doctors' reports regarding the teratogenicity of a drug.

Antimicrobials

Antibiotics

Considered safer: penicillin, amphotericin, clindamycin, erythromycin, miconazole, nitrifurantoin, nystatin, cephalosporins

Considered risky: aminoglycosides, streptomycin, trimethoprim (folate agonist)

Contraindicated in pregnancy: tetracycline

Antiviral Drugs

Considered safer: AZT, alpha-interferon

Considered risky: acyclovir, ganciclovir, amantadine

Contraindicated in pregnancy: Ribavirin, trifluridine, vidarabine, idoxuridine

Antifungals

Considered safer: clotrimazole, miconazole, nystatin, amphotericin B

Contraindicated in pregnancy: griseofulvin

Antiparasitics

Considered safer: chloroquine, pyrantel pomoate, thiabendazole

Use with caution: mebendazole, metronidazole

Considered risky: quinine (category D), sulfadiazine, pyrimethamine (folic acid agonist)

Contraindicated in pregnancy: lindane (endocrine disruptor)

Antituberculin Drugs

Considered safer: ethambutrol

Considered risky: rifampin, pyrazinamide, isoniazid (neurological symptoms)

Contraindicated in pregnancy: streptomycin D

Some viruses appear to cause birth defects during the first ten weeks of gestation; however, there is little documentation on developmental disorders caused by exposure later in the pregnancy. Cytomegalovirus can cause defects in brain, eyes, liver, and spleen. Rubella readily crosses the placenta and, depending on time of exposure, can result in brain disorders, dental, hearing, sight, and heart defects. Risk of defects decreases from exposure in first month (50 percent) to exposure in fifth month (6 percent). Herpes simplex is related to mental retardation, poor brain development, and disrupted development of eyes, liver, and spleen. Antiviral drugs can give a baby protection against the transmission of herpes and cytomegalovirus and can even prevent the baby from catching HIV from an infected mother.

Pain Medications and Anesthesia

Some women find they must have emergency surgery during their pregnancy. The use of anesthesia during surgery and pain medication often concerns a pregnant mother. Fortunately the exposure to anesthetics requires only a very short period, usually a few hours, and most general anesthetics produce no reports of malformations associated with such short-term use. There seems to be a greater risk of problems, including miscarriages, among nurses who are exposed to waste anesthetics (airborne in surgical rooms) on a regular basis.

Drugs Used for Surgery and Postsurgery

Anesthetics

Considered safer (for surgical use): thiopental, ketamine, succinylcholine, nitrous oxide

Considered risky: halothane

Pain Relievers

Considered safer: acetaminophen, codeine, lidocaine, morphine

Considered risky: aspirin, ibuprofen, other NSAIDs

Use in pregnancy contraindicated: aspirin and NSAIDs in the last trimester

Antinausea

Considered safer: cyclizine, meclizine

Only when necessary: prochlorperazine, promethazine

Psychiatric Conditions

A significant portion of our population uses antidepressants, tranquilizers, antipsychotics, or sleeping medications. Many of these include women of childbearing age who may wonder if they can continue using their antidepressant or other psychiatric medication during pregnancy. One concern with psychiatric drugs is that they affect CNS neurotransmitters and therefore have the capacity to change neural function in the developing baby when taken for long periods. However, there have been no studies to observe children longitudinally for developmental effects and so we must depend upon reports of birth defects for indications of safety. Mothers with certain psychiatric illnesses, such as schizophrenia, are more likely to have babies with birth defects even without taking medications (Elia, Katz, and Simpson 1987).

The categories below reflect patient and physician reports only—not studies. However, we must issue a caution regarding the use of CNS-altering drugs throughout a pregnancy. These drugs work by altering brain chemistry. In a developing fetus or a nursing infant altered brain chemistry can alter brain structure and function.

Certain psychiatric drugs may also affect the developing fetus' hormonal balance. For instance, phenobarbital exposure during fetal life can cause permanent changes in the child's sexual functioning due to improper hormonal programming in the fetal brain (Riley and Voorhees 1986; Cunningham, et al. 1997).

Psychiatric Drugs

Antidepressants

Considered safer: fluoxetine, paroxeline, sertraline, bupriopion, sertraline

Considered risky and only when necessary: tricyclics, amitriptyline, amoxapine, clomipramine, imipramine, nortriptyline, lithium

Contraindicated in pregnancy: MAO inhibitors

Antipsychotics
Considered safer: chlorpromazine, clozapine,
Considered risky and only when necessary: mesoridazine

Tranquilizers
Considered risky: clonazepam, lorazepam
Use only when necessary: alprazolam, diazepam, chloriazepoxide

Sedatives
Considered safer: Ambien
Considered risky: Placidyl
Use only when necessary: Nembutal
Contraindicated in pregnancy: Dalmane, Halcion

Hormones and Contraceptives

All hormonal drugs are contraindicated in pregnancy (FDA Category X) including estrogen, androgens, progesterones, and contraceptive medications. Hormones have the potential to alter the development of the baby's genitals, cause cancer in reproductive organs later in life, result in functional sexual disorders, and increase the chance of masculinization of female children and feminization of male children.

If you have become pregnant while taking contraceptives, as a few women do, don't worry. Recent studies have found no evidence of obvious fetal harm in babies exposed during the first few weeks. However, in the second and third trimesters the potential for genital malformations and sexual dysfunction increases greatly. Again, these studies focus on birth defects rather than on effects related to the sexual functioning of the individual after puberty.

There may be an advantage to stopping birth control as soon as possible once a woman discovers she is pregnant. Genital growth and sexual determination occur within the first eight weeks of pregnancy and hormones such as the estrogens and progesterones in birth control pills may interfere with these processes in a negative way.

Cancer

Cancer patients in life-threatening situations must be treated even though most cancer drugs cause an increase in birth defects and brain malformations in animals. These effects have also been reported in humans (Cunningham, et al. 1997; Glanz 1994). Some experts feel the risk of fetal effects can be reduced significantly by avoiding use of these drugs during the first trimester. There is no doubt that in most cases the benefit to the mother exceeds the risk to the child. Additionally, the choice of anticancer drugs may depend solely on the type of cancer involved.

Antineoplastic Drugs

Only when necessary: Taxol, paclitaxel, cyclosphosphamide
Contraindicated in pregnancy: aminopterin, methotrexate
Contraindicated in breast-feeding: Methotrexate, Taxol, paclitaxel

Skin Disorders

Acne, while seemingly a minor problem, can be a disfiguring disorder requiring the use of strong and developmentally damaging medications for treatment. Accutane (isotretinoin) is an oral vitamin derivative that can cause serious birth defects such as facial malformation, heart defects, thymus gland defects, brain malformations, and developmental disorders such as reduced IQ. Women who are taking Accutane are cautioned to use contraception for the entire period of treatment with Accutane starting one month before starting the drug and continuing for one month after treatment has ended. This advice is also given to women who are not currently sexually active, because they can become sexually active very quickly—before their birth control has had time to work.

Tretinoin or Retin-A is applied directly to the skin and shows no concentrations in the bloodstream. Studies of women who used the drug during pregnancy showed no unusual percentage of fetal abnormalities (Jick, Terris, and Jick 1993). Therefore, it has been designated a Category B drug.

Etretinate, however, another Vitamin A derivative used for psoriasis, remains in the body for as long as two years after the termination of therapy. Serious birth defects including brain abnormalities have been observed from the use of this drug within a year of conception. Therefore, experts advise that pregnancy be postponed and actively avoided for at least two years after the cessation of treatment. Cunningham, et al. (1997) advises doctors to completely avoid prescribing this medication to women who intend to conceive.

Skin Treatments

Considered safer: Topical drugs only, tretinoin, Retin-A

Contraindicated for pregnancy: isotretinoin, Accutane, etretinate

Contraindicated for women who may become pregnant: etretinate

Toxoplasmosis

Toxoplasmosis presents a serious threat to the fetus and can be easily prevented through good hygiene during pregnancy. The most common route of exposure is contact with kitty litter, mouse droppings, and uncooked meat. Pregnant mothers should have another family member clean or dispose of cat litter. All meat should be cooked thoroughly. Hands, utensils, and kitchen surfaces should be cleaned well after preparing raw meat for cooking. Turn off the water faucet with a paper or cloth towel to avoid recontaminating your hands, and wipe the faucet handle with a soapy cloth before handling again. Place the soiled towel or paper in the laundry or trash.

Mice should be controlled, as well. Use gloves, or get someone else to clean up mouse droppings, and quickly discard exterminated rodents. See chapter 7 for information on rodent control.

Diabetes

Diabetes can exist in a mother prior to pregnancy or may develop during a pregnancy. Offspring of women with diabetes have approximately twice the risks of obvious birth defects (6 percent instead of 3 percent), but this is considered strongly related to how well the mother controls her blood sugar levels (Miller, et al. 1981). In a diabetic, controlling blood sugar level significantly reduces any risks to the fetus. The higher the blood sugar, the greater the risk. In fact, birth defects seem to occur more frequently in mothers who maintain poor control before they become pregnant.

Uncontrolled diabetes can lead to delivery of large babies, miscarriage, stillbirth, newborn respiratory distress, excessive amniotic fluid, and high blood pressure in the mother which can retard the baby's growth. Women are best advised to get their diabetes under control prior to conception and then continue vigilant control during pregnancy by using a diabetic diet, exercise, and of course, the insulin or other medication prescribed by their physician. Blood glucose monitors requiring a finger prick and a drop of blood provide the most accurate method of evaluating sugar levels on a daily basis. Insulin for diabetes is considered safe for use during pregnancy, and many experts recommend that diabetic pregnant women be controlled with insulin rather than oral diabetic agents.

Diabetes Medication
Considered safer: insulin
Considered risky: Diabinese, Glucophage, Micronase

Epilepsy

In approximately 40 percent of the women who have epilepsy while pregnant, the disorder actually improves during the pregnancy, while only 10 percent become more severely affected. Women with seizure disorders have a two to three times higher risk of having a baby with an obvious birth defect. This usually amounts to a 7–9 percent risk, indicating that the vast majority of these babies, just over 90 percent, are normal. However, many experts think genetic predisposition plays a part in the incidence of birth defects since mothers who are not medicated also are at higher risk. Almost all medications used for seizure controls increase the risk of birth defects, possibly because they use up folic acid excessively (Cunningham, et al. 1997).

Several fetal malformation syndromes are association with anti-convulsant drugs. The most common symptoms are cranial and facial deformities, mental deficiency, growth retardation, limb defects, and cleft palate. These syndromes result from use of hydantoin (Dilantin, phenytoin, mephenytoin, ethotoin), carbamazepine, trimethadione, and valproic acid. As many as 30 percent of infants exposed to phenytoin during their fetal life have physical malformations. Use of phenobarbital during pregnancy has been shown to reduce cognitive performance in the offspring. The risk of birth defects and developmental disorders appears to rise with the number of anti-epileptic medications the mother is taking. Avoiding these drugs in the first trimester seems to lower the risk of obvious birth defects (Annegers, et al. 1978).

However, the risk to mother and baby often justifies the necessity of medicating the mother and only a physician is qualified to make this decision. Some epileptic medications offer less risk to the baby than others and your doctor should be consulted about this. Studies show there may be some benefit to epileptic mothers taking folic acid prior to and during pregnancy to help avoid problems (Cunningham, et al., 1997).

Epileptic Medications
Most experts recommend that women who take valproic acid to prevent seizures be changed to an alternate antiseizure medication well in advance of pregnancy.

Considered safer: None
Considered risky: phenytoin, phenobarbital, carbamazepine
Contraindicated in pregnancy: valproic acid

Hypoglycemia

Pregnant mothers with a history of hypoglycemia should eat frequent, small meals during the day to prevent serious drops in blood sugar that can affect their baby negatively. The developing baby's brain needs nutrients to grow and to maintain existing cells. Nutrients in the form of glucose are vital for use by the baby's brain. Chronic or persistent low blood sugar in the mother can result in the loss of fetal brain cells. The degree of damage depends upon how many brain cells have died and whether the brain growth in an area is able to compensate for the loss. Your doctor can recommend the appropriate hypoglycemic diet to reduce episodes of hypoglycemia during pregnancy.

Heart Problems

Maternal heart problems affect a fetus when the mother's heart has trouble taking on the extra load of pregnancy, and many newborns of heart patients are smaller and born early. Since the heart must pump as much as 40 percent more blood during pregnancy, mothers with heart problems may need to restrict their activities as the pregnancy progresses so that the baby will receive adequate circulation.

Fetal Warfarin Syndrome, which occurs from maternal use of coumarin for heart disorders, occurs in 15 to 20 percent of babies exposed during the first trimester. These babies can show developmental delays, brain damage, reduced brain size, visual abnormalities, growth retardation, and facial and bone abnormalities. Doctors typically switch a pregnant mother from coumarin type drugs to injectable blood thinners such as heparin which have been found not to cross the placenta.

Heart Medications

Considered safer: heparin drugs, digoxin

Considered risky: propranolol

Contraindicated in pregnancy: warfarin, Coumadin, ACE inhibitors

The ACE inhibitors drugs (angiotensin-converting enzyme inhibitors) used for hypertension are suspected teratogens associated with kidney malfunctioning and stillbirth and are contraindicated during pregnancy. These include but are not limited to: enalapril, lisinopril, ramipril, fosinopril, and so forth.

Asthma

Pregnant women with asthma often experience breathing problems that require the use of inhaled medications. Asthma can cause problems in a developing baby when oxygen to the fetus is reduced during acute attacks. Therefore, controlling asthmatic attacks gives your baby the best opportunity to develop healthily. Most of the inhaled medications such as broncodilators and topical steroids are considered safe for use during pregnancy. These substances usually act on the lung and bronchial tissues upon contact rather than on entering the mother's bloodstream. Most of these substances have not been studied for effects on the fetus. However, there have been no reports of birth defects resulting from first trimester use. No specific testing or research has been conducted regarding developmental disorders originating from use during the second and third trimesters.

There is little evidence that subcutaneous administration of epinephrine in the event of an asthmatic emergency will harm the baby. In fact, not treating severe asthma can be dangerous to both mother and baby.

Asthma Medications

Considered safer: topical corticosteroids, cromolyn, terbutaline, beta-adrenergic inhaler

Simple Solutions
For Medicines and Medical Conditions

- Discuss with your doctor and educate yourself on the fetal effects of any prescription medications you may have to take during pregnancy and lactation.

- Avoid taking any over-the-counter medications during pregnancy and lactation.

- If you are taking any medications that appear on the FDA's Drug Category X and you discover that you are pregnant, call your doctor immediately.

- Work with your doctor to choose medications and dosages for a physical condition that will minimize fetal risk.

- Recognize that "increased risk" does not mean that your baby will definitely be affected by a medication or by your medical condition. It just means that the percentage of risk is higher and that your pregnancy needs to be monitored more carefully.
- If you are using Accutane for a skin condition, you must use contraception beginning one month before treatment until one month after treatment, whether you are sexually active or not.
- Control stress during pregnancy and lactation.
- Avoid mega-vitamins. Instead, take vitamins in moderate amounts.
- Avoid herbal medications because many are known for or are being investigated for adverse fetal effects.
- Control any medical condition carefully during pregnancy because a healthy mother is the best guarantee for a healthy baby.

Toxic Stress and the Developing Baby

Pregnancy can be a stressful time even when you are excited and happy about your coming baby. Lifestyles change, your body changes, finances can become strained, and in-laws, friends, and total strangers begin to offer advice.

Your body's reaction to stress is to channel blood flow to the heart, lungs, and large muscles so that you are prepared to fight or flee a danger. This process diverts circulation from the rest of the body. During periods of stress or anxiety, blood flow to the uterus decreases as much as 60 percent, so your baby gets less oxygen and nutrients. Extended periods of reduced oxygen and nutrients can inhibit the baby's brain growth and development by killing brain cells.

Stress hormones in the mother's bloodstream pass through the placenta to the baby. Adrenaline, also known as epinephrine, appears to have long-term effects on a baby's brain development. Significant amounts of these hormones can restrict the baby's use of nutrients, and can act like toxic chemicals on the baby's brain, changing structure and function because of fast neuronal development during pregnancy. Exposing the growing brain cells to epinephrine can affect the way a baby will respond to stress during her life by changing the way that the central nervous system's neurons transmit information.

Pregnancy-Specific Stressors

Money for prenatal care and baby supplies	Fears about parenting
Job and maternity leave concerns	Concerns about exposures
Concerns about physical appearance	Pregnancy complications
Not enough support from family or spouse	Infections and illnesses
Conflicts with family or in-laws	Concerns about older children
Insurance or government red tape	Conflicts with spouse
Mood changes or strange cravings	Added weight to carry
Excitement about the coming baby	

In fact, a recent study evaluated 120 children under the age of four for effects associated with their mothers' stress during pregnancy (Wadhwa 1998). High levels of prenatal stress were correlated with behavioral problems and temperamental dispositions.

Stress hormones, including epinephrine and cortisol, disrupt normal sexual development in the fetus by blocking fetal testosterone production. Since adequate testosterone to the baby's brain appears necessary to produce male sexual behaviors, little boys may be feminized when their mothers suffer continuing stress during pregnancy.

Simple Solutions For Combating Stress During Pregnancy

- Avoid allowing a stressful situation to go on for long periods.
- If you are at odds with a person or situation in your life, either settle the problem or get away from it.
- Learn to say "So what!" to things that don't really matter.
- Make connections with individuals who are supportive.
- Talk to someone you trust about your concerns. Your mouth is your pressure valve to let off steam.
- Make a list of activities (reading, mild exercise, music, warm baths, shopping, driving, singing, etc.) that have helped you

relax in the past and use them to reduce your stress during your pregnancy.

- Use deep breathing, imagery, relaxation tapes, or therapeutic music to keep yourself calm.

- Resolve to be calm and peaceful during this time for your baby's health.

- Avoid worry; do something about the things you can, and let the other things go.

- Develop a healthy spiritual life.

- Seek counseling if you can't resolve a situation on your own.

Avoiding Antibiotics

Until recently, antibiotics were hailed as "miracle" drugs of the twentieth century. However, much like the overuse of pesticides has created superbugs, the overuse of antibiotics has created superbacteria which are resistant to almost every drug. Like all living creatures, bacteria show adaptive immunity to their environment by adjusting and mutating to survive.

As a society we demand from our medical professionals quick, fast relief. Doctors often prescribe antibiotics when they are not warranted, simply because patients can go elsewhere to get what they want. Sometimes doctors prescribe antibiotics to prevent infections even before they happen. These chemicals offer inexpensive and rapid solutions for our fast-paced world. Unfortunately, the overuse of antibiotic drugs mandated the creation of even stronger, more powerful antibiotics to replace those the germs have overcome. The germs may be winning the race. The drug companies that produce new drugs did not foresee that the need for "superantibiotics" would develop so quickly. An entire generation of antibiotics has now been researched and manufactured, and there already are diseases that are completely resistant to all existing antibiotics.

Pregnant mothers will want to be especially cautious in their use of antibiotics. Several are damaging to the fetus, although others have demonstrated considerable safety over time. However, studies have not been conducted to determine subsequent developmental disorders that may not show up until school age. Be sure any doctor you see knows you are pregnant before prescribing for you.

Simple Solutions
To Reduce Your Need
for Antibiotics

- Keep your body healthy with exercise and a balanced diet. Get adequate vitamins and minerals from natural sources, or take a low-dose vitamin and mineral supplement. Exercise mildly during pregnancy and lactation.

- Control stress. Stress suppresses your immunity to infection.

- Reduce your chemical exposure. Any chemical your body must process uses up your immune system's capacity to fight off infections, so you become more susceptible.

- Avoid anything that sets off your asthma or allergies. These disorders often lead to bacterial infection if untreated.

- Wash your skin cuts with soap and water and apply antibiotic ointment.

- Wash your hands during and after any excursions out of the house. This really can prevent colds and flu. Keep fingers away from eyes, nose, and mouth during flu and cold season. Avoid touching door handles with bare hands.

- If your physician does prescribe an antibiotic, ask if the medication is truly necessary. Be aware that overgrowth of fungi in your vagina, nails, and digestive system can occur because antibiotics destroy even the good bacteria in your system; this is especially true of the powerful "floxin" antibiotics. Take lactobacillus acidophilus, which stays in your digestive tract, to replace your natural flora. You can find this at a health food store. Or buy yogurt labeled "contains live acidophilus cultures."

- Use uncooked garlic at the first sign of illness. The military used garlic to fight infections before the discovery of antibiotics. Real garlic is best (although some experts like the concentrated kind) and, taken with hot peppers, it can improve resistance. Make a delicious medicative salsa with canned tomatoes, red onions, fresh garlic, and chili peppers to be served with chips.

- Zinc lozenges reduce length and severity of colds. Zinc is necessary in pregnancy but because it is a metal it should be limited to small quantities and very short-term use.

- Bladder, not kidney, infections often respond well to cranberry juice which prevents bacteria from adhering to the bladder wall. If symptoms don't respond within 24 hours or a fever develops, call your doctor since the kidneys can become involved and cause serious threat to the baby.

- Vitamin C in doses of 500 mg per day may help you recover faster.

Hypervitaminosis and the Developing Baby

Vitamins in moderate amounts can help you give birth to a healthy, happy baby. Most prenatal vitamins are listed as Category A in the FDA's medication list, meaning they have been shown as safe for use during pregnancy.

Megavitamins, however, present a problem for the developing fetus. As with any medication, taking too much of a vitamin makes it toxic. Some vitamins tend to accumulate in the mother and then in the fetus, creating a toxic situation. The fat soluble vitamins, A and D, build up when taken in concentrations higher than what can be used immediately by the mother's body. This results in a condition known as hypervitaminosis. High doses of Vitamin A or Vitamin D taken during pregnancy can produce birth defects, seizures, and retarded mental development The recommended daily allowance (RDA) for Vitamin D during pregnancy and lactation for the human is 400–600 IU.

Since Vitamin A stays in the mother's body for several weeks, doses exceeding 5000 IU per day should not be taken either by women who are pregnant or by those who may conceive. Eating a well-balanced diet supplies Vitamin A in quantities of about 7500 IU per day which easily exceeds the RDA of 5000 IU for pregnancy and 6000 for breast-feeding.

Nonprescription Drugs

Very few nonprescription drugs have been demonstrated to be safe for fetal development or for breast-feeding. In fact, most are classified Category C, meaning no adequate studies with pregnant women have been conducted. In almost every case, the manufacturer advises a woman to consult her doctor before using the drugs during pregnancy or breast-feeding. However, most pregnant women continue to use them on a regular basis. Some of these drugs cross the blood-brain barrier and the placenta readily and have CNS effects. Others contain aspirin (see the section on aspirin below), steroids, or stimulants, all of which should be avoided during fetal and/or infant development. Women who are pregnant or breast-feeding should consult their obstetrician or pediatrician before using any over-the-counter drug.

Medications with Specific Potential for Disrupting Development

The following sections discuss over-the-counter medications that have proved to be disruptive to the developing fetus.

Pesticide Medications for Scabies And Lice

Some over-the-counter treatments for body infestations contain substances that are known endocrine disruptors that can cause reproductive effects in the fetus and affect sexual structure and functioning in the child. Medications that contain synthetic pyrethroids such as permethrin should be avoided during pregnancy. Some of these medications have pyrethum extract, which should be avoided since the active factor, pyrethrin, has been implicated as an endocrine disruptor.

Medications with Stimulating Action

Some nonprescription medications contain stimulants including ephedra, caffeine, and pseudoephedrine. Many of these nonprescription medications are pain relievers and decongestants. Since stimulants may cause a reduction in fetal blood circulation and a release of stress hormones, they should be avoided during pregnancy. Ask your doctor before using them.

Respiratory Medications

Avoid during pregnancy: pseudoephedrine, guaifenesin

Herbal Medications

Herbal medications should not be taken by a pregnant or breast-feeding woman until she first consults her doctor. Unfortunately, most doctors have not studied herbal medications and may not know how to advise you. Most herbal medications contain substances that have not been tested for use during fetal development or breast-feeding. Some contain substances that can have developmental consequences for the fetus or infant. For instance, St.-John's Wort is an extremely popular herbal medication which, according to research, has antidepressant effects. However, St.-John's Wort is a monoamine oxidase inhibitor, a type of antidepressant not recommended for pregnancy due to its potentially dangerous effects on the developing baby's brain. It alters brain chemistry and should not be taken by pregnant or breast-feeding women.

Other herbal medications contain stimulants that simulate the same physiological reactions in the body as stress does. Medications that contain ephedrine, ma haung, and ginseng are sympathetic nervous system stimulants that could reduce circulation to the baby, thus reducing nutrients and oxygen at a time when the baby's brain is particularly sensitive to a lack of oxygen and nutrition. Additionally, anything that simulates stress has the potential to release stress steroids in your body, which can affect your baby's development.

Several other herbal medications with demonstrated developmental effects may not be safe during pregnancy. Herbal medicines suspected to cause problems in the fetus include echinachea, licorice, comfrey, and senna.

Since no one tests these medicines on pregnant women, avoiding them totally makes the most sense. Just because a substance is natural doesn't make it safe. Many of the most powerful medications on the market originate from natural sources.

Medications Containing Aspirin and Other NSAIDs

Many nonprescription drugs contain aspirin, acetylsalicylic acid. Aspirin use during the third trimester is contraindicated because it can cause bleeding in the baby and the mother during childbirth. Although aspirin falls into Category C in the first trimester, according to the FDA guidelines, it is an acid that can accumulate in the embryo during the first few weeks of pregnancy. Aspirin use during the first half of pregnancy has been shown to have negative effects on IQ later in childhood, although subsequent research has failed to support this. Girls seemed to be affected more than boys, suggesting some interaction with hormones. Aspirin use during pregnancy is also associated with pulmonary hypertension as a result of premature closure of an important artery duct in the fetus (Briggs, Freeman, and Yaffe 1994).

 Simple Solutions To Avoid Nonprescription Drugs

- For sore throats, gargle four to five times a day with one teaspoon of salt to a cup of warm water. Salt dehydrates and kills germs.

- Use tepid, not hot, baths to reduce fever but don't let a fever persist.

- For itchy skin, add one to two cups of oatmeal to your bath.

- To calm a bug bite, make a paste of natural meat tenderizer and apply.

- Ask your partner for a rubdown and keep your fever down to help body aches.

- For coughs, mix honey and lemon and take by the spoonful.

- Chicken soup, cool mist vaporizer, and increased liquids ease congestion.

- For diarrhea, drink clear liquids such as broth and soda for several hours, then eat crackers, rice, dry toast.

- For a too stuffed stomach, eat a little pineapple which contains enzymes that help you to digest protein.

- For upset stomach, drink a cup of ginger tea with a little sugar, or drink clear soda until stomach settles, then eat crackers, bread.

Nonsteroidal anti-inflammatory drugs (NSAIDs) are chemically similar to aspirin and pregnant mothers should avoid them early in the pregnancy and during the last trimester for the same reasons they should avoid aspirin. The safest drug to take for pain, fever, and inflammation during pregnancy according to doctors and most medical guides is acetaminophen, brand name Tylenol.

NSAIDs to Avoid During Pregnancy and Breast-Feeding

Before you take any medication, check to see if it contains any of the following (note that this list is not complete):

Ibuprofen	Aspirin	Alka Seltzer
Naproxen Sodium	Bayer aspirin	Excedrin
Nuprin	BC powder	Ecotrin
Naprosen	Vanquish	St. Joseph's aspirin
Motrin	YSP aspirin	Goody's powder
Aleve	Advil	Orudis

Medications Containing Metals

A few nonprescription drugs contain significant levels of metals including bismuth, gold, selenium, and aluminum (see chapter 6 for a discussion about metals). Many metals have a tendency to collect in nerve tissue, especially in the CNS, and cause neurological damage. Heavy or continued use of drugs or products containing metals is not advisable for pregnant women. As a precaution, check drug and product labels for these substances and check with your doctor before taking them. Pepto-Bismol is one example of a commonly used non-prescription medication that contains metals. Pepto-Bismol contains the metal bismuth.

Antacids seem like such safe drugs to use. However, many of these have metals in them that can accumulate in fetal brain tissue much like lead. Although occasional use, supervised by your doctor, may be okay, mothers who have heavy bouts of nausea and heart-burn during pregnancy or breast-feeding may overdo it.

Medications Containing Steroids

Many oral and topical medications, such as hydrocortisone, con-tain corticosteroids that have been found to be teratogenic in animals. Continued use even of topical cortisone preparations may cause prob-lems for a developing fetus. Note that even the manufacturers urge caution. Although most corticosteroids fall under a Category C desig-nation, use during pregnancy should be avoided unless your doctor determines that the benefit to you outweighs the risk to your baby. Use during breast-feeding is not recommended since corticosteroids pass readily through breast milk. For oral prescription cortisone use, manufacturers advise mothers not to nurse during the time they take the medication. Cortisone can be found in anti-itch creams, sham-poos, and some over-the-counter anti-inflammatory lotions.

Alcohol-Free Medications

Women who are pregnant or breast-feeding need to know that many liquid prescription and nonprescription drugs contain signifi-cant amounts of alcohol that can affect your baby's neurological and intellectual functioning. Experts contend that no level of alcohol is safe during brain development. Therefore, you should avoid taking medications that contain alcohol while you are pregnant or breast-feeding and avoid giving medications that contain alcohol to your infant.

Many medications have been formulated specifically to exclude the use of alcohol. A comprehensive list can be obtained from the

Physicians' Desk Reference for Nonprescription Drugs (1997), found in any library and some bookstores, or by talking with your physician or pharmacist. Also read labels before you buy over-the-counter medications. Alcohol may be listed in the ingredients as ethanol.

Medications and chemicals to which a pregnant mother is exposed obviously have a direct impact on the unborn baby. But what about after the baby is born? Does the physical separation of mother and infant provide a safety net that ensures the baby will not receive the same substances as his/her mother? As you will see, what happens when the mother breast-feeds is another story.

Breast-Feeding and Baby Food

Pediatricians agree that breast milk is, in most cases, the ideal food for newborns and babies. However, just recently a blood pesticide study conducted on Middle Eastern citizens startled researchers. In the Middle East, pesticides are considered valued possessions. Because agriculture has become dependent upon pesticides for continued production of food, Middle Easterners hide their pesticide caches under their beds. As a result, these people have shockingly high levels of toxins in their blood. Only one group of Middle Easterners was found to have low pesticide blood levels. That group was comprised of mothers who had breast-fed!

What happened? Because of its high fat content, breast milk is the perfect repository for toxic pesticides. So the mothers simply passed the chemicals on to their newborns.

Breast-feeding can be an emotionally charged issue that produces guilt. Although it provides the ideal nutrient for newborns, breast milk can also be a chemical cesspool. As mammals, breast-feeding is the natural way to feed human young. In today's world, however, we are forced to confront and deal with the unnatural. Nevertheless, there are ways to ensure that your breast milk provides a healthy food for your baby.

Breast Milk Is Natural Food

First and foremost, mother's milk is genetically programmed to foster the newborn's proper growth and development. The essential fatty acids present in human milk are key components of brain cell membranes and promote optimal brain development (Hamosh 1996). Breast milk also contains digestive enzymes that enable the newborn, who has an immature pancreas, to digest food adequately.

Whether breast milk is, in fact, inherently nutritional is a matter of some disagreement. Some experts contend that mother's milk is nutritionally adequate even when the mother's nutrition is not. Others suggest that the vitamin and mineral quality of breast milk is related to the mother's vitamin and mineral intake (Coveney 1985). One recent study showed that the majority of lactating mothers do not take in enough calories to keep themselves and their breast milk nutritionally adequate.

No matter which contingent is correct, common sense tells us that the more nutrients a lactating mother takes in, the more nutrients will be available to her nursing infant. After all, how can the baby obtain the vitamins and minerals he/she needs if the mother isn't making them available?

We also know that there are some nutritional necessities that breast milk will not provide for the newborn. For instance, Vitamin D, needed for proper growth and development, is not present in breast milk since it is produced by skin when exposed to sunlight. In order to produce an adequate amount of Vitamin D, human skin must be exposed to sunlight for at least ten minutes a day, which is something many newborns and infants do not get. Therefore, many pediatricians recommend that breast-feeding mothers give their infants Vitamin D supplements, usually in the form of liquid drops, starting at about two weeks of age.

Iron, necessary to produce red blood cells, is another supplement pediatricians recommend mothers give to their breast-fed infants. Unlike Vitamin D, our bodies do not make iron: Instead we must rely on food for this essential mineral. A healthy, full-term infant is actually born with an iron supply taken from his/her mother. By the time the newborn is around four-months old, however, he/she has already depleted this store and must rely upon supplements, usually in the form of iron drops or iron-fortified formula. Although breast milk does contain iron, the amounts are not high enough to keep up the adequate levels that infants must constantly maintain. Research has shown that infants who are anemic can suffer deficiencies in intelligence and development.

Breast-feeding mothers who adhere to strictly vegetarian diets may need to take additional vitamins and minerals as well. Under any of the circumstances discussed above, it is always best to consult your doctor or your baby's pediatrician for guidance.

Protection Against Pathogens

Breast milk boosts the newborn's immune system, making it better able to resist infection and disease. Scientists have found that the incidence of various infections, diseases, and metabolic disorders occur less frequently in nursing infants than in formula-fed infants (Kacew 1993). Breast-fed infants also tend to suffer fewer ear, gastrointestinal, and respiratory infections. In geographic areas where bacterial controls are lax or absent, professionals often recommend that mothers breast-feed their babies for longer periods of time. Some reports have indicated that infant mortality rates increase when breast-feeding declines (Rogan et al. 1991).

Don't assume, however, that your breast-fed baby will not get sick. When doctors talk about immunity from disease, they are not necessarily talking about cold and flu bugs. Although breast-feeding may boost your baby's immune system, there are hundreds of cold viruses alone, and it is highly unlikely that there is a mother anywhere who is immune to all of them. Increasing numbers of infants attend day care where they are routinely exposed to viruses that often result in higher incidences of ear and respiratory infections not seen in children who stay at home.

The immunities provided by breast-milk are essential mostly in areas where infectious diseases are life-threatening problems. Mothers in industrialized nations may face extremely different circumstances than in underdeveloped countries with regard to breast-feeding benefits. For example, a woman in an undeveloped country may face significant risks of infection that a woman in the United States generally doesn't need to worry about. In developed countries like the United States, diseases of these kinds are prevented by immunizations. So, even if your baby does breast-feed, she/he must still receive her immunizations on time, since breast-feeding is not foolproof.

Bonding

Additionally, breast-feeding is thought to facilitate the mother-infant bond. Bonding is thought to result from the close interaction that occurs during breast-feeding when mother and infant form an attachment to one another. Bonding, therefore, is biologically desirable since it causes mothers to protect their offspring and offspring to stay close to their mothers.

In recent years, the issue of bonding and attachment has received much press in the United States where juvenile crime and child abuse are at all time highs. Proponents of bonding suggest that infants who bond with caregivers during the first three years of life are more likely, in general, to become productive members of society. These findings have added a new emotionally charged element to the option of breast-feeding. Expectant parents now wonder if they will bond properly with their infant if, for some reason, they are unable to breast-feed or decide not to do it. Parents of rebellious teenagers who did not breast-feed now obsess about whether they bonded or not. The answer to all this worrying lies in understanding what happens during the bonding process.

Eating activates the parasympathetic nervous system (our energy conservation system) which engenders relaxation and comfort while turning off the sympathetic nervous system (our fight or flight system) which activates alertness, distancing, and withdrawal. In fact, eating in close proximity promotes bonding and diminishes fear and discomfort between individuals. That's why business people eat with their clients and why meetings are held at lunch or dinnertime.

So, is breast-feeding a terrific way to bond with your baby? Definitely! Is it the only way to bond with your baby? No! Just consider all the mothers who have bottle-fed their infants in the past five or six decades when breast-feeding was out of style, so to speak. Were they not attached to their children and vice versa? What about fathers who can't breast-feed? Does that mean they don't love their children as much as mothers love them, or that they aren't loved as much by their children? We don't think so. In fact, there are many circumstances under which bonding can take place. And breast-feeding alone probably won't produce the loving attachment for which most parents yearn.

Simple Solutions For Establishing a Bond with Your Baby

- Always hold your baby during feeding rather than propping the bottle up on a blanket.

- Make tender eye contact with your baby whenever possible, especially while feeding.

- Stroke your baby's bare skin lovingly while feeding to make physical contact. Even when you aren't feeding, caress your baby as much as possible. Give your infant daily baby massages.
- Talk or sing softly to your baby while feeding and anytime you are together and awake.
- Attend to your infant's needs promptly so she/he will connect comfort and relief with your presence and touch.
- Sleep with your baby. Although this is still controversial in our society that highly values independence, many experts contend that sharing a bed with your baby will promote the baby's sense of security and overall well-being.
- Hold your baby. Don't be afraid your newborn will get spoiled. Experts agree this is impossible. In fact, some suggest that parents should "wear" their babies as much as possible, carrying them in backpacks or frontpacks especially designed to carry babies close to the adult body.

When Breast-Feeding Is Not Ideal

There are times when parents have to ask themselves if breast-feeding is the right choice for their baby. In some instances, the negative effects it could have on a baby may outweigh the many advantages. In these cases, guilt must be pushed aside. After all, what is good for someone else's baby may not be good for yours.

Medical Conditions

There are circumstances when human milk may not be suitable for mothers and/or infants with certain medical conditions. For instance, infants with some metabolic conditions, should not breast-feed (Coveney 1985). Mothers who are being treated medically for any health condition should speak with their doctor or their baby's pediatrician before breast-feeding. Mothers with AIDS are also advised not to breast-feed their infants since the virus can be transmitted via breast milk.

Medications and Breast-Feeding

Over 50 percent of mothers today breast-feed their babies, up from the 37 percent who breast-fed in the '70s. Some mothers who want to breast-feed are women who must take medications for serious health problems. They should know that the vast majority of medications pass into breast milk, in amounts ranging from a percentage of the mother's blood level to several times higher than the amount the mother receives (Cunningham, et. al. 1997).

Many medications considered okay during pregnancy contain warnings against use by a nursing mother (PDR 1997). This makes absolutely no sense considering that the same drugs that cross into breast milk, also pass through the placenta to the baby while the baby's developing brain and other organs are even more susceptible.

Caution: When you take a medication during breast-feeding, in most cases, you are also exposing your baby to the medication. We want to caution mothers against taking unnecessary medications when breast-feeding. In fact, for many medications listed in the *Physicians' Family Guide to Prescription Drugs* (1996), the mother is advised to choose between breast-feeding or taking the medication. Bear in mind (1) most medications have not been tested for effects on newborns and (2) for many, if not most, medications there is simply no available data. If you must take a medication that may affect your baby adversely, talk with your pediatrician about using a formula during that period of time when you are taking the medication.

Simple Solutions
When Taking Medications During
Breast-Feeding

- Stop breast-feeding during the time you are taking the necessary medication. Talk to your doctor about how to keep your breast milk flowing while you are taking the medications. Many medications are contraindicated for breast-feeding.
- Ask your doctor if you should stop the medication for the period you are breast-feeding.
- Your doctor may be able to substitute a medication with less potential for harm to your infant.
- Depending on the way the medication works, the doctor may advise you to take the dose at a time when your infant will receive the least amount.

Medications cross into breast milk often in different concentrations than those in the mother's bloodstream. Just like environmental toxins, medications may be more or less attracted to breast milk, that is, they are attracted to the fat in breast milk.

If a medication is particularly fat soluble, much higher concentrations may show up in breast milk where the mother's blood deposits the substance. If it is less fat soluble, more of it may stay in the mother's body with less going to the baby. For many medications these facts are available, but for many others they are not.

For most drugs, the time of peak concentration in the bloodstream, and sometimes in the breast milk, is known. The drug's half-life may also be known. For acetaminophen, peak milk concentration occurs at approximately two hours after ingestion. The half-life in milk is 2.6 hours. That means that within approximately two and one-half hours, half of the breast milk concentration is gone. In another two and one-half hours three fourths is gone. Every medication has a different half-life. However, the implication is that, if you must take medication and you must breast-feed, you can schedule your dosages so that your baby is exposed to the least amount of medicine possible (Briggs, Freeman, and Yaffe 1994).

Sometimes the best time to take medication is immediately *after* a breast-feeding session. Another option would be for the mother to take her medication after breast-feeding, and then feed the baby formula for the next feeding session to give the medication time to exit her system and reduce the milk concentration. Your physician or your baby's pediatrician should have access to information about the half-life and blood and milk concentrations of your medication and should be willing to advise you and work with you to offer the baby the safest solution.

Psychoactive drugs, like antidepressants and tranquilizers, affect the central nervous system and so may be of major consequence during breast-feeding. They can have either direct or indirect effects on the baby's still developing brain. Direct effects are seen when the drug crosses the blood-brain barrier and alters the functioning of brain cells, information transmittal, or brain chemistry. Indirect effects occur when the medication affects some part of the body that in turn affects brain tissue, for example, by reducing the amount of blood to the brain as a stimulating drug might do.

Because an infant's immune system is immature, toxic substances may remain in his/her body for extended periods while being metabolized and eliminated. And, as we have pointed out before, new cells that control different brain functions are still being created, and huge numbers of brain cells continue to be myelinated during the same period an infant is breast-fed. Many drugs have the potential to interfere with myelination. Since most drugs cross into breast milk and since so few studies exist for medications to see if they end up in breast milk, it is reasonable to assume that they do.

Mothers who are exposed to radioactive pharmaceuticals for diagnostic purposes should be advised not to breast-feed for a specified period depending on the specific drugs used. Medications containing ethanol, or alcohol, should be avoided, and nonalcohol-based medications substituted. Mothers undergoing pharmaceutical treatment for cancer should not breast-feed.

Recreational Drugs

Every expert agrees that mothers should stay away from recreational drugs during pregnancy. This also holds true if you decide to breast-feed your baby since the drugs will contaminate your milk. Chapter 3 explains the dangers of recreational drug use during your baby's growth and development.

Infants exposed to cigarette smoke during fetal development and later via breast milk or passive smoking exhibit lower birth weights and increased incidence of ear and respiratory infections. Nursing infants of smoking mothers show adult level urinary cotinine excretion and 10 times the cotinine levels seen in formula-fed infants of smoking mothers (Schulte-Hobein, et al. 1992). (Cotinine is just one of the hundreds of chemicals found in cigarette smoke.) Recently there has been some suggestion among researchers that smoking during pregnancy and breast-feeding can predispose a child to nicotine addiction later in life.

Alcohol is a recreational drug. Mothers who breast-feed should not drink and, inversely, mothers who drink should not breast-feed after drinking. Alcohol is neurotoxic to a developing brain and even though the baby is no longer a fetus, she/he can still suffer increased neurological effects from the mother's alcohol intake. Even though much brain growth has taken place, the infant's tiny brain grows at a phenomenal rate during the first two years of life, concurrent with nursing. Chronic exposure to alcohol through breast milk has been shown to have an adverse effect on the psychomotor performance of babies (Little, et al. 1989).

Chemical Contamination of Breast Milk

It makes sense that, along with drugs and alcohol, harmful chemicals should be avoided during lactation. We have already explained how chemicals are stored in body fat and how, when fat is broken down during pregnancy, these chemicals tag along, contaminating the fetus' food supply (Aranda and Stern 1983). The same is true for breast milk. In fact, breast-feeding is the best way to rid your body of chemicals.

Lactation causes a mother's fat tissue to break down to aid in the production of breast milk. This accounts for the added benefit of weight loss many women think they're getting when they decide to breast-feed their infants. Unfortunately, the breakdown of fat tissue also results in the release of chemicals that may have been stored in the mother's body for years. Studies have shown that nursing mothers can discharge as much as 20 percent or more of their lifetime chemical stores (Pottkotter 1994). Unfortunately, those chemicals go directly to the nursing infant's tiny body.

And it's not just the fat-soluble, stored chemicals that you need to worry about since even those chemicals that leave your body relatively quickly still can contaminate your breast milk. In fact, breast milk is the preferred route of excretion for many toxins.

Solvents, like tetrachloroethylene, cross over into breast milk at three times the level seen in the mother's blood. Because alcohol is a solvent and produces psychomotor effects in breast-fed infants, using other solvents while breast-feeding is definitely inadvisable because it is likely that they too will cross over into breast milk.

Using other chemicals with known neurotoxic effects is also not wise especially because they end up in breast milk in such heavy quantities. For some pesticides such as Dieldrin and DDT, the amount in breast milk can be up to seven times that in the mother's blood, while PCBs can cross into breast milk at levels four to ten times greater. Breast-fed infants whose mothers ingested PCB-contaminated rice in Japan in 1968 suffered serious neurological consequences (Reggiani and Bruppacher 1985).

Who Is Contaminated?

We know that chemicals and the vulnerable developing baby do not mix. We also know that even if we stringently avoid chemicals from this day forward, our bodies may still contain stored chemicals that can contaminate our breast milk. The question now has to be: How do I know the extent of my chemical body burden and what do I do about it?

Sadly enough, studies conducted all over the world demonstrate that everyone on the planet carries a chemical body burden to some extent. Most of us have been exposed to chemicals since conception through sources like our mothers' bodies and milk supplies, the food we eat, and even the air we breathe. Because of these varied sources of exposure, chemical burdens vary widely.

Breast-Feeding

If your breast milk is healthy and you want and have the opportunity to breast-feed, nothing could be better and healthier for your baby.

Simple Solutions To Determine Breast Milk Chemical Load

If any of the following factors apply to you, you may want to get your breast milk tested for contamination levels prior to breast-feeding. Many women are getting tested just to be safe.

- Have you worked around any chemicals on a regular basis in the last few years?
- Have you used chemicals in your home, farm, or office heavily or on a regular basis?
- Are you living in a geographic area that is known to be highly contaminated?
- Have you been exposed in any way to chemical leaks?
- Do you play golf regularly (most golf courses are sprayed heavily) or do you swim in chemically treated swimming pools?

Other factors also contribute to chemical body load and the subsequent content of breast milk. Some of these include maternal age, lifestyle, history, weight, work, diet, fat intake, exercise, previous exposures, and geographic location. For instance, the age of the mother may affect her chemical body burden since she has had more time to accumulate chemicals. Weight can also contribute to body burden since more chemicals have more places to be stored. Exercise, on the other hand, can relieve body burden since fat tissue is broken down, releasing with it stored chemicals.

Now that you have considered all the ways you may have been exposed to chemicals, what do you do next? Well, that's up to you. Although most obstetricians and pediatricians argue that the advantages of breast-feeding largely outweigh the dangers of chemical contamination, in our opinion, it is important to remember that broad generalizations, when considering your baby's optimal growth and development, should not always be relied upon because individual chemical burdens and exposures can vary widely. For example, some experts suggest that women routinely exposed to chemicals on the job must seriously consider whether breast-feeding is the best choice for their baby.

We must also remember that neither our governments nor the scientific community have undertaken large-scale studies on the developmental effects of chemicals. Much of what we do know is the result of accidents or animal research. Therefore, most health professionals really have no solid basis on which to advise a mother to breast-feed without considering what harmful substances in her body and environment will be passed on to her baby. As one research group so aptly put it, "no evidence of harm" is not the same as "evidence of no harm" (Paitrast, Keller, and Elves 1998).

Contaminants Found in Breast Milk

All over the world breast milk samples are taken for research purposes since it tends to be a good indicator of chemical body burden. Although much of this research was meant to study the persistence of chemicals in the body, it is used here to show you the common chemicals a typical baby may be exposed to during pregnancy and breast-feeding.

The most common chemicals found in breast milk samples worldwide are pesticides. According to WHO, breast milk routinely contains pesticides such as DDT, DDE, chlordane, dieldrin, and heptachlor. Other studies contend that many of these chemicals are regularly found in breast milk "at levels that would prevent its sale as a commercial food for infants" (Rogan, et al. 1991).

Ongoing research indicates that breast milk pesticide concentrations are declining over time in areas where organochlorines were banned. Breast milk studies in Canada have recently shown a decrease in hexachlorobenzene, DDT, heptachlor epoxide, dieldrin, some chlorinated benzenes, and PCBs. Canadian breast milk contamination appears to be one of the lowest among the industrialized nations (Davies, et al. 1993).

In countries that banned PCBs almost two decades ago, PCBs are still found in levels that exceed "safe" limits. PCBs in breast milk are linked with reduced newborn neurological capacity. Testing among toddlers 18 to 24 months old showed scores 4–9 points lower on Bayley Scales for breast-fed children contaminated with PCBs or DDE. Where mothers lived and ate food grown next to a stream polluted with PCBs from a factory upstream, their breast-fed babies showed a significant predisposition to developing various diseases (Rogan and Gladen 1991).

In some of these situations, an infant breast-fed for twelve months would receive around 10 percent of the cumulative exposure dose/per body weight that would be received by an adult with fifty years exposure. That would amount to 1.7 times the concentration of the chemical in the mother.

Breast Implants and Breast-Feeding

Mothers who have silicone breast implants are advised not to breast-feed their babies. Studies have shown that these implants can leach silicone that can make its way into breast milk. Babies who drink silicone-tainted breast milk have been found to develop swallowing problems. The long-term risks have not been determined at this time (Levin and Ilowite 1994).

Breast Milk Testing

Women who want their breast milk tested can do so at any time. A small amount of fluid can be pressed from the nipple of any woman, even those who are not breast-feeding or who have never been pregnant. At the time of testing, that small amount of fluid is enough to get a good idea of how much contamination your baby would receive from your breast milk if you were to nurse. The technicians at the labs that test for breast milk contaminants can check you and let you know within hours what the chemical levels in your breast milk might be.

The next step is to compare those levels with the levels recommended by the FDA for baby formula. If your levels are too high, you must decide whether the benefit of feeding your infant with breast milk outweighs the risk. It is not an easy decision, and it is one that only you can make.

Reducing Breast Milk Pollutants

In chapter 3, there is a discussion of the many ways chemicals can be expelled from our bodies prior to pregnancy. You may remember that some of these detoxification techniques include weight loss and saunas, two practices that should not be undertaken during pregnancy or during breast-feeding since the chemicals released from mother's body would contaminate her breast milk. If you haven't read this book before becoming pregnant or breast-feeding, don't be alarmed. There are still ways you can easily and significantly reduce the amount of chemicals your body passes on to your baby.

Simple Solutions
To Reduce the Chemicals in Your
Breast Milk

- Don't lose a lot of weight after pregnancy. Breast-feeding in itself causes weight loss but at a measured level.
- Take in sufficient calories so your body doesn't break down excess fat.
- Don't add to your body's chemical load. Avoid pesticides, chemically contaminated food, and household cleaners.
- Don't continue to work in a toxic environment.
- Don't exercise strenuously.
- Avoid unnecessary medications.
- If you sustain a heavy chemical exposure, alternate breast-feeding with bottle feeding. Call your doctor.
- Make use of the natural antioxidants in foods (chapter 1) to help tie up toxins and move them quickly out of your body.

Avoid Heavy or Rapid Weight Loss

One of the concerns most mothers face after pregnancy is weight loss. In fact, one of the many reasons women favor breast-feeding is due, in part, to its weight-loss potential. Unfortunately, if your body has stored chemicals, and medical science tells us that everyone does, losing weight can cause the fat-soluble chemicals your body has been carrying around for years to be released into your breast milk. Many medical experts recommend that nursing mothers not lose weight until after lactation and that they should maintain a strict dietary regimen to avoid weight loss.

This is not to suggest that losing a few pounds will be detrimental to your baby. So don't frantically weigh yourself whenever you think you may have shed a pound or two. This is simply a recommendation that significant weight loss can be harmful if you have a significant load of toxics stored. The more weight you lose, the more chemicals may be passed on to your nursing baby.

This issue also brings up the subject of exercise which many new mothers rely on not only to loose weight but to stay healthy, increase energy levels, and reduce stress. During pregnancy and lactation, exercise can have a positive effect on mother and baby if it is done in moderation. Excessive amounts of exercise can release stored chemicals by breaking down body fat. So if you do exercise, remember to maintain proper caloric intake to keep your body from having to burn fat for energy.

Diet

Many of the chemicals stored in our bodies get there through the food we consume. Obviously, before pregnancy is a good time to begin eating organically to reduce your overall accumulation of chemicals. During pregnancy and lactation, mothers should also strive to eat chemically free, not only to keep their chemical body burdens from increasing, but also to avoid any chemicals from reaching their babies via the placenta or breast milk.

In addition, reducing fat intake will reduce the chemical contamination of breast milk since fat-soluble chemical residues are obviously higher in fatty foods that contain stored chemicals. One research group suggests that a lower dietary fat intake will reduce lifetime chemical stores, thus reducing chemical contamination of breast milk (Schlaud, et al. 1995). A balance should be reached with a moderate level of fat in the diet, not too much so that more chemicals are taken in and not too little so that fat stores are broken down. You can gauge this by weight loss. Significant weight loss may mean you need to add a little more fat to your diet.

Avoid Chemicals

Not all of the chemicals routinely found in breast milk come from contaminated food and water. In fact, most of the large chemical exposures we come into contact with every day come from nonfood sources like household cleaners or carpet. Even the chemicals we use to make ourselves beautiful can be absorbed or inhaled by the mother and then by the nursing infant. We have tried to highlight many of the dangerous and varied chemical exposures that the average person sustains on a regular basis (see chapters 4, 5, 6, 7, 8, and 10).

We have also tried to list chemical alternatives that are relatively easy and inexpensive, so pick out as many as you feel you can handle and use them. Remember, any chemical you avoid can't harm your baby.

Infant Formulas

Commercial infant formulas will never completely duplicate breast milk which has human enzymes and chemical compositions, many of which haven't even been identified yet. For all that, formula feeding is an acceptable alternative to ensure an infant's proper nutrition when mothers decide not to or are unable to breast-feed or they need to supplement their milk supply. There are a variety of infant formulas on the market that are generally categorized as cow-based, soy-based, or specialized formulas.

Scientific studies undertaken by health groups, the EPA, and the FDA (National Research Council 1993) show that cow's milk–based formulas have nondetectable levels of pesticides. This is due to milk fat being replaced with vegetable oil and to the multiple processing steps that formula undergoes. This is one reason we feel that mothers who learn or suspect they have high chemical body loads can feel good about feeding their babies formula. There are other reasons, too.

Babies don't have to be breast-fed in order to bond with their caregivers. And, indeed, it is possible for a breast-fed infant not to bond with a parent who is distant, neglectful, or who thinks nursing is the only step needed to facilitate bonding. Breast-feeding does not necessarily keep a baby from getting sick. Breast milk does provide the baby with the mother's immunities to disease which, in many parts of the world, is essential for the infant's survival. It will not, however, keep a baby from ever getting sick, especially if the baby is routinely exposed to other sick children.

We don't want it to seem as if we are opposed to breast-feeding. Nothing could be further from the truth. We simply want to dispel many of the myths and gray areas surrounding the breast-feeding versus formula-feeding battle that often leads to unnecessary guilt in mothers who decide not to breast-feed or don't want to do it for an entire year. We want these mothers to know that they can be assured that their infant can receive alternative yet sufficient nutrition and nurturing.

Cow's Milk-Based Formulas

Cow's milk-based formulas are obviously derived from the milk produced by lactating cows. To make the formula easier for the infant to digest, the milk fat is replaced with vegetable oils and the milk protein is hydrolyzed or partially predigested. Formula does take more time to be digested than breast milk, which has special digestive enzymes.

In addition to the lactose that is added to formula to make it comparable to the sugar content of breast milk, needed vitamins and minerals, such as Vitamin D and iron, which aren't available in breast milk, are added to commercial formulas. Therefore, if your baby drinks formula alone or uses it as a supplement, he/she may not need extra vitamins and minerals. Also, keep in mind that your baby needs iron for optimal growth and development so low-iron formulas should not be used unless specified by your pediatrician. Studies have finally proved mother-in-laws around the world wrong. Iron does not cause constipation or colic and serious ramifications can occur if your baby doesn't maintain adequate iron stores (Pottkotter 1994).

Research has also shown that formula feeding does not predispose an infant to allergies such as exema or contact dermatitis. In most cases, these allergies are related to conditions like asthma or environmental contaminants. One baby we know developed contact dermatitis only after wearing polyester clothing. When his mother switched to all-cotton clothing and bedding, the condition disappeared.

Soy-Based Formulas

Soy-based formulas are made from soy protein and sucrose rather than lactose. This formula is suggested for infants who are lactose intolerant, either permanently or during instances of diarrhea. Soy formula is also used by strict vegetarian families who do not want to use products made from animals.

Soy formulas do take a little more time to be digested than breast milk or cow's milk–based formulas. Soy formulas also tend to have slight traces of pesticide residues, probably due to chemicals used on soy beans during the growing process. Most of these chemicals, however, are filtered out during processing.

Soy-based products often contain phytoestrogens (Setchell, et al. 1997). Used as directed, soy formulas provide the infant with a daily dose rate of a total of 150 isoflavones at approximately 3 mg/kg body weight, maintained at a constant level between zero to four months of age. Supplementing the diet of a four-month-old infant with a single daily serving of cereal can increase isoflavone intake by over 25 percent depending upon the brand.

This rate of isoflavone intake is much greater than that shown in adult humans to alter reproductive hormones. Researchers are suggesting that more studies on the effects of soy isoflavones on human babies should be conducted due to their concern that ingesting too much of these substances may act as endocrine disruptors.

Formula and Lead

Many people think that babies who are fed with formula are exposed to lead. This is true in some cases, but the lead comes from the water used to mix the formula, not from the formula itself (Shannon and Graef 1989). To avoid contaminating your baby's formula with lead and other harmful metals, follow the practices described in chapter 4.

Milk

At about one year of age, babies outgrow their need for formula and can begin drinking cow's milk if they are not allergic to it. Unfortunately, most commercial cow's milk contains a genetically bioengineered hormone rBGH (recombinant bovine growth hormone) or rBST (recombinant bovine somatotropin) that causes cows to produce 10–20 percent more milk. These hormones contain IGF-1, a growth hormone, which is not destroyed by pasteurization. In cows, these hormones can result in horrible side effects including mastitis, bone lesions in feet, knees, and legs, reproductive problems, and cystic ovaries. Furthermore, exposure to significant amounts of IGF-1 may sensitize the breast tissue of female infants, making them more likely to develop cancer when exposed to endocrine-disrupting pesticides later in life. It is, obviously, an endocrine disruptor.

Unlike cow's milk–based formulas, the milk fat in commercial cow's milk is not removed and can contain pesticides. Luckily, large supermarkets are beginning to carry organic milk products. This is milk that has been taken from cows who have been fed only organic food and who have not been given harmful hormones and antibiotics. Pregnant women, lactating mothers, and toddlers should try to consume only organic dairy products or dairy products that do not contain harmful hormones. The Pure Food Campaign (800-253-0681 or 202-775-1132) has a list of companies who have pledged in writing not to use rBGH dairy products or who use certified organic dairy products.

Baby Food

Commercial baby foods and cereals routinely show slight or nondetectable levels of pesticide residues mostly because of the processing steps employed to eliminate chemicals from the finished product (National Research Council 1993). For example, apples used to produce baby applesauce are washed, blanched (to preserve color), peeled, pressed (for juice), finished (removal of fibrous or indigestible material), and heated (for sterilization). Many commercial infant foods today are even free of additives and preservatives and many are fortified with vitamins and minerals like Vitamin C and iron. However, some contain high levels of nitrates. Organically grown and processed baby foods are also available at health food stores and many large retail supermarkets.

Make Your Own Baby Food

Many parents choose to make their own baby food because they enjoy doing it and because they feel it is more nutritious, which may or may not be true. Opinions vary on whether produce sold in markets is more nutritious than food that has already been processed. Market produce is most often picked before ripening to make the long trips to your grocery store. This means it has been harvested before it attained its nutritional peak. So, produce bought at market tends to lack the nutrients of produce that has been harvested and processed when ripe.

Often, frozen produce or produce in jars has the same problem. Many large companies can get their food ripe since it is processed quickly. Processing does decrease the amounts of nutrients available yet it tends to preserve what is left when it is frozen or canned. So it is impossible to really know how much nutritional value "fresh" as opposed to processed produce has.

Another factor you must consider if you make your own baby food is the chemical pesticide residues on the food available at your market. Commercial baby food has nondetectable pesticide levels due to the steps it undergoes during processing. The food you prepare at home will not go through these steps and may contain pesticides if you have not bought organic produce. If you can't buy organic produce and still want to make your baby's food, be sure to wash it thoroughly with cool tap water or bottled water, scrub it with a vegetable brush, and peel if possible. These steps combined with cooking should reduce your baby's pesticide exposure significantly. Keep in mind that systemic pesticides can't be washed off and it is impossible to know if surface or systemic pesticides or both have been used on your food.

Homemade Baby Food

We think it's a great idea to make your baby's food if you have the time and you like to do it. But if you don't, don't sweat it. Commercial baby food is nutritious and virtually chemical-free if it doesn't include additives and preservatives. Listed below are a few basic baby foods anyone can make.

Simple Solutions
For Making Your Own Baby Food

- Steam organic vegetables and mash, no sugar or salt is needed.

- Steam or stew fruits and mix some together for variety.
- Well-cooked meats can be ground in a food processor with a little water.
- Mash a banana or an avocado.
- Cut organically grown raw fruits and vegetables into tiny pieces that babies that can gum, or chew.

Mothers in some parts of the world chew their babies' food before giving it to them. There are many baby food recipes and cookbooks available on the Internet or at your local library or book store. One terrific and easy to use recipe book is Vicki Lansky's *Feed Me, I'm Yours* (1986).

Caution: Little-Known Danger!

Infants, children, and adolescents should avoid foods labeled as containing glutamate, aspartame, and cysteine. These substances are hidden in so many foods that it would be easy for a small child to receive a harmful dose from ingesting several foods that contain them in one day.

These substances are excitotoxins and there is concern in the scientific community that the immature brain may be especially susceptible. (Excitotoxins are chemicals that are so stimulating to nerve cells that they can overstimulate them to the point of destroying the cell.) Glutamate, for instance, in relatively small amounts can cause hypothalamic damage in immature animals which may go unnoticed, but which may result in skeletal shortening, obesity, and reproductive failure. The hypothalamus controls metabolic functions and mediates in the stress response.

Clean food, pure breast milk, and safe formula are not the only ways to protect an infant during this period of rapid brain development. Baby products that have passed safety standards to prevent accidents, poisonings, and other incidents often contain materials that can affect your baby's development. Since there are countless choices among baby products, how can you know which are the safest? Chapter 10 addresses this question.

Personal Hygiene and Baby Products

A funny thing happened to this book on the way to the printer. An exceptionally talented artist, contracted to create the book cover, came up with a clever and attractive design: a baby in a spacesuit. The little guy was peering out of the helmet all safe and snug from the toxins of our polluted earth.

The only problem? Spacesuits are made of plastics. Several layers, in fact. Plastics outgas chemicals that just happen to contain developmental disruptors. The cover was cute, well-intentioned, and would have attracted a lot of readers, but this little faux pas really underscored the importance of the information we are giving you. It also highlights the fact that hardly anyone, including artists, professionals, and parents, knows much about developmental toxins!

Hygiene and Beauty Products

Bath times for baby and you are good opportunities to begin using chemical-free products. Most commercial soaps and shampoos contain a wide variety of chemical detergents, fragrances, preservatives, and colors that can retard a baby's optimal growth and development. Even commercial baby soaps and shampoos that claim to be gentle often contain added chemicals that make them "gentle."

For these reasons, you should use chemical-free shampoos and soaps on your baby and on yourself, especially if you are pregnant or nursing. Chemical-free products can be found at any health food store and at an ever-increasing number of supermarkets and drug-stores. But remember to read labels. Just because it is in a health food store doesn't mean the product is chemical-free.

Searching the aisles and reading lengthy product labels, how-ever, can be time-consuming and a hassle for those of us who have jobs and kids. Luckily there are books available like *The Safe Shopper's Bible* (Steinman and Epstein 1995), in which harmful chemical products are identified and the names of alternative products are supplied. This book is a valuable resource for home products and goes into much greater detail than we can here.

Artificial Fragrances

Manufacturers of consumer hygienic products are not required to list fragrance ingredients, so they can protect their trade secrets. As a result, when we buy shampoo or lotion, we don't realize that the products may contain many toxic chemicals in the fragrance alone. In fact, one fragrance can contain hundreds of chemicals (Steinman and Epstein 1995).

Fragrance Chemicals

To give you an idea of how toxic fragrance chemicals can be, some common ones and their effects are listed below.

- **Methylene chloride**, produced from methane gas. This solvent is a known carcinogen and a suspected endocrine toxicant, neurotoxicant, respiratory toxicant, and reproductive toxicant.
- **Toluene**, petroleum derivative that is a known developmental toxicant and a suspected reproductive toxicant, immunotoxicant, and neurotoxicant.
- **Formaldehyde**, a known carcinogen and neurotoxicant and a suspected developmental toxicant.
- **Ethyl alcohol**, recognized developmental toxicant.
- **Farnesol**, suspected neurotoxicant.
- **Eugenol**, suspected neurotoxicant.
- **Colophony** (rosin), suspected immunotoxicant.

Luckily, many manufacturers are beginning to meet the grow-ing demand for safe products. In many drug and grocery stores, not to mention health food stores, you can now find fragrance-free products and products with natural fragrances. Avoid products labeled "unscented," however, since they may actually contain a mild fragrance used to cover up chemical odors.

Artificial Preservatives

Synthetic preservatives are used in consumer hygiene products to promote shelf life. Most of these chemical preservatives are known toxins. For example, BHA (butylated hydroxyanisole) is a known carcinogen and a suspected neurotoxin. BHT (butylated hydroxytoluene) is a suspected neurotoxin, among other things (see chapter 4). Some preservatives use formaldehyde-releasing chemicals, which often result in the formation of nitrosamines, known carcinogens. Listed below are some common preservatives and their possible effects. This is by no means a complete list. We just want to give you some idea of how dangerous chemicals are added to the seemingly harmless substances we all use every day.

Common Preservatives and Their Developmental Effects

Diethanolamine (DEA)/ Triethanolamine (TEA). These are wetting agents used in many cosmetics, lotions, shampoos, and conditioners. They are suspected neurotoxicants and can react with nitrites to produce nitrosamines.

2-Bromo-2-Nitropropane-1, 3-Diol (Bronopol). This is a suspected gastrointestinal or liver toxicant that can break down into formaldehyde and cause formation of nitrosamines. Many adult and baby lotions, shampoos, and conditioners contain this chemical. It is also found in many cosmetics.

DMDM hydantoin. This is a suspected neurotoxicant and respiratory toxicant that can break down into formaldehyde and can cause the formation of nitrosamines. It is found in shampoos, conditioners, and lotions.

Padimate-O (octyl dimethyl PABA). This is used in cosmetics, particularly in sunscreens. It can break down into formaldehyde and cause the formation of nitrosamines.

Quaternium 15. This can break down into formaldehyde causing the formation of nitrosamines. It is found in shampoos, conditioners, lotions, and cosmetics.

1,4-dioxane is a known carcinogen. According to the exhaustive research done by Steinman and Epstein, the authors of *The Safe Shopper's Bible* (1995), 1,4-dioxane can often be found in chemicals like polyethylene glycol, oxynal, polysorbate 60 or 80, and in chemicals that end with the suffix "eth" (as in sodium laureth sulfate). Many shampoos, conditioners, hair sprays, hair styling products, and some toothpastes and mouth washes contain this chemical.

Benzyl alcohol (phenylcarbinol). This is a suspected neurotoxicant.

Thimerosal (merthiolate). This is a recognized developmental toxicant and a suspected skin and sense organ toxicant. This is a mercury compound found in some eyedrops.

Parabens. These are recognized skin and sense organ toxicants. They are found in conditioners, shampoos, lotions, and cosmetics.

Urea. This is a suspected neurotoxicant. It is found in cosmetics, especially in facial powders and powdered blushes.

Artificial Colors

Most hygiene and baby products contain artificial colors. As with the artificial fragrances and preservatives discussed previously, artificial colors are often made with known toxins. For instance, coal tar colors like D&C Orange 15, 17, D&C Red 9, 19, and FD&C Blue 1, commonly used in cosmetics, are recognized carcinogens and suspected skin and sense organ toxicants that should be avoided.

Chemical-free cosmetics can be found in many health food stores. They lack the variety you would find elsewhere, but the benefits are obvious.

Hair and Body Care

Most adults are concerned with their personal appearance. Just look in our bathrooms and you will usually find varieties of soaps, body washes, shampoos, conditioners, hair sprays, and hair gels that we use on a daily basis. We don't realize, however, that the harsh, sometimes toxic, chemicals contained in these products destroy the natural oils our skin and hair produce and need and, at the same time, contaminate our bodies.

Most commercial soaps and shampoos contain harmful chemicals such as formaldehyde, coal tars, nitrosamine-producing products, propylene glycol, lauryl sulfate, laureth sulfate, and quaternium-15, many of which can affect development or brain functioning.

Antibacterial soaps and hand gels may contain harmful chemical agents such as triclosan, also used as a pesticide (Steinman and Epstein 1995). Many soaps and shampoos contain phenol, an endocrine disruptor, although some manufacturers are voluntarily eliminating it from their products.

Propylene glycol, for instance, is a solvent used in hygienic products to absorb excess water. It harms the heart, kidneys, and CNS. Pregnant laboratory animals exposed to high levels of propylene glycol had offspring with birth defects. Male animals suffered reduced sperm count (ATSDR 1996). Propylene glycol is so widely used that it is probably contained in almost every conventional liquid, commercial hygienic product, e.g., shampoos, conditioners, hair colors (dyes), lotions, antiperspirants, cosmetics, and deodorants.

Talc/Powder

Although most pediatricians agree that babies need to be bathed only about twice a week, their faces, necks, and hands probably need to be cleansed every day or every hour depending upon the spit-up rate. That makes for a lot of chemicals applied to a baby's skin. Pregnant mothers and mothers of infants especially will want to use chemical-reduced shampoos that are available in health food stores.

Talc should not be used on babies. Not only is it a carcinogen, it can also be inhaled and cause respiratory problems, which in some cases has led to infant death (Harbison 1998). Talc powder can also contain asbestos. Studies have shown that women who use talc on their genital areas also have an increased risk of ovarian cancer (Harlow, et al. 1992). Powders made from cornstarch are available, although some experts say cornstarch, being effective as a fungicide, can contribute to the growth of bacteria. Powders of any kind can also cause clogged pores and vaginal irritation in girls.

Lotion/Oils

Lotion and oils are used primarily to relieve dry and flaking skin. These skin problems are often the result of water and chemical cleaning agents that rob the skin of its natural oils. It is ironic that the chemicals we use to clean our bodies destroy moisture that has to be replaced, most commonly, by the use of more chemicals.

Most commercial lotions contain chemical dyes, fragrances, and preservatives. Many also contain oil in the form of petroleum. Needless to say, you should not use these products on your baby or yourself if you are pregnant or nursing. The chemicals in these products are readily inhaled and absorbed by the body. The need for moisture-restoring products can be decreased if you avoid chemical soaps and shampoos. Also, babies bathed only two or so times a week instead of every day probably won't need lotion.

If you think you do need lotions, try chemical-free brands with all-natural ingredients. They can be obtained at health food, drug, and grocery stores and should be reasonably priced because there are so many on the market.

Common chemicals found in lotions include petroleum derivatives, paraffin wax, mineral oil, microcrystalline wax, glycerin (glycerol), sodium lactate/lactic acid, and urea. Commercial lotions also contain chemicals including diethanolamine (DEA), triethanolamine (TEA), and formaldehyde.

They also often have synthetic fragrances and dyes. Using these products during pregnancy can add to your baby's chemical exposure and body load. Chemical-free lotions can be obtained at health food stores as well as some drug and grocery stores.

Lanolin

Lanolin is not inherently harmful and can be good for the skin if you aren't allergic to it. Lanolin can become a health problem because of the many pesticides and endocrine disruptors such as DDT, dieldrin, lindane, and diazinon that may contaminate it. Nursing mothers should never use products containing lanolin on their nipples for relief of dry or cracked skin because their infants will ingest the lanolin during feeding. In addition, any chemical pesticide residue present on the mother's skin will be more readily absorbed when lanolin is applied. Oily substances of any kind help toxic materials move through skin.

Cosmetics

Most chemicals contained in cosmetics have not been tested for safety. Cosmetics can contain many synthetic fragrances, preservatives, flavors, and colors like those previously discussed. The chemicals found in cosmetics can become even more dangerous when makeup is reapplied several times a day. Lipstick containing lanolin, artificial colors, and preservatives should be avoided because lipstick is often ingested.

Feminine Hygiene

Any product bleached by chlorine can contain harmful dioxins, which are known carcinogens, endocrine disruptors, and developmental toxins. Various chemical additives, surfactants (surface-active substances), and fragrances are added to tampons, increasing their toxicity. This holds true for most tampons, panty liners, and menstrual pads.

Tampon use is no small issue. Many women use tampons during their entire menstrual cycle and throughout their entire fertile life. Just add that up. Most women have approximately five days of flow approximately 12.6 times per year. That makes a total of 63 days per year. Between the ages of 14 and 50, a woman can use more than 10,000 tampons and her body can be in direct contact with tampons and dioxins for more than a total of six years. Women who are pregnant, breast-feeding, or who intend to conceive should avoid chlorine-bleached tampons because dioxins accumulate in the mother's tissue and pass easily to the fetus and into breast milk. In addition, plastic and cardboard tampon applicators have been reported to cause tiny cuts and abrasions in delicate vaginal tissue. This makes it easy for chemicals to enter the body.

There are alternatives to chlorine-bleached tampons and pads. One hundred percent cotton, fragrance-free tampons and pads (some organically grown) are bleached with hydrogen peroxide, oxygen, or just left natural. Tampax, from Procter and Gamble, has a 100 percent cotton tampon on which they use an "elemental chlorine-free" bleaching process that supposedly doesn't produce detectable dioxin levels. Some relatively safe tampon alternatives such as natural sea sponges and washable cotton pads are available at some health food stores.

Some Natural Product Websites

- Terrafemme (all long fiber cotton and peroxide bleached): www.web.net/terrafemme/
- Natrcare (oxygen bleached and all cotton): www.indra.com/natracare/
- Organic Essentials (organic cotton, peroxide bleached): www.organicessentials.com/

Deodorants/Antiperspirants

Commercial deodorants and antiperspirants contain multiple chemicals, some of which we have highlighted as toxic in this chapter, such as propylene glycol, talc, and many synthetic fragrances. In addition, many deodorants contain aluminum which is a suspected neurotoxicant and a possible link to Alzheimer's disease (Millichap 1993).

All-natural deodorants and antiperspirants are available at health food stores. Remember that even unscented products may still contain chemical fragrance. Avoid aerosols because the propelling agents are toxic chemicals.

Toothpaste/Mouthwash

Most toothpastes and mouthwashes contain fluoride to aid in the prevention of cavities, although some recent studies suggest that this is untrue. Fluoride is a suspected developmental and neurological toxicant (Environmental Defense Fund 1998). Extremely large amounts of fluoride ingestion at once can even cause death (Rosenstock and Cullen 1994).

Many pediatricians and dentists suggest that parents begin brushing their child's teeth (or tooth) as soon as they (or it) appear. You should probably avoid using a fluoride toothpaste on your infant especially since he/she is likely receiving fluoride through breast milk and water. Fluoride-free toothpastes for children are available at health food stores. If you feel the need to use toothpaste with fluoride, limit the amount to only a pea-sized drop once a day.

Mouthwashes containing alcohol, a neurotoxin, should be avoided by pregnant and nursing mothers. They should also be kept well away from children. Children have become seriously ill and some have died after drinking mouthwash (Shulman and Wells 1997). In addition, many mouthwashes contain synthetic dyes like Blue 1, Green 3, and Yellow 5. Both toothpaste and mouthwash often contain chemical flavorings like saccharin, a recognized carcinogen and suspected developmental and reproductive toxicant.

Like most of the other hygienic products we have discussed, all-natural toothpastes and mouthwashes are available at health food stores. A paste made of baking soda and water is also an effective and inexpensive alternative.

Hair and Nail Color

All women should avoid most commercial hair colors because studies have identified an increased ovarian cancer risk for women who dye their hair, especially the darker shades like brown, red, and black (Tzonou, et al. 1993). The use of chemical hair colors has also been associated with an increased risk of breast cancer, suggesting they may be endocrine disruptors (Kinlen, et al. 1977). Phenylenediamine, found in many hair coloring products, is a known carcinogen and a suspected mutagen, immunotoxicant, and skin and sense organ toxicant (Harbison 1998; Environmental Defense Fund 1998).

Even women who use hydrogen peroxide to lighten their hair can suffer health problems. In large quantities, hydrogen peroxide is a suspected neurotoxicant. Hair colors and kits for permanents also contain many toxic chemicals, including solvents. Women who plan to conceive, are pregnant, or are breast-feeding should avoid coloring, lightening, or perming their hair unless they are positive they are using safe substances.

Simple Solutions For Hair Coloring

* Henna
* Chamomile
* Other plant-based hair colors

These are available at health food stores. Make sure they do not contain added chemical preservatives or fragrances.

Nail polish and nail polish remover should be avoided by pregnant or nursing women. They contain many harmful solvents such as toluene and acetone. Acetone causes birth defects, nerve damage, and reproduction problems in laboratory animals. In these forms, acetone can enter and accumulate in your body through skin absorption and inhalation. Nail polish and polish remover products should never be used around developing children.

Simple Solutions For Buying Personal Care Products

* Buy all-natural personal care products (shampoo, lotion, cosmetics, etc.) whenever possible. This may mean a trip to your local health food store. But remember to carefully read the label on any product you consider, since even the products sold at health food stores can contain harmful chemicals.

* You might want to purchase a copy of *The Safe Shopper's Guide: A Consumer's Guide to Nontoxic Household Products, Cosmetics, and Food* by David Steinman and Samuel Epstein, M.D. (1995). This book rates various products according to their chemical content and it provides an easy and quick way to find safer products for yourself and your family.

* Buy lanolin and PABA-free products.

- Use a fluoride-free toothpaste on your child until he/she is old enough to rinse.
- Use cornstarch rather than talc on yourself and your baby.
- Buy all-cotton, naturally bleached clothing, bedding, diapers, and hygienic supplies.
- Go all natural by avoiding chemical hair colors and nail polish.

Baby-Care Products

Baby-care products are big business. There are multiple brands of bottles, diapers, toys, and clothing, each claiming to be the one your baby will prefer. Indeed, today's parents-to-be spend hours researching the safety and worth of anything labeled "baby." And rightfully so since everyone wants his/her baby to be as happy and as healthy as possible.

Bottles

One product, besides diapers of course, that all babies have in common is bottles. Even most nursing infants use a bottle eventually, especially if they attend day care or go to Grandma's house to be baby-sat. Plastic bottles are now the norm and they do offer many benefits. They don't break, they are easier to obtain, and they are cheaper than glass bottles. However, they also contain chemicals that can leach into the liquid placed in them. (See chapter 4, for a discussion on the harmful health effects plasticizers can have on the developing infant.)

The best way to avoid harmful plasticizers in this situation is to use glass bottles. Glass bottles are nontoxic and have the added benefit of being recyclable. However, being glass, they can break and for that reason it is important to hold your baby's bottle when she/he is eating. Holding your baby during the feeding is also a great way for you or another caregiver to bond with the baby.

Even if you do decide to use glass bottles, the rubber or plastic nipples they come with still present a problem with harmful chemicals. Rubber nipples can release chemicals and nitrosamines when sucked on, and plastic nipples release harmful chemicals (Havery and Fazzio 1983). To reduce your baby's exposure to these chemicals, you should initially boil nipples in water for about five minutes, remove them with tongs, and rinse them thoroughly with cold water. Remember to use bottled water when boiling and rinsing, and stainless steel or glass pots to keep further chemical exposure to a minimum. Also, you should replace rubber or plastic nipples immediately when they begin to feel sticky or gummy.

Because of the cost and availability of glass bottles, you might find that you prefer to use plastic. If you do, buy only hard plastic bottles. Stay away from the more flexible bottles because they probably contain more chemicals. For the same reason, avoid bottles that use disposable plastic bags.

Next, don't use plastic bottles to store fluids of any kind for more than an hour. The longer the liquid is left in, the more chemicals can leach into your baby's drink. If you have to, carry powdered formula and glass-bottled water, and mix the two when your baby is hungry. Pediatricians agree that babies don't need warmed liquids. However, many babies, especially those who nurse, learn to prefer liquid that is about the temperature of breast milk. It is probably not a good idea to give your baby very cold fluids because they have a tendency to shock the body. It is possible to buy battery-powered bottle warmers or those powered by a car cigarette lighter. Use glass bottles, or if plastic bottles are a must, use the harder plastic and do not store liquid for more than one hour.

Toys/Teethers

Plastic toys and teethers should be avoided because harmful chemicals can be ingested when your baby chews on them. In addition, most teething toys are made from soft plastic, which makes the chemicals in them more abundant and unstable.

It seems as though every available toy and teether is made of plastic. However, many baby specialty stores carry natural cloth toys that babies can chew on. You may find yourself getting pretty creative to fulfill your baby's need to chew on something but once she/he stops putting everything in sight in her/his mouth, a few hard plastic toys are okay. If your baby is teething, let her/him chew on your finger or a cool, damp rag.

Simple Solution
For Toys and Teethers

- Use natural cloth toys and teethers. Don't let your baby chew or suck on soft plastic that will leach chemicals into his/her mouth.

Pacifiers

Like nipples, pacifiers can release toxic chemicals. If you want to give your infant a pacifier, be sure to boil and rinse it first as you would a rubber or plastic nipple to minimize chemical exposure. Also, replace the baby's pacifier every few weeks especially if it becomes sticky.

Diapers

Ever since disposable diapers were first introduced, there has been controversy over whether their benefits outweigh the damage they may do to the environment compared to traditional cloth diapers. Recent studies, however, suggest that both diapering methods can be equally harmful to the environment although in slightly different ways.

Most commercial disposable diapers are not biodegradable and, therefore, add to landfill space although not as much as other forms of trash. Most also contain wetness-absorbing chemical gels that harm the environment. These chemicals do, however, enable parents to use fewer diapers, which helps with the landfill volume issue.

Commercial diapers usually have been bleached with chlorine and thus may contain dioxin that could be absorbed by your baby. Many diapers also have cute little pictures made from harmful dyes as well as added chemical fragrances. Makers of the most popular disposable diaper brands vehemently stress that study after study has shown that their diapers contain no detectable chemical residues.

Cloth diapers can also be cause for environmental concern. The energy and water needed to clean cloth diapers is one issue, and the harmful detergents and bleaches most parents and diaper services use to clean cloth diapers can also be detrimental to soil and water. This cleaning can also leave chemical residues on the diapers that can harm your baby the next time they are used.

Some cloth diapers also contain synthetic fibers that release toxic chemicals your baby can inhale or absorb. Even 100 percent cotton diapers could contain pesticide residues or dioxin if they were bleached (and they probably were) with chlorine. Also, the plastic diaper covers many parents put over their babies' cloth diapers can emit chemicals. Another issue to keep in mind is that many day care centers won't accept babies who wear cloth diapers.

In researching this book, the authors found that the cloth versus disposable diaper controversy is one of the many situations where the benefits of each method can have almost as many negatives as the other. Whichever diapering method you choose, here are a few tips we have compiled from different experts to keep your baby's chemical exposure at a minimum.

Simple Solutions
For Disposable Diapers

- "Green" disposable diapers are available at many health food stores. These diapers are often free of chemical dyes, fragrances, and absorbing gels. One brand, Tushies, is also biodegradable and uses cotton and wood pulp cellulose to absorb wetness. (800-34IM DRY or 800-344-6379)
- Change your baby's diaper as frequently as possible. Even though many diaper manufacturers claim that dioxins are not present, it never hurts to stay on the safe side and decrease the amount of chemicals that could be leached out of your baby's diaper when she/he wets.
- Try to avoid scented, colored, and decorated diapers because these contain chemicals that can harm your baby. If you want to dress up your baby's plain diaper, simply buy solid or patterned cotton diaper covers.
- Stay away from the plastic bags made especially for disposable diaper removal. Besides being made of harmful chemicals, most of these contain chemical dyes and fragrances, all of which pollute indoor air. Instead, invest in a trashcan with a lid and dispose of your trash frequently.

Simple Solutions
For Cloth Diapers

- Use only 100 percent cotton diapers and wash them several times before using them to remove or reduce chemical residues.

- Don't use harmful detergents and chlorine bleaches to launder your baby's cloth diapers. These chemicals leave behind residues that your baby can inhale or absorb. Wash the diapers in hot water with baking soda or vinegar. They can then be placed in the sun to whiten. All of these procedures kill bacteria.

- Avoid using plastic diaper covers. Instead, try using two cloth diapers and checking for leaks more often.

- Don't use disposable paper liners in your baby's cloth diaper. They have probably been bleached with chlorine and contain harmful dioxins.
- Don't use plastic bags or deodorizer cakes in your diaper pails. These will emit chemicals that will pollute your indoor air and your baby's diapers.

Diaper Rash Ointment

Zinc is a common ingredient in diaper rash ointments. Although humans need a certain amount of zinc to stay healthy, too much can cause serious repercussions. Zinc is a known respiratory toxicant and a suspected developmental toxicant, immunotoxicant, and reproductive toxicant. Laboratory animals exposed to excessive amounts of zinc suffer from infertility and have smaller babies (ATSDR 1994).

The amount of zinc that may be absorbed by your baby from a diaper rash ointment containing zinc may not be significant by itself; however, it is important to keep in mind that there are many other zinc sources to which you and your baby may be exposed. Zinc is also used as a rust preventative, and zinc coating on pipes may make its way into your water supply. It is also used in paints, rubber, dyes, and dietary supplements. The RDA (recommended daily allowance) of zinc for men is 15mg, 12mg for women, and 5 mg for infants.

Baby Wipes

Commercial baby wipes often contain chemical cleaning agents, dyes, and fragrances that can be harmful to developing babies. They probably also contain dioxins because most have been bleached with chlorine. The good news is that you can get your baby just as clean without commercial baby wipes and save money in the process. All you have to do is use a damp washrag, paper towels, or toilet tissue (use all-natural if possible). You can even keep a spray bottle of water on hand and lightly mist your baby's bottom at changing time. Buy a small spray bottle with a lid and travel-sized tissue for your diaper bag. Even stainless steel spray bottles are available so you don't have to worry about storing liquid in plastic containers. Nothing could be easier and more baby-friendly.

Baby Bedding

When buying baby bedding, it is important to keep in mind the many chemicals that are found in the home. For instance, if at all possible, plastic or vinyl mattress and covers should be avoided. This may be difficult since the majority of affordable mattresses have plastic covers and synthetic padding. You will want to completely encase a plastic mattress in sheets even on the bottom to reduce chemical emissions. Natural fabrics and cotton cushions, batting, and pillow forms can be obtained from most fabric stores. Infants should not have a pillow until at least two years of age.

Also try to avoid mattresses, mattress covers, sheets, and blankets that have been stain-proofed and water-proofed. Baby cribs and furniture should be made from solid hardwood or metal.

When stocking your baby room, remember to think natural. Some parents make many of their own baby supplies. This is a great way for fathers and grandparents to participate in the pregnancy and for mothers to fulfill their biological need to prepare their nests.

Clothing

Synthetic fabrics contain toxic chemicals. For example, nylon is a form of plastic and can contain hydrocarbons and petrochemicals such as phenol and benzene which are developmentally toxic. Polyesters emit small amounts of formaldehyde which can outgas even after multiple washings. When it comes to synthetic clothing, babies and pregnant mothers are a real concern.

However, natural fabrics can present problems too. Made from the fibers of plants or the coats of animals, they may be contaminated with pesticides or treated with chemicals to make them resistant to stains and stretching. "No iron" or "permanent press" labels indicate that the fabric was chemically treated, usually with a formaldehyde finish. Moth-resistant fabrics may have been treated with paradichlorobenzene or naphthalene, both of which are developmental toxins.

Most cotton fabrics used for clothing and bedding have been made from chemically grown and/or processed cotton. This is particularly ironic considering that one reason people opt to buy all-cotton clothing is to avoid harmful chemicals. Unfortunately, conventionally grown cotton clothes carry with them residues of the chemical pesticides and dyes with which they have been treated. These chemicals can then be inhaled and absorbed by the body during use, especially when perspiration takes place.

The good news is that more and more cotton farmers are giving up chemicals and embracing organic methods and are producing the same yields as their conventional counterparts. Therefore, it is possible to buy organic cotton clothing that is chemical-free, either from pesticides or synthetic dyes. Some manufacturers are even using natural dyes. In fact, many U.S. textile companies now bleach their cotton with hydrogen peroxide to avoid harmful dioxins.

Nowadays, organic cotton can even be grown in colors so that dyes and bleaches aren't needed. As an added benefit, rather than fading, naturally colored cotton becomes brighter and more colorful with each washing.

Wool fabric comes from sheep and other animals including goats (mohair and cashmere), rabbit fur (combed from the living rabbit's coat), camel, llama, alpaca, and vicuna. It can, however, contain pesticide residues and is often treated with chemical dyes and moth repellants. Most infants and children find wool too scratchy to endure anyway.

One hundred percent silk provides one of the most comfortable materials for body wear and the price has been dropping substantially. Washable forms are now available. Ramie is made from an East Asian nettle. The fabric appears loosely woven and airy and is used both for summer clothing and upholstery fabrics. Note that, like any other fabric, both silk and ramie may contain chemical dyes and treatments.

Simple Solution
To Decrease Chemical Exposures
To Fabrics

Because buying all-natural, chemical-free, organically grown fabric may not always be a realistic option, here is a procedure you can take to decrease exposure to chemicals via fabric.

- Wash clothing and bedding in baking soda several times before using. Remember, this doesn't work with polyester because breakdown is slower. Polyester should be avoided whenever possible.

Flame-Retardant Clothing

The majority of infant and children's sleepwear and bedding is flame-retardant. Unfortunately, most of the chemicals used to make cloth flame-retardant are toxic and many have not been tested for safety. One common flame-retardant, deca-bromo-diphenyl oxide, is a suspected carcinogen and developmental toxicant (Environmental Defense Fund 1998). Tetrakis compounds, flame-retardant chemicals used on cotton, flannel, and rayon, outgas formaldehyde often at levels as high as 500 ppm. Chronic exposures of 0.1 ppm can result in headaches, dizziness, nasal congestion, scratchy eyes and throat, and immune system damage.

Is flame-retardant clothing really necessary? Flame-retardant clothing was created to prevent children's pajamas from catching fire as they stood in front of open gas-burning heaters. Many homes continue to heat with these kind of heaters or portable electric heaters and children avoid burns when parents purchase flame-retardant night clothing. However, we are concerned that little is being done to find healthy alternatives to the toxic chemicals used in these garments.

Final Thoughts

Well, there it is. We have touched on all the major and some minor ways that you can provide your developing baby with the safest possible environment. But let's be realistic. Having both been pregnant ourselves, we know that what we have described is an ideal situation, a goal to strive for rather than conditions that everyone or even most can achieve perfectly.

No one's pregnancy is perfect and you won't be able to keep your body and your baby's body free of all chemicals. Simply do the best you can and be proud of any efforts you make. And remember, your baby's brain is plastic and renewable and continues to develop well into early childhood. So if any significant exposures do occur, the possible effects often can be overcome even before they show up.

Sound strange? Many scientists don't think so.

Windows of Opportunity

Janie, now seven years old, was a high risk for a developmental disorder because her mother used heroin throughout the pregnancy. Although children who experience this kind of drug exposure prenatally often have serious mental impairment and behavioral problems, to date Janie shows only mild developmental disorders and seems to be a bright, well-adjusted child. The reason she is doing so well is that after being adopted by her grandparents, from the time of her birth Janie received extra attention, mental and physical challenges, and verbal reinforcement from several members of her family. They took turns providing intellectual and cognitive stimulation to her all through her infancy. Everyone, including Janie's therapist, credits the child's relative lack of problems to her enriched environment during infancy.

In today's world, no pregnancy is perfect, even though most pregnant mothers try to stay healthy for the benefit of the developing baby. Because it is impossible to assess accurately how much chemical exposure a fetus has sustained, we feel that many, if not most, babies are at risk for some type of toxic effects, no matter how subtle. From the statistics available for birth defects, developmental disorders, and functional defects, we estimate that as many as 50 percent or more of the world's children have been negatively affected by pre- and postnatal chemical exposure. In some very polluted areas of the world, the incidence of observable birth defects reaches 100 percent (Laseter 1998).

Experts Advise Infant Stimulation

Professionals at a pediatric roundtable meeting, including Dr. Berry Brazelton, determined that infants who have a less-than-perfect experience in the womb benefit from early developmental intervention while their brains remain malleable and actively developing.

The benefits of an enriched environment in infancy may not become fully visible until the child begins to talk in sentences. However, in one study, older infants given early stimulation were developmentally three months ahead of other babies (Gunzenhauser 1987).

As previously mentioned, many neurological effects in a developing baby caused by chemical exposure can be turned around in the period of brain growth from birth to two years when the brain is still very pliable. And even if you have done a good job protecting your baby during pregnancy, he/she will still benefit from these exercises. You'll just have a brighter baby.

Therefore, to intercept chemical effects on development and to reprogram the brain to compensate for some amount of exposure, we are providing a simple program of early intervention strategies that any parent can implement.

Intercepting Developmental Disorders

The silver lining to the black cloud of chemical exposure during pregnancy is that many developmental and functional disorders often can be overcome through learning and experience. Although some of these approaches are those you would follow in rearing your child anyway, you will want to pay special attention to any child who has experienced exposure in fetal life. And, of course, part of the program must involve protecting the child from additional chemical exposure during infancy and breast-feeding.

Charlie Solis is a specialist in reprogramming functions. He uses several techniques to repattern the brains of young children whom others have given up on. Some of the children he worked with were so severely delayed developmentally or so defective that they relied on machines to help them sustain life. Today, many of these severely disabled children are now functioning in ordinary classrooms.

Although specialists are required in severe cases, some techniques can be used by average parents to help their children build neural connections to help overcome any potential problems. Because so many new synapses are forming just after birth, areas of weakness in brain growth can receive compensation. In some cases, even a child who is moving toward autism can be turned around if caught early enough. The developing brain looks for ways and opportunities to compensate for neural damage. However, when the brain compensates for injury it doesn't always do so in a manner that is beneficial for the individual. So it must be guided into the appropriate rewiring.

Delayed Effects

The full effects of toxic interference during fetal development or early infancy may not surface until the child is school age and must perform intellectual tasks or control his/her behavior for extended periods. In fact, by the time most developmental disorders are discovered (usually through teacher complaints), poor behavioral control is well established, which makes it difficult to retrain the child developmentally. We recommend very early intervention to prevent rather than waiting to cure these problems.

Developmental retraining can take place at any time in life. However, the earlier the better; the optimal time occurs when new connections in the brain are proliferating rapidly—from birth to age two. During this time, new glial cells are forming, heavy myelination of nerve cells is building neural efficiency and speed, and billions of new connections are being created in response to the demands of the baby's environment.

The next best time to retrain a child developmentally is from age two to age six and so on, with the retraining process becoming a little harder and a little less successful as time progresses. Some Down's syndrome children who received early intervention have even been able to attend college.

At the first sign of any developmental problems, get help from a professional. Don't wait until the issue has solidified and the child has developed maladaptive habits. Such habits can make it harder to retrain the child and more likely that she/he will suffer some damage to self-esteem.

Normal infants given enrichment move through developmental stages faster, and appear more enthusiastic, spirited, and alert than other children. They verbalize more frequently and acquire reaching skills earlier. Enrichment seems to provide an excellent basis for intelligence.

Effects of Early Intervention

Pre-term infants who are massaged and exercised are
- 47 percent higher in weight gain
- Released from hospital an average six days earlier
- More socially responsive
- More active
- More alert
- Higher scoring on developmental tests
- More efficient in processing and using food energy

Brain stimulation must take place for certain perceptual and intellectual systems to operate effectively. Certain aspects of both anatomical and neurochemical brain development result from appropriate stimulation. For instance, the visual system must have suitable experiences if the visual area of the brain is to function normally. If inadequate stimulation occurs, those areas deteriorate. Likewise, poorly developed areas can be stimulated to function more effectively or to take over functions that other affected areas cannot. In fact, some neural cells may compete for synaptic space and the type of cell that gets the most stimulation may get the most space. In general, enriched conditions create a heavier, thicker brain with substantial increase in occipital lobes (Spreen, Risser, and Edgall 1995). This is due to the greater number of connections, neural cell density, and the overall size of neural cells. Every new experience a child has, no matter how small, causes a whole series of new connections to be formed within her/his brain.

The goal of developmental stimulation is to provide your baby with rich and varied experiences since this is the stuff brains are made of. Be cautious and sensitive to your baby's response to stimulation. Some babies are more temperamental and more sensitive, so they need and like less stimulation than other babies do.

Windows of Opportunity

In the young child, several critical or sensitive developmental periods exist when encouraging brain growth can help to overcome developmental deficiencies. Developmental experts disagree about the exact timing, so these periods are approximate.

- Development of competence: from ten to eighteen months. (In this study, competence was measured according to language ability, abstract thinking and sensory discrepancies.)
- Language acquisition: from birth to age five to six.
- Social bonding development: from birth to age four to five.
- Psychomotor skills: from birth to age four to five.

For Your Information

The three parental techniques most effective for enriching development are as follows:

- Designing a safe environment that captures a child's interest
- Being available to your child for comfort and consultation
- Disciplining and controlling her/him in a timely and consistent manner

The environmental factors that stimulate infant development the most are visual stimulation and lots of physical contact with a loving adult (Anselmo 1987).

Respond to Your New Baby's Needs Promptly

Responding quickly when your baby cries during the first few months gives the child a secure emotional base upon which to build a lifetime of emotions. A quick response stimulates the emotional part of the brain to develop and teaches the baby that she/he has some control over her/his environment. Not only does the baby receive security from the stimulus, it also helps the infant brain to develop new connections. Infants who learn that their needs will be met tend to cry less after the age of three months. Handling your baby gently in no way will overstimulate him/her. In fact, the baby should be handled constantly from birth on. Not holding the baby is a form of neglect and such neglect can reduce electrical activity in the brain's left frontal lobe, which seems to limit a baby's ability to experience positive emotions such as joy, and may lead to depression in later life (Dawson, et al. 1997).

Talk to Your Baby as Much as Possible

During the later months of pregnancy, your baby will be able to hear your voice inside your womb. Once the baby arrives, talk to him or her; your voice will be recognized. Make eye contact and smile while talking. Babies respond to the high-pitched tones of parent language, called "parentese," even more than to normal tones.

Most parents begin talking to a new infant in parentese and adjust their language according to the baby's abilities as he/she grows. This stimulates the language areas of the baby's brain. The parents' speech should be responsive to the interests of the child. Babies whose parents talk with them a great deal develop the most language competence by age two. Use simple, concrete language to describe the object or activity that the baby attends to.

Foreign Language Preparation

Teaching young children foreign languages can begin simply by singing songs to them in other languages. We taught the children in our family songs like "Frere Jacques" and "Dites Moi" to build their faculties for French. Children learn pleasantly from music, and the songs tend to force correct pronunciation of the words (Gunzenhauser 1987).

If you can, teach your baby fragments of other languages. The best time for a child to learn a language stretches from birth to about five or six years of age. Hearing language stimulates language areas of the brain. Later, it becomes progressively harder to learn a second language and its rules. Some experts suggest that learning several languages only requires setting up a predisposition for each language during the language acquisition period between the ages of one and three. Dr. Nico Spinelli (1987) suggests that the child learn to pronounce correctly "a few perfectly learned sentences of a second language containing all of the important phonemes" or "fifty or more words" of several different languages. Later, your child can learn any of those languages more easily because her/his brain will have been primed to learn the related sounds.

Give Your Baby Extra Loving Attention

Treat your baby as a very special individual. Allow her/him to interact with affectionate relatives and friends on a regular basis; they can help take part in the training of this tiny brain. Recognize that toys don't take the place of human interactions. Young children seem to benefit most from the attention of a few familiar caregivers.

The critical period to foster the development of social bonding may extend from birth to age three, although some researchers have found that maternal deprivation after the age of six months was responsible for affectionless and conscienceless individuals.

Some say social development begins at four to six weeks; others claim the period immediately following birth strongly affects later bonding and attachment. In general, it seems that lack of constant infant-parent contact during the first two years may affect the child's ability to form affectionate bonds.

Provide Adequate Nutrition

After weaning from the breast or formula, you must watch that your child continues to get adequate nutrition. She/he must have adequate protein to grow properly and continue to build brain cells (Anselmo 1987). Children who are mild to moderately malnourished have fewer brain cells, are more vulnerable to toxins, and score lower on mental function tests. Breast-feeding mothers should make sure they obtain a healthy diet so their nursing babies will be well-nourished. Good quality protein can be obtained very inexpensively by substituting whole grains and legumes for meat when meat proves too expensive.

Provide Consistent and Positive Discipline and Reinforcement

Children who learn social limits early in life establish patterns of self-control that prevent poor behavior. They establish brain connections that help them to control their actions, to feel secure, and to experience less fear. A properly socialized child draws other people to interact with him/her in a way that facilitates learning. Poor discipline, however, fosters the development of the connections in the brain that create poor self-discipline.

The first rule of disciplining an infant or toddler is to use distraction first. With small children, two and under, simply move or lead the baby away from an area or activity he/she should avoid and when the child returns, lead him/her away again, firmly but lovingly. Give the child a toy or another activity as a substitute.

Next, use reinforcement to increase the responses you want. When your child performs a "good" behavior, reward him/her with praise, approval, or a desired activity. Different rewards work for different children. To determine what makes a good reward for your child, observe what he/she chooses when given a choice. Does your child beam when approval is given, does he/she ask for treats, or want to turn the light switch on and off?

Ask your child to do something *only one time*. If he/she fails to follow your instructions, lead him physically through the desired behavior. Don't give up on your request when the child protests, expresses anger, screams, or throws a tantrum. If you give up, that only reinforces the behavior and teaches the child that protesting works.

If you say "no," you should mean it. If you are going to acquiesce to your child after saying no, why not just say "yes" in the beginning. Say "no" only when you intend to make it stick, otherwise you teach the child to whine, argue, or throw a fit. The child also learns that there are no limits and that everything is negotiable.

Guidelines for Using Discipline Effectively

Discipline should fit your child and should be in the mildest effective form. Disapproval absolutely crushes some children while others remain unaffected. Others find time-out distressing but some enjoy the solitude. Many tantrum-throwing children respond well to brief physical restraint. Wrap your arms around the child for a few minutes until some self-control is reestablished. This approach also works well for small children who run through public spaces such as restaurants getting into everything.

To identify the appropriate discipline for your child, you must use a consequence she/he does not like such as losing a toy or being ignored. Use discipline to discourage poor behavior.

- Discipline should be immediate. You must respond to negative behaviors quickly and consistently, every time. Make punishment brief and be careful not to reward the child during punishment.

- Teach "instead" behaviors. Discipline is useless unless you teach appropriate behavior. Always tell your child what she/he should do when you intervene to discipline poor behavior.

- Always discipline with love and a desire to teach. Discipline should never be an outlet for your anger. An overstressed parent in the habit of spanking may hit a child too hard because of his/her own internal pressures. For that reason it is always a good idea to avoid using physical punishment as a discipline tool.

Protect Your Child from Abuse

The infant brain's response to abuse or a fearful environment is to develop hypersensitive fear responses. The result is a fearful child who fails to interact with her/his environment in ways that stimulate brain growth. Abuse in the first two years appears to be the most damaging. Even newborns can feel pain and can learn fearfulness. Developmental disorders are made worse by environmental factors such as poor child-rearing practices, abuse or neglect, and stressful home conditions.

Offer Your Baby Varied Learning Situations

Infants exposed to an enriched visual environment have larger occipital lobes, to process visual material. Help your baby become involved in activities that both mesh with his/her level of developing skills and that interest him/her. Take your child places, give him/her visual stimulation, objects to see, faces to watch, expressions to contemplate. Never assume that a thing is too small to teach a child.

For the young human, every situation is a learning situation with hundreds of new details to incorporate from every person, place, and activity. Parents who teach "on the go" take time out to explain and describe when the baby exhibits interest in an object or situation. Take an interest in your baby's activities and be helpful and encouraging. Your goal is to help your baby develop an interest in the world.

When our little Ramsey was an infant, we often took him with us on shopping excursions. We would hold him and let him touch and stroke items of different textures while we, at first, held his hand gently to help him control his hand pressure. Then we would repeat the name of the object and describe it in simple terms. He quickly learned to handle objects with care and to remember object names.

Some infants are so "easy" that parents often forget they benefit from attention, while more difficult infants require a parent to be attentive, patient, and flexible. Timid or withdrawn infants need quiet and calm much of the time and they need their parents to introduce new people and experiences slowly. These babies like to set their own pace and shouldn't be pressured to do things too quickly.

The way you interact with your baby also determines whether she/he will benefit from enrichment. Adjust your pattern of interaction to your baby's response. Increase your interaction when the baby shows interest and reduce it when she/he loses interest. When the baby looks away give her/him time to recover and then gently initiate more interaction.

Simple Solutions
For Brain-Stimulating Learning
Experiences

Babies need lots of auditory and visual stimulation. Encourage your baby's brain development by naming, describing, defining, and categorizing all the objects the baby can see.

- Touch and name everything, including body parts, articles of clothing, furniture, objects in the natural world, pictures in books, and people.
- Hold your baby where she/he can look out from your arms and also see your face. Then point to and name objects on which the baby can focus.
- As the child can understand more, describe in simple language the purpose, color, size, or shape of the object. Identify sounds she/he can hear, carry the child to the source of the sounds and show what is producing the sound and describe it.
- Introduce your baby to written language early.
- When your baby can attend to objects, place brightly colored letters and words in his/her environment.
- By the age of two, a baby should understand that words have meaning and that letters combine to make words.
- Point to simple words that have meaning for the child such as *cat* and *hat*, and say the word, then point to a corresponding picture. Most picture books for children make this an easy task.

Simple Solutions
To Stimulate the Baby's Senses

- Allow your baby to touch different textures, shapes, liquids, solids, and even mist. Hanging colored toys from above the baby's bed in infancy allows the infant to develop depth perception and motor coordination as he/she reaches for them.

- Your baby can hear well at birth but an infant's sensory thresholds are higher than an adult's. It takes more stimulus for babies to perceive effectively.

- He/she needs to hear lots of auditory stimulation, human voices and interesting sounds.

- Your baby can differentiate smells at birth. She/he will like the same smells that everyone else does. Babies enjoy vanilla and strawberry odors and dislike the smell of rotten eggs and fish. Encourage your baby to sniff and identify smells.
- Taste is well developed at birth, and babies like sweet foods. By the time your baby is two years old, you should have introduced many different tastes to the child.
- Your baby's brain will connect visual and tactile information during the first year of life, so he/she needs to touch objects as they are being seen.
- Massaging your baby provides tactile sensory areas of the brain with stimulation.

Anselmo (1987); Santrock (1992)

Read to your baby from infancy until she/he can read to you. While you read, hold and touch the baby lovingly. Encourage the baby to touch the pictures with her/his fingers as soon as she/he can while following the story. Games like peek-a-boo and "this little piggy" provide the baby with information about sequences, imitation, and anticipation of outcomes.

The Business of Brain Development

Think about your child's learning in these terms. Every time your child sees, hears, or otherwise perceives a new experience, object, or detail, her/his brain cells send out arms that make innumerable connections with other brain cells, thus establishing a memory and a learning experience that the child can draw on later. Every sight, sound, taste, smell, or feeling translates into brain growth and new connections. Depending on how you help your baby interpret experiences, these connections create a sense of awe, excitement with the world, and self-confidence or they can foster a sense of fear and anxiety. If you give your baby a wide and colorful range of experience, this helps to overcome problems in brain development that may have taken place during fetal life.

Play Is Serious Business

Play is your child's developmental work. It is his/her job, and the baby is paid with brain growth and millions of neural connections.

Give your baby the freedom to explore and play in a safe area that provides the opportunity to interact socially and physically with objects in the environment. Confining the child for large parts of the day in playpens or cribs limits exploration and squanders the opportunity to build new neural connections.

Your baby's physical environment should both facilitate exploration and provide various shapes, colors, and textures that stimulate all the senses. Include objects that make noises or respond to the child's actions in some way.

Allow your baby to play at some of the adult tasks he/she sees you perform, such as washing dishes, dressing up, brushing hair, digging in the ground for planting. Allow the child to manipulate objects such as unopened food cans for stacking, unbreakable dishes, cooking utensils, hairbrushes, and combs. When he/she stacks or matches objects, learning to discriminate real-world objects according to their characteristics is taking place. Even the poorest child will, if allowed, create playthings from everyday items and activities.

Help Your Baby Create

Encourage imagination and creativity. Allowing your child to play pretend games builds brain connections that create imagination.

Encourage your child's artistic talents by giving him/her crayons and paint when she/he is old enough. Give the child plenty of space to draw once she/he can manipulate a writing tool and supply many different colors to use. Participate in artistic activities of your own with the baby and proudly display his/her creations around your home.

The Mozart Effect

Researchers have found that playing Mozart to young infants stimulates their brain development. In fact, some states have recommended that hospitals send a Mozart tape home with all new babies. Although we certainly appreciate Mozart, his compositions are not likely to be the only music that stimulates babies' brains. However, for young children, music should be fairly calming, rather than loud and overstimulating.

Music helps to develop the right hemisphere of the brain. Provide your baby with all types of music. One woman we know played the piano softly at night once her babies had gone to bed. It was soothing and made falling asleep a pleasant experience for the children.

Sing to your baby and encourage him/her to sing with you. Often, babies can "sing" before they can talk. Use music like the ABC song to teach stories, language, rhymes, etc. Your child can begin playing with simple musical instruments such as castanets and drums as early as one year of age.

Psychomotor Development

Make sure your baby crawls and goes through all the normal psychomotor stages to stimulate the motor centers in his brain. As soon as the baby begins to crawl, encourage him/her to move around by placing toys and safe interesting objects on the floor. If the baby tries to skip the crawling stage and goes straight to walking, you will want to help him learn to crawl afterwards. Skipping the crawling stage is not advisable because certain language areas of the baby's brain require this stimulation to develop properly. Crawling facilitates the development of brain patterns for alternating and sequencing skills, something your child uses to understand how things work in the world. Sometimes, children who learn how to walk without first going through a crawling stage develop dyslexia. Many such children have greatly improved or been cured by learning how to crawl in the way an infant does.

Play games with your child that require physical coordination such as rolling, and later throwing, a ball. Throw bean bags or other soft objects toward targets. Play pat-a-cake and other games that require your baby to perform rhythmic coordinated movement.

Teach Problem Solving and Encourage Competence

You will want to help your baby develop an understanding of physical laws and problem solving. As the child grows, give her/him small problems to solve that fit the child's skill level (How do you get the Popsicle out of the package?). Teach reasoning by pointing out the consequences of actions. (When you hit the kitty, the kitty doesn't want to play with you anymore.) You want to encourage just the right amount of independence by allowing your baby to attempt some things on his/her own. At later stages don't anticipate your child's every need so he/she will learn to ask for what he wants. Requesting help is a method of problem solving. You then become a resource to help your baby when he/she attempts a too difficult task. Mistakes should be treated as part of the learning process rather than a reason for punishment.

Activities That Interfere with Brain Development

- Waking your sleeping infant to provide stimulation. Babies' brains and bodies grow when they sleep.

- Caging children in a crib or playpen once they can move about on their own. Limit such confinement to a maximum of thirty minutes.

- Focusing on a single skill before the age of three blocks development in other brain areas. Provide a balance of activities.

- Leaving your baby in a single location. Move him/her around the house with you.

- Arguing loudly and frequently around your baby. Too much emotionally intense auditory stimulation disrupts development and causes babies to become fearful and hypersensitive.

- Allowing a child to leave tasks incomplete. When your child abandons a project help him/her go back and finish it.

- Resenting your baby. Spend enough time away from your baby so that when you are being the caregiver, you want to be with him or her.

- Reading to your baby when he/she exhibits no interest is counterproductive and could turn the child against the activity.

- Punishing your child without giving him/her information regarding appropriate behavior is valueless.

- Solving problems for your child when allowing him or her to solve them would provide a learning situation.

- Confusing your child by giving her/him too many choices.

- Trying to force a left-handed child to use her/his right hand.

Continue Protecting Your Baby from Harmful Chemicals

Your baby's nervous system grows at a rapid rate during the first two years of life, growing the myelinating sheaths for the nerve cells that control motor function, speech, behavior, thought patterns, and all the other functions of the brain. New connections are being formed minute by minute. This gives your baby's brain every opportunity to reclaim functions that may have been altered or affected in the womb by adverse conditions. Making the most of this opportunity requires that you continue your vigilance in maintaining a chemically reduced environment for your baby as she/he grows.

 Simple Solutions
To Assist Sensory, Perceptual, and
Motor Development

From Birth to One Month

- Babies need to see human faces often at close range.
- Play Mozart tapes for your baby.
- Hang bright colored objects within 8 to 10 inches of your baby's face.
- Use interesting patterns for bedding, fabrics, and walls.
- Imitate baby's sounds. This can triple the number of sounds baby makes.
- Introduce your baby to pleasant smells like flowers and fruit.

From Two to Three Months

- Provide bright objects for your baby to touch.
- Make his/her area bright with pictures and well-attached mirrors.
- Allow baby to accompany you when you are doing household chores. Use an infant seat that permits a vertical view of the room.
- Introduce your baby to soft music of all types when awake.

From Four to Six Months

- Hold your baby about seven inches from a mirror where he/she can see the image responding to his/her own movements.
- Give your baby brightly colored toys to grasp and throw.
- Introduce your baby to new tastes in tiny amounts.

From Six to Nine Months

- Provide large (2 inch minimum) colored, noisy, droppable toys.
- Allow the baby to operate simple mechanisms like a light switch.

- Play hide-and-seek with your face or an object.
- Hold the baby so she/he can pat a mirror and make sounds at the image.
- Make funny faces to encourage your baby to imitate you.
- Touch and name everything the baby sees and hears.
- Give the baby paper to tear.

From Nine to Twelve Months

- Show your baby large pictures in a book and name the objects.
- Take your baby out to see animals, people, objects, and movement.
- Roll a ball to the baby and encourage him/her to roll it back.
- Show your baby how to stack objects.
- Demonstrate rhythmic movement to music by clapping, bobbing your head, or moving your feet.

Simple Solutions To Encourage Tactile Development

From Birth to One Month

- Hold, caress, and cuddle your baby.
- Keep him/her warm.
- During baths, use a soft cotton cloth with warm water to gently stimulate the baby's skin.
- Gently massage your baby's body.

From Two to Three Months

- Caress your baby while bathing and during diaper changes.
- Comb your baby's hair with a soft brush.
- Use gentle massage to relax a fussy baby.

From Four to Nine Months

- Give your baby soft cloth or wooden toys of various textures.
- Place your nude baby on soft rugs or fabrics and move his/her arms and legs
- Gently hold your baby's hand and help him/her touch the objects he/she sees in a store.

- Let your baby have finger foods of different sizes and textures.
- Allow your baby to "catch" running water and splash in the bath.
- Give your baby sticky tape to play with.

From Nine to Twelve Months

- Let your baby squeeze and play with food.
- Allow him/her to touch cold and warm objects. Describe which is which.
- Help your baby touch natural surfaces like tree bark, soil, and raindrops. Name them for her/him.
- Let your baby feel a breeze or a soft wind blowing on him/her.

 Simple Solutions For Bonding and Social Development

From One to Four Months

- Respond promptly to your baby's cries and needs.
- Look at, hold, stroke, talk with, play with, carry, and rock your baby.
- Be emotionally involved with your baby.
- Touch and look at your baby frequently. Making eye contact with him/her is important.
- Provide interaction with a limited number of significant others.
- Use toys to interact with your baby.

From Four to Eight Months

- Share your baby's quiet periods by holding and rocking her/him.
- Sooth, stroke, and sing to your baby when she/he feels upset and uncomfortable.
- Learn to read your baby's emotions from her/his sounds and actions. Then, respond to the emotion your baby displays.
- Encourage, but do not force, your baby to interact with relatives.

From Eight to Twelve Months

- Talk to and play with your baby frequently.
- Play turn-taking games and imitation games such as pat-a-cake.
- Verbalize limits by telling the baby, "No, no."
- Help your baby to make choices. Limit the choices to two or three at most.
- Reassure your baby often.
- Shift your baby's attention to new activities when she/he becomes upset.

From Twelve to Eighteen Months

- Push for independence by allowing your baby to practice making choices
- Provide help with tasks only if your baby needs it.
- Give your baby tasks she/he can accomplish without help.
- Continue to set limits for your baby.

From Eighteen to Twenty-Four Months

- Help your toddler to make a distinction between self and others.
- Allow your toddler to expand his/her interactions with other children and safe adults.
- Provide your toddler with a positive self-image by giving him/her approval.
- Allow your toddler to sort objects.
- Begin teaching your baby appropriate social behaviors.

Santrock (1992); White (1985); Anselmo (1987); Whaley and Wong (1989)

Whether or not your child requires this type of attention, he or she deserves it. After all, this is literally the chance of a lifetime to help build a person with tender, loving care. Your baby, an extension of yourself, yet entirely a separate individual, is someone to whom you will always be connected through the special bond between parent and child.

Guide to Common Chemicals and Developmental Effects

You Can Change the World

We humans have outsmarted ourselves in this century. We have created 100,000 synthetic substances and placed them in products that we use every day, dumped them into our drinking supply, added them to our foods, and applied them to the earth that provides our food. In most cases, we have done these things without testing the substances to see if they will harm us and our children.

Synthetic chemicals are not, in themselves, evil entities. They have been extremely useful in our society. This book, the paper it is printed on, and the ink that forms the words are created either with synthetic chemicals or via chemical processing. However, the gross misuse, mishandling, and misunderstanding of chemicals are currently leading to a health crisis on our planet. Synthetic chemicals don't belong in our food, water, soil, air, personal products, or our bodies. Now that we do understand the consequences of such indiscriminate use of these materials, we can use our technical knowledge and resources to formulate safer substances to replace the dangerous ones.

We all must share the responsibility for the current state of affairs because we all have used and financially supported these products. But because many of these choices are under our control, we can turn this situation around, now, by taking action. Here's how you can change the world for the better.

Simple Solutions For Changing the World

- **Stop purchasing toxic chemicals.** The alternatives offered in this book are clean and inexpensive. By using nontoxic substances you will send a message to chemical manufacturers that toxic chemicals are not marketable. Only then will changes be made.

- **Vote for leaders who support environmental controls.** Instruct your government representatives to block harmful chemical production. Get to the polls and make your voice heard.

- **Avoid jobs where toxic chemicals are used.** Or suggest to your employer ways to make the workplace safer.

- **Educate others.** The more knowledgeable individuals are, the less contamination there will be. Focus on teaching your children about chemicals so they will build a better future for their own children. Provide information to health professionals who have the power to broadcast such information to large parts of the population.

- **Create healthy babies.** Be sure your babies will be smart and able to learn well by avoiding the use of synthetic chemicals and other teratogens.

How Health Professionals Can Help

One purpose of this book is to expand the knowledge of professionals so they will recognize that even if an adult parent does not experience symptoms from a chemical exposure, her or his child can be affected in the womb in ways that have important behavioral and neuropsychological consequences.

A health professional's job is to listen to the patient, believe the patient, consider his/her concerns, research the problem, and provide solutions within the framework of the professional's expertise. Biological and social evaluations can help determine the level of danger a woman may be experiencing during her pregnancy. Part of a health professional's job is to inform patients about laboratory tests that can help them make informed decisions regarding risks to their baby. The patient then depends upon the professional to interpret the results and help her decide how to reduce her baby's risk.

Biological monitoring. Tests on blood, urine, and exhaled air can determine a mother's body load of a hazardous substance. Volatile organic compounds (VOC) can currently be measured in blood samples. Some other VOCs like benzene and toluene produce metabolites that show up in urine samples. Blood tests can also measure the presence of organophosphate pesticides, and both blood and urine tests are used to measure for the presence of lead.

Social monitoring. Tests and social evaluations by mental health professionals can help determine a pregnant woman's emotional stress load. We recommend that every pregnant woman be evaluated for stress. Then, health professionals can advise these mothers-to-be about reducing stress during pregnancy and breastfeeding.

Health professionals have several ways to help protect the unborn fetus. Clearly, they must advise the patient. Then, if dangers are involved, with the patient's permission, they may contact the patient's employer or labor organization, inform the appropriate governmental authority if unresolved work issues threaten the patient's pregnancy, and/or contact experts for more information.

How Government Can Help

Ideally, most societies want to preserve their heritage and future through healthy, productive children. Because low-income pregnant women must often work in high-risk situations, governments must take measures to protect unborn children.

Children with developmental disorders who are also born into poverty not only face a difficult life, they also require much help from society. A child with ADHD, behavioral problems, birth defects, or a learning disorder often requires thousands of dollars in health care and special education. And, as an adult, he or she may find it harder to advance at work and thus will contribute less to the tax base. A more reasonable and humane approach for a society would be to protect the developing baby to the fullest so that healthy development and growth can take place.

Although few of us want more government intervention in society, this may be one area where state support is needed. Pregnant mothers who cannot continue their present occupation or who have a high-risk pregnancy must either be provided low-risk employment or, in some cases, given adequate financial assistance during the pregnancy so the fetus and developing child will have a safe environment in which to grow. Current government programs may not provide adequately for the developing child whose mother has no mate and has other children to rear. Government assistance offers financially minimal and ego-deflating means to a pregnant woman to avoid a toxic pregnancy. Also, young married couples often need two salaries to pay their bills and support even a minimal lifestyle. Therefore, such couples may also need help too in protecting their unborn children.

Some Western industrialized countries already acknowledge this need. In Finland and France, liberal maternity leaves are provided for women who need to stay away from the job during their pregnancies. These countries are making a wise investment in their futures.

Since 1990 many different states in the United States have passed Toxic Use Reduction laws requiring firms to list the toxic substances used in their products along with plans to replace, reduce, or eliminate the chemicals from production. Industry can meet these requirements by substituting safer chemicals, redeveloping products by using safe materials, using nontoxic production processes, improving maintenance and operations, and recycling toxic substances. The best of all options takes place when firms undertake chemical reduction voluntarily. In fact, some food packagers are currently voluntarily eliminating phenol, an endocrine disruptor from their products. Although the motive for these acts may be fear of liability, this still represents a move in the right direction.

In some countries, regulatory agencies have established safety protocols for working with toxic chemicals and have the power to write citations and stop work in a company if conditions are hazardous. However, safe conditions may not exist even in a company with a clean record. Often facilities are cleaned up just to meet the inspection standards and then are allowed to degrade rapidly to pre-inspection conditions soon after. Some inspections focus only on safety hazards while new production processes are bringing in new chemicals every month.

Presently, most governmental guidelines for industry fail to take a conservative approach when a teratogenic *potential* exists from chemicals that, although not subject to adequate research, are highly suspect. We believe that pregnant mothers should receive education and cautious protective measures in light of the possible consequences to their unborn children.

Industry has much to gain from protecting pregnant workers. Insurance claims and expenses can be better controlled when birth defects related to job factors are minimized. Mothers who have healthy children are likely to have better attendance rates. Companies should consider insurance policies that include pregnancy as a covered disability when environmental conditions demand time off. In some cases, the job of protecting the unborn child may fall to labor unions that can encourage employers to improve conditions for workers. And, ultimately, it falls to the expectant mother to make decisions about the safety of her baby.

It is up to us all working together to decide that our babies are the most important mark we leave upon this earth. Once that decision is made, we must work, as individuals and as a community, to change the direction in which we have been traveling for the past century. Our technology is now advanced enough to provide us all with the safety we need in products and production techniques. Our human brains have proven brilliant enough to solve many seemingly intractable problems. Now let's solve this one, while we still have time.

Guide to Common Chemicals and Developmental Effects

This chart includes approximately 300 substances and drugs out of 100,000 or more in use. It is not meant to be complete; rather, we hope it will give readers some information regarding chemicals which can affect the developing fetus or infant. Bear in mind that exposure to a chemical on this list does not mean that in all cases there will be a developmental effect. It means that the risk is increased and that such effects have been reported in humans or has occurred in laboratory animals. "Risk of neurological impairment" means there is no specific information on fetal effects but since the substance causes neurological impairment in exposed adults and since all chemicals tested to date cross the placenta and many cross into breast milk, both the fetus and infant can be assumed to be at risk.

Substance/(Related Substances/Other Names)	Developmental Effect or Risk	Classification; Common Use
2,4,5-T (Agent Orange, 2,4-D)	Reported endocrine disruptor, suspected carcinogen, reproductive toxin and neurotoxin; may be due to dioxin impurities	Herbicide; agriculture, parks
2,4- dichlorophenol	Suspected endocrine disruptor	Herbicide, fungicide; wood preservatives
4-nitrotoluene	Suspected endocrine disruptor and neurotoxin	Solvent; solvent mixtures
Accutane	Category X Drug—Do Not Use During Pregnancy or Breast-feeding; severe birth defects	Anti-acne; medical

OC pesticide (organochlorine pesticide in the same group with DDT and lindane.)
OP pesticide (organophosphate pesticide in the same group with Malathion and Diazinon.)

Chemical	Effect	Use
Acetone (Acetate, dimethyl ketone, dimethy formaldehyde, methy ketone, propanone)	Suspected neurotoxin	Solvent; nail polish removers, paints and solvent mixtures, particleboard, art materials, cosmetics, dermatological preparations, pharmaceuticals, flea collars, shoe polish, suntan lotions, pesticides, cleaners, etc.
Acrylamide	Risk of neurological impairment, probable carcinogen	Plastic; grout, adhesive, oil recovery
Adoxycarb	Risk of neurological impairment	Carbamate pesticide; pest control
Alachlor	Reported endocrine disruptor, carcinogen	Pesticide; banned in U.S./Canada
Alcohol	Neurological impairment	Solvent; beverages, liquid medicals
Aldicarb	Reported endocrine disruptor	Systemic carbamate pesticide
Aldrin	Carcinogen, suspected developmental, reproductive, and endocrine toxin and neurotoxin	OC pesticide; pest control
Alpha-naphthylamine	Carcinogen	Solvent; production of antioxidants, dyes, and herbicides
Allyxycarb	Many carbamates are suspected endocrine disruptors and reproductive toxins	Carbamate pesticide; insects, mites

Substance/(Related Substances/Other Names)	Developmental Effect or Risk	Classification; Common Use
Aluminum	Suspected neurotoxin	Metal; antacids, antiperspirants, inks, textiles, insulation, occupational, conductive fillers in plastics
Aminocarb	Many carbamates are suspected endocrine disruptors and reproductive toxins	Carbamate pesticide; pest control
Amitrole	Reported endocrine disruptor	Herbicide; weed control
Androderm	Category X Drug—Do Not Use During Pregnancy or Breast-feeding; abnormal genitalia in female fetus, possible masculinization of female fetus	Male hormone; medical
Android/Android Capsules	Category X Drug—Do Not Use During Pregnancy or Breast-feeding; possible masculinization of female fetus	Male Hormone; cancer RX
Antimony	Risk of neurological impairment with significant accumulations	Metal; batteries, solder, pipe metal, pewter
Aquasol A Casules	Category X Drug—Do Not Use During Pregnancy or Breast-feeding; can cause neurological malformations	High Potency Vitamin A
Arsenic	Risk of neurological impairment	Metal; pesticides, animal feed additives, wood preservative, riot control gas, metal pickling

Arsine	Carcinogen and developmental toxin, suspected endocrine toxin and neurotoxin	Arsenic gas; smelting, transisters
Aspirin	Category D in last trimester; avoid when breast-feeding	Pain reliever/NSAID; OTC medications
Atrazine	Reported endocrine disruptor	Herbicide; weed control
Aygestin	Category X Drug—Do Not Use During Pregnancy; masculinization of female fetus	Hormone/Progestin; medical
Baygon (Propoxur)	Suspected reproductive toxin and neurotoxin, suspected carcinogen	Carbamate pesticide; agriculture
Bellergal-S	Category X Drug—Do Not Use During Pregnancy or Breast-feeding	Autonomic stabilizer; medical
Benomyl	Reported endocrine disruptor, inhibits brain development and growth	Pesticide; fungus
Benzene	Decrease in sperm motility, testicular damage, risk of neurological impairment, carcinogen, developmental and reproductive toxin, suspected endocrine toxin	Solvent; sealants, laundry starch, scatter rugs, bathmats, lubricating oil, automotive
Benzene hexachloride (Gamma lindane)	Carcinogen, suspected developmental, endocrine and reproductive toxin and neurotoxin	Pesticide/solvent; pest control
Benzidine	Carcinogen, suspected neurotoxin	Aromatic amine; imported dyes and dyed products, contaminated water and waste sites

Substance/(Related Substances/Other Names)	Developmental Effect or Risk	Classification; Common Use
Benzo(a)pyrene	Testicular damage, carcinogen, suspected developmental and endocrine toxin	Aromatic hydrocarbon; cigarette smoke, coal tar, auto exhaust
Benzophenone (alpha-oxodipheylmethane)	Suspected endocrine disruptor	Solvent; hair mousse, pigments, inks
Beta-HCH	Reported endocrine disruptor	Pesticide; pest control
Bismuth (Pepto-Bismol, Helidac)	Risk of neurological impairment with accumulation or high use; do not use during breast-feeding; may harm infant	Metal; medication for colon disorders
Bisphenol A	Reported endocrine disruptor	Plasticizer; plastics, epoxy resins, teeth coatings, dental fillings, linings of food cans
Boric acid	Suspected reproductive toxin and neurotoxin	Pesticide; pesticide products, circuit board, flame retardants in cotton
Boron	Reduced sperm count, testicular damage, risk of neurological damage	Metal; conductive agents, insulating fibers
Brevicon (Norinyl)	Category X Drug—Do Not Use During Pregnancy or Breast-feeding	Hormone/contraceptive; medical
Carbamates	Risk of neurological impairment, inhibit brain enzymes that prevent overstimulization of brain cells, suspected process in cerebral palsy	Pesticide; pest control

Chemical	Developmental Effects	Source/Use
Cadmium	Reported endocrine disruptor, reduced fertility, testicular damage	Heavy metal; electroplating, pigments, alloys, nickel cadmium (NiCad) batteries
Cafergot (Ergotamine tartrate)	Category X Drug—Do Not Use During Pregnancy or Breast-feeding; risk of fetal growth retardation	Headache RX; medical
Carbamazepine (Tegretol, Atretol)	Risk of microcephaly, developmental delay, meningomyelocele	Anti-seizure drug; medical
Carbaryl (Sevin)	Reported endocrine disruptor, abnormal sperm morphology, testicular damage	Pesticide; pest control
Carbon disulfide	Reduced sperm count, decreased sperm motility, neurological impairment; affects all nervous system functions in exposed adults, one of the most neurotoxic solvents	Solvent; agriculture, rayon processing, cellophane, and rubber
Carbon monoxide	Testicular damage, risk of neurological impairment	Hydrocarbon gas; combustion of carbon materials
Carbon tetrachloride (Tetrachloromethane, Halon 104, Freon 10)	Testicular damage, carcinogen, suspected developmental and endocrine toxin and neurotoxin	Solvent; paints, cleaners, paint removers, lab chemicals, pharmaceuticals, solvent mixtures, propellants
Casodex	Category X Drug—Do Not Use During Pregnancy	Anti-androgen/cancer use; medical
Chlordane	Reported endocrine disruptor, neurological impairment	OC pesticide; pest control, termite control

Substance/(Related Substances/Other Names)	Developmental Effect or Risk	Classification; Common Use
Chlordecone (Kepone)	Reduced sperm count and motility, testicular damage, neurological impairment, carcinogen, developmental toxin, suspected endocrine disruptor	OC pesticide; contaminated soil and fish near waste sites, not made in U.S.
Chloroform (Trichloromethane, methane trichloride)	Carcinogen, suspected developmental, endocrine, and reproductive toxin and neurotoxin	Solvent; tap water, cleaners, propellants, dry cleaning, industrial processes, laundry starch, cleaning products
Chlorpropham	Many carbamates are suspected endocrine disruptors and reproductive toxins	Carbamate pesticide; systemic pest control
Chlorpyrifos (Dursban)	Suspected endocrine disruptor	OP pesticide; pest control for insects, fleas
Chloromethyl methyl ether	Carcinogin	Solvent; plastics
Chloroprene	Reduced sperm count, abnormal morphology, decreased libido, suspected carcinogen, developmental, endocrine, and reproductive toxin and neurotoxin	Solvent; adhesives for carpet/furniture, manufacture of neoprene rubber
Chromium	Risk of neurological degeneration, suspected carcinogen	Metal; antacids, KC1 solution, radiological contrast medium
Cis-platinum	Carcinogen	Metal; chemotherapy

Climara	Category X Drug—Do Not Use During Pregnancy or Breast-feeding; birth defects, reproductive effects, may cause cancer in offspring's later life	Hormone; medical
Clomid	Category X Drug—Do Not Use During Pregnancy; caution in breast-feeding	Fertility agent; medical
Copper	Risk of myelin damage, neuron degeneration, cerebellum effects	Metal; welding, pipe cutting, mining
Coumadin	Category X Drug—Do Not Use During Pregnancy; birth defects, neurological abnormalities and impairment	Blood thinner; medical
Cypermethrin	Reported endocrine disruptor	Pesticide; pest control
Cytotec	Category X Drug—Do Not Use During Pregnancy or Breast-feeding; risk of spontaneous abortion	Ulcer preventative; medical
DDT and metabolites	Reported endocrine disruptor, risk of neurological impairment	OC pesticide; agriculture in some countries, imports, still manufactured in U.S. for export even though use is banned
D.H.E. 45 (Dihydroergotamine mesylate)	Category X Drug—Do Not Use During Pregnancy or Breast-feeding; fetal growth retardation possible	Headache RX; medical

Substance/(Related Substances/Other Names)	Developmental Effect or Risk	Classification; Common Use
Danocrine Capsules	Category X Drug—Do Not Use During Pregnancy or Breast-feeding; masculinization and genital malformation in female fetus, inhibits development	Steroid hormone; medical
Delatestryl	Category X Drug—Do Not Use During Pregnancy or Breast-feeding; masculinization and genital malformation in female fetus	Male hormone; medical
Demeton	Suspected neurotoxin	Systemic pest control
Demulen	Category X Drug—Do Not Use During Pregnancy; avoid during breast-feeding	Hormone/contraceptive; medical
Depo-Provera	Category X Drug—Do Not Use During Pregnancy; birth defects, masculinization and genital malformations in female fetus	Hormone/contraceptive; medical
Desogen	Category X Drug—Do Not Use During Pregnancy; avoid during breast-feeding	Hormone/contraceptive; medical
Diazinon	Suspected developmental toxin and neurotoxin	OP pesticide; pest control for lawns, golf courses
Dibromochloropropane (DBCP)	Reduced sperm count, azoospermia, hormonal changes, reported endocrine disruptor	Pesticide; pest control

Chemical	Effects	Uses
Dichloromethane	Carcinogen, suspected endocrine disruptor, reproductive toxin and neurotoxin	Solvent; art materials, personal products, cleaners, auto products, pesticides, laundry aids, finishes, sealants, etc.
Dicofol	Reported endocrine disruptor	Pesticide; pest control
Didrex	Category X Drug—Do Not Use During Pregnancy or Breast-feeding; birth defects, embryotoxic	Amphetamine; weight loss
Dieldrin	Reported endocrine disruptor	OC pesticide; pest control, banned in some countries
Diethylhexyl adipate	Carcinogen, suspected endocrine disruptor	Plasticizer/additive; finishes, pigments, inks
Diethylstilbestrol	Category X Drug—Do Not Use During Pregnancy	Anti-nausea; medical
Dimecron (Phosphamidon)	Suspected carcinogen and neurotoxin	OP pesticide; pest control
Dimethoate	Suspected carcinogen, developmental toxin and neurotoxin	Systemic pesticide; insects
Dimethylaminopropionitrile (DMAPN)	Suspected neurotoxin	Industrial catalyst; polyurethane foam
Dimethyl dichlorovinyl phosphate (DDVP, Dichlorvos)	Reduced sperm count, carcinogen, suspected developmental and reproductive toxin and neurotoxin	Pesticide; pest control, insects, fleas

Substance/(Related Substances/Other Names)	Developmental Effect or Risk	Classification; Common Use
Dioxin	Endocrine disruptor, neurological impairment	Pollutant; released from chlorine processing and products, plastics, burning of chlorine products, chemical plants, transformers, bleaching
Doral	Category X Drug—Do Not Use During Pregnancy or Breast-feeding; birth defects, CNS depressant	Sleep aid; medical
EPN	Suspected neurotoxin	OP pesticide; pest control
Efudex	Category X Drug—Do Not Use During Pregnancy or Breast-feeding; birth defects	Skin cancer RX; medical
Electroplating/soldering	Risk of neurological impairment	Metal processing; jewelry, metal works
Endosulfan	Reported endocrine disruptor, neurotoxic	OC pesticide; pest control
Endrin	Recognized developmental toxin, suspected endocrine and reproductive toxin and neurotoxin	OC pesticide; pest control
Epichlorohydrin	Testicular damage, carcinogen, suspected endocrine and reproductive toxin and neurotoxin	Solvent; paper, pulp, printing, flame retardants, stains, varnishes

Ergomar	Category X Drug—Do Not Use During Pregnancy; caution in breast-feeding; stimulates uterine contractions	Migraine RX; medical
Esfenvalerate	Reported endocrine disruptor	Pesticide; pest control
Estrace	Category X Drug—Do Not Use During Pregnancy; avoid during breast-feeding	Hormone; medical
Estraderm	Category X Drug—Do Not Use During Pregnancy; avoid during breast-feeding; risk of cancer later in offspring's life, reproductive and genital defects	Hormone; medical
Estratab	Category X Drug—Do Not Use During Pregnancy; avoid during breast-feeding; risk of cancer later in offspring's life, reproductive and genital defects	Hormone; medical
Estratest	Category X Drug—Do Not Use During Pregnancy or Breast-feeding	Male/Female Hormone; medical
Estrogens	Category X Drug—Do Not Use During Pregnancy or Breast-feeding; reduced sperm count, risk of cancer later in offspring's life, reproductive and genital defects	Steroid hormones; medical
Ethane	Anesthetic gases have been associated with fetal growth retardation	Anesthetic gas; medical uses
Ethylan	Neurotoxic	OC pesticide; pest control

Substance/(Related Substances/Other Names)	Developmental Effect or Risk	Classification; Common Use
Ethylene oxide	Testicular damage, neurological impairment	Gas; medical equipment sterilization, production of ethylene glycol, polyesters and detergents
Ethylene dibromide (EDB) (Dibromoethane)	Abnormal sperm motility, testicular damage, developmental toxin, suspected neurotoxin	Pesticide; polystyrene and latex production, laboratory use
Ethylene glycol ethers	Decreased sperm motility, testicular damage	Solvent; antifreeze, prints, plastics industry, photo developing
Ethylparathion	Reported endocrine disruptor	OP pesticide; pest control
Fenvalerate	Reported endocrine disruptor	Pesticide; pest control
Floroplex	Category X Drug—Do Not Use During Pregnancy or Breast-feeding; mutagenic and may be carcinogenic, teratogenic and embryotoxic in animals, birth defects	Keratosis RX; medical
Floropryl ophthalmic	Category X Drug—Do Not Use During Pregnancy or Breast-feeding; can alter brain chemistry	Glaucoma RX; medical
Formaldehyde	Potential carcinogen	Gas/preservative; plastics

Freons (Nitromethane, fluoroalkanes, fluorotrichloromethane, 1,1,2,2-tetrachloro-1,2-difluoroethane)	Carcinogen, suspected neurotoxin	Solvent; refrigeration in autos, etc.
Furans	Reported endocrine disruptor	Organochorine pollutant; by-product of chlorine, released by burning bleaches, chemical manufacturing, plastics
Gallium arsenide	Neurotoxin	Arsenic compound; semiconductor manufacture
Gold, organic	Risk of damage to hypothalamus, tremor	Metal; gold therapy for arthritis, asthma, lupus
Griseofulvin (Fulvicin, Grisactin, Grifulvin)	Birth defects in animals, sperm suppression in animal studies, Do Not Use During Pregnancy	Antifungal; medical
HCB (Hexachlorobenzene)	Reported endocrine disruptor	Solvent/OC pesticide; by-product of chlorines, organochlorines, pesticides, fungicides
Halcion	Category X Drug—Do Not Use During Pregnancy or Breast-feeding; birth defects, CNS depressant, neonatal flaccidity	Sleep aid; medical

Substance/(Related Substances/Other Names)	Developmental Effect or Risk	Classification; Common Use
Halotestin	Category X Drug—Do Not Use During Pregnancy or Breast-feeding; possible carcinogen, masculization of female fetus	Male hormone; medical
Halothane	Anesthetic gases have been associated with fetal growth retardation	Anesthetic gas; hospitals, veterinary clinics
Heat	Decreased sperm count	Environmental condition; sauna, hot baths, elevated body temperature, climatic conditions
h-epoxide	Reported endocrine disruptor	Pesticide; pest control
Heptachlor	Reported endocrine disruptor	OC pesticide; pest control
Hexane	Risk of neurological impairment, suspected developmental toxin, degeneration of nerve axons	Solvent; gasoline, glue, lacquers, used to extract essences and vegetable oils, pharmaceuticals, cleaners
Hormones (all) (testosterone, estrogen, progesterone)	Category X Drugs—Do Not Use During Pregnancy	Steroids; medical
Humegon	Category X Drug—Do Not Use During Pregnancy; avoid during breast-feeding; can cause fetal harm	Fertility agent; medical

Humorsol	Category X Drug—Do Not Use During Pregnancy or Breast-feeding; alters brain chemistry	Glaucoma RX; medical
Iron	Accumulations carry risk of neurological degeneration, demyelination and intellectual impairment	Metal; iron oxide fumes, industry
Kelthane	Reported endocrine disruptor	Pesticide; pest control
Kepone	Reported endocrine disruptor	OC pesticide; pest control
Lead	Reported endocrine disruptor, decreased sperm count/motility in adult, testicular damage, abnormal sperm, damage to myelin sheath, crosses blood-brain barrier, placenta, and into breast milk, alters and deforms sperm, neurological and intellectual impairment, offspring at risk for brain tumors if parents work with lead	Heavy metal; solvents, leaded gas, mining, welding, steel manufacturing, art, printing, electronics, cleaning fluids
Lescol	Category X Drug—Do Not Use During Pregnancy or Breast-feeding; fetal harm and neurological changes associated with drugs in this class	Cholesterol RX; medical
Levlen/Tri-Levlen	Category X Drug—Do Not Use During Pregnancy; avoid during breast-feeding	Hormone/contraceptive; medical
Lindane	Reported endocrine disruptor	OC pesticide; pest control

Substance/(Related Substances/Other Names)	Developmental Effect or Risk	Classification; Common Use
Lo/Ovral (Ovral, Ovrette)	Category X Drug—Do Not Use During Pregnancy	Hormone/contraceptive; medical
Lupron Depot (Lupron, Lupron Depot-Ped, Lupron Depot 3.75 mg.)	Category X Drug—Do Not Use During Pregnancy or Breast-feeding; major fetal abnormalities in animals, increased fetal mortality, reduced weight, may have endocrine effects on fetus	Synthetic hormone; medical
MBK (Methyl-butyl-ketone)	Neurological impairment	Solvent; resins, oils, print and plastic industry
MEK (Methyl-ethyl-ketone)	Neurological impairment	Solvent; solvent mixtures, thinners, removers for adhesives, lacquers
Malathion	Reported endocrine disruptor	OP pesticide; pest control lawns
Mancozeb	Reported endocrine disruptor	Pesticide; pest control for fungus
Maneb	Reported endocrine disruptor	Carbamate pesticide; pest control for fungus
Manganese	Decreased libido, impotence, testicular damage, neurological impairment in large amounts	Metal; dry cell batteries, germicides pesticides, fertilizers, animal food, mining, welding, steel alloy plants
Megace Suspension	Category X Drug—Do Not Use During Pregnancy or Breast-feeding; genital abnormalities, reproductive capability impaired, endocrine effects	Hormone; medical

Chemical	Developmental Effects	Uses
Menest	Category X Drug—Do Not Use During Pregnancy	Synthetic hormone; medical
Mercury	Reported endocrine disruptor, motor and cognitive impairment	Metal; folk medicines, some Chinese patent medicines, dental, laboratory, furnaces, metal recovery, agriculture, production of chlorine and fluorescent lighting, temperature devices
Methamidophos	Suspected neurotoxin	Systemic pest control
Methanol	Neurological impairment, suspected developmental toxin and neurotoxin	Solvent; antifreeze, paint and removers, pesticides, cosmetics, soaps, semiconductors, electroplating, solvent mixtures and cleaners, household chemicals, inks, circuit board manufacturing, antibacterials
Methomyl	Reported endocrine disruptor	Systemic pest control
Methotrexate/Rheumatrex	Category X Drug—Do Not Use During Pregnancy or Breast-feeding; increased fetal death, birth defects, may be mutagenic, may affect sperm	Cancer RX; medical
Methoxychlor	Reported endocrine disruptor	OC pesticide; pest control
Methylene chloride (Chloromethane, dichloromethane)	Risk of neurological impairment	Solvent; see dichloromethane

Substance/(Related Substances/Other Names)	Developmental Effect or Risk	Classification; Common Use
Methyl bromide	Neurological impairment, developmental toxin, suspected reproductive effects	Pesticide; agricultural
Methyl chloride	Neurological impairment	Solvent; industrial solvents, refrigerants, insecticide propellants, foods
Methyl isobutyl ketone	Neurological complaints from adults at high doses	Solvent; paint, glue
Methyl mercury	Neurological impairment, motor and cognitive impairment, recognized developmental toxin; crosses into breast milk	Organic metal; seed treatments, paint, electrical, contaminated shellfish, pharmaceutical industries
Methyl methacrylate	Neurological impairment, suspected developmental and reproductive toxin	Plastic; adhesives, pharmaceutical
Methyl-n-butyl ketone	Neurological impairment	Solvent; thinners, removers for adhesives, lacquers, gums, varnishes
Metiram	Reported endocrine disruptor	Pesticide; pest control for fungus
Metribuzin	Reported endocrine disruptor	Pesticide; pest control for weeds
Metrodin	Category X Drug—Do Not Use During Pregnancy	Fertility agent; medical

Mevacor	Category X Drug—Do Not Use During Pregnancy or Breast-feeding; birth defects, may affect sperm, may be carcinogenic	Cholesterol RX; medical
Mevinphos (Phosdrin)	Suspected neurotoxin	OP pesticide; pest control
Micronor (Modicon, Ortho-Novum)	Category X Drug—Do Not Use During Pregnancy; avoid when breast-feeding	Hormone/contraceptive; medical
Mineral spirits (Naptha)	Suspected neurotoxin and endocrine disruptor	Solvent; cleaners, paint removers, cleansing creams, eye makeup, polishes, hairspray, pesticides, lubricants, laundry presoaks, art materials
Mirex	Reported endocrine disruptor	OC pesticide; pest control, banned in some countries
Mithracin	Category X Drug—Do Not Use During Pregnancy or Breast-feeding; possibility of birth defects, affects sperm	Cancer RX; medical
N-butyl benzene (Butylpropane)	Suspected endocrine disruptor	Solvent; solvents for paints, adhesives, etc.
Nickel	Carcinogen, risk of neurological impairment, suspected developmental, reproductive, and neurotoxin	Metal; electroplating
Nitrofen	Reported endocrine disruptor	Pesticide; pest control for weeds

Substance/(Related Substances/Other Names)	Developmental Effect or Risk	Classification; Common Use
Nitrous Oxide	Anesthetic gases have been associated with fetal growth retardation	Anesthetic gas; dental and medical use
Nor-Q	Category X Drug—Do Not Use During Pregnancy; avoid when breast-feeding	Hormone/contraceptive; medical
Nordette-21	Category X Drug—Do Not Use During Pregnancy; avoid when breast-feeding	Hormone/contraceptive; medical
Norplant	Category X Drug—Do Not Use During Pregnancy; avoid when breast-feeding	Hormone/contraceptive; medical
Octachlorostyrene	Reported endocrine disruptor	Solvent; released from processing organochlorine and from burning of chlorinated and organic wastes
Ogen/Ogen tablets	Category X Drug—Do Not Use During Pregnancy; avoid when breast-feeding; birth defects, reproductive disorders, cancer in offspring's later life	Hormone; medical
Oreton	Category X Drug—Do Not Use During Pregnancy; may be carcinogenic; masculinization of female fetus, may affect sperm	Male hormone; medical
Organic mercurials	Neurological impairment	Organic metal; contaminated fish, air, soil, water near waste sites

Organochlorine insecticides	Neurological impairment, some are reported endocrine disruptors, many are proven or suspected carcinogens	Pesticide; pest control, agriculture, imported merchandise and foods
Organophosphates	Risk of neurological impairment, inhibits enzymes that prevent overstimulation of brain cells, suspected process in cerebral palsy, some are reported endocrine disrupters	Pesticide; pest control, agriculture, sprayed worksites, pesticide manufacture
Organotin compounds (diethytin, trimethyltin, triethyltin)	Risk of neurological impairment, destroys myelin	Metal; solder, dental amalgam, pesticides, disinfectants, marine paints, plastic and polyvinyl chloride stabilizer
Ortho Dienestrol Cream	Category X Drug—Do Not Use During Pregnancy; caution in breast-feeding; birth defects, endocrine effects, may cause cancer in later life	Hormone; medical
Ortho-Cept	Category X Drug—Do Not Use During Pregnancy; avoid when breast-feeding	Hormone/contraceptive; medical
Ortho-cyclen/ Ortho-Tri-Cyclen	Category X Drug—Do Not Use During Pregnancy; avoid when breast-feeding	Hormone/contraceptive; medical
Ortho-Est	Category X Drug—Do Not Use During Pregnancy; avoid when breast-feeding; cancer in later life in both male and female offspring, reproductive organ defects	Hormone; medical

Substance/(Related Substances/Other Names)	Developmental Effect or Risk	Classification; Common Use
Ovcon	Category X Drug—Do Not Use During Pregnancy; avoid when breast-feeding	Hormone/contraceptive; medical
Oxandrin	Category X Drug—Do Not Use During Pregnancy or Breast-feeding; masculinization of female fetus, birth defects, fertility of fetus altered	Synthetic testosterone; medical
Oxychlordane	Reported endocrine disruptor	OC pesticide; pest control, banned some nations
PCP (Pentachlorophenol)	Suspected developmental, endocrine, and reproductive toxin and neurotoxin	Solvent/pesticide; rubber, plywood, preservative, pest control, microbials
PCP	Neurological damage	Hallucinogen; street drug and veterinary use
PBBs	Recogized developmental toxin and carcinogen, endocrine disruptor, suspected neurotoxin, testicular damage	Pollutants; banned, background exposure
PCBs (over 100 different PCBs)	Reported endocrine disruptor	Organochlorine pollutant; fire resistant coatings, plastics, electrical transformers and equipment, environmental toxin
PMB	Category X Drug—Do Not Use During Pregnancy or Breast-feeding; cancer in later life, birth defects, may be carcinogenic	Hormone; medical

Chemical	Developmental Effects	Uses
Parathion	Carcinogen, suspected developmental, endocrine and reproductive toxin and neurotoxin	OP pesticide; pest control, insects, mites
Pentachlorophenol	Reported endocrine disruptor	Pesticide; pest control for fungus, textiles, wood preservatives
Perchloroethylene (Tetrachloroethylene)	Risk of neurological impairment, changes brain chemistry, mutagen	Solvent; dry cleaning, solvent mixtures
Pergonal	Category X Drug—Do Not Use During Pregnancy	Fertility agent; medical
Permethrin	Reported endocrine disruptor	Pesticide; pest control, animal products, lice control
Phenols (Penta phenols to Nonyl phenols)	Reported endocrine disruptor	Surfactants; detergents, pesticides, textile mills, paper mills, toiletries, spermicides, cosmetics, plastics, soaps, latex paint, lubricating oils
Phenytoin	Risk for learning disability, reduced IQ, facial and cranial abnormalities	Anti-seizure drug; medical
Phosphine	Suspected neurotoxin	Gas; welding, semiconductor manufacture, foods, grain fumigation

Substance/(Related Substances/Other Names)	Developmental Effect or Risk	Classification; Common Use
Phthalates (includes the following phthalates: Butyl benzyl, BBP; Di-ethylhexyl; DEHP; Di-n-butyl, DBP; Di-n-pentyl, DPP; Di-hexyl, DHP; Di-propyl, DproP; Dicyclohexyl, DCHP; Diethy, DEP)	Reported endocrine disruptors	Plasticizers; paints, ink, adhesives, PVC, vinyl rain wear, upholstery toys, bottle caps, heat-seal coatings on foods, laminates, pesticides, paper and paperboard, floor tiles, polyurethanes, cellulose film, plastics, beauty products, molded plastics, i.e., toothbrushes and car parts
Polybrominated biphenyls (PBBs)	Reported endocrine disruptor, testicular damage	See PBBs
Pravachol	Category X Drug—Do Not Use During Pregnancy or Breast-feeding; may be carcinogenic, skeletal malformations possible	Cholesterol RX; medical
Premarin w/Methyltestosterone	Category X Drug—Do Not Use During Pregnancy	Male/female hormones; medical
Premarin (Vaginal Cream, IV, Tablets)	Category X Drug—Do Not Use During Pregnancy	Hormone; medical
Premphase	Category X Drug—Do Not Use During Pregnancy; risk of reproductive defects and cancer in later life	Hormone/Est/Progest; medical for postmenopausal symptoms

Prempro	Category X Drug—Do Not Use During Pregnancy; risk of reproductive defects and cancer in later life	Hormone/Est/Progest; medical for postmenopausal symptoms
Profasi	Category X Drug—Do Not Use During Pregnancy	Fertility agent; medical
Proscar	Category X Drug—Do Not Use During Pregnancy or Breast-feeding; abnormalities of male genitalia, decrease in fertility, this drug is not intended for use in women	Male cancer RX; medical
ProSom	Category X Drug—Do Not Use During Pregnancy or Breast-feeding; CNS depressant, birth defects, withdrawal in newborn	Sleep aid; medical
Pseudoephedrine	Manufacturer recommends mothers either avoid drug while nursing or discontinue nursing while taking the drug; stimulant effects can simulate stress	Decongestant; nonprescription drug
Pyrethrins	Risk of neurological impairment	Pesticide; organic pesticides
Pyrethroids (synthetic)	Reported endocrine disruptor, risk of neurological impairment	Pesticide; animal sprays, etc.
Pyridoxine (abuse)	Neurological impairment with high doses or abuse by mother; do not exceed recommended daily requirement	Vitamin; nutritional supplement

Substance/(Related Substances/Other Names)	Developmental Effect or Risk	Classification; Common Use
Quadrinal	Category X Drug—Do Not Use During Pregnancy or Breast-feeding; birth defects, neonatal goiter, hemorrhage, respiratory effects	Asthma RX; medical
Radioactive Iodine	Category X Drug—Do Not Use During Pregnancy; radiation is known to affect intellectual and neurological functioning	Thyroid RX; medical
Radiation, ionizing	Decreased sperm count, testicular damage, neurological impairment	Diagnostic/cancer; RX medical facilities
Restoril	Category X Drug—Do Not Use During Pregnancy; birth defects, CNS depression, skeletal abnormalities, use with caution when breast-feeding	Sleep aid; medical
Ronnel	Suspected developmental toxin and neurotoxin	OP pesticide; pest control, insects, mites
Sansert	Category X Drug—Do Not Use During Pregnancy	Headache RX; medical
Sarin (Fuserin)	Suspected neurotoxin	OP pesticide; pest control
Selenium	Suspected developmental and reproductive toxin and neurotoxin	Metal; photochemicals, oxidizing agents, dandruff shampoos

Name	Developmental Effects	Common Uses
Sevin (Carbaryl)	Suspected carcinogen, developmental, endocrine and reproductive toxin and neurotoxin	Carbamate pesticide; pest control, garden, animals, flea and tick collars
Solvent Mixtures	Neurological impairment, offspring at risk for brain tumors if parents work with solvents	Solvent; cleaners, thinners
Stilphostrol	Category X Drug—Do Not Use During Pregnancy	Hormone/cancer RX; medical
Styrene	Risk of neurological impairment	Solvent; plastic production, floor waxes, polish, paints, putty, cleaners, varnish, tobacco smoke, automotive exhaust, food containers
Styrene (dimers and trimers)	Reported endocrine disruptor	Solvent; same as above
Supprelin	Category X Drug—Do Not Use During Pregnancy	Hormone inhibitor; medical
Synarel Nasal	Category X Drug—Do Not Use During Pregnancy	Synthetic hormone; medical
Synarel	Category X Drug—Do Not Use During Pregnancy	Synthetic hormone; medical
TDE (DDD)	Carcinogen, suspected endocrine toxin and neurotoxin	OC pesticide; pest control
Tegison	Category X Drug—Do Not Use During Pregnancy	Retinoid/psoriasis RX; medical

Substance/(Related Substances/Other Names)	Developmental Effect or Risk	Classification; Common Use
Tellurium	Suspected neurotoxin	Metal; mining, alloys, rubber, stainless steel, metal industry
Telone (Dichloropropene)	Carcinogen, suspected neurotoxin	OC pesticide; pest control, soil fumigant, fungicide, polystyrene and latex production
Testoderm	Category X Drug—Do Not Use During Pregnancy; must not be used in women	Male hormone; medical
Tetrahydrofuran (Diethylene oxide, epoxybutane, tetramethylene oxide)	Many furans are known endocrine disruptors, risk of neurological impairment	Solvent; used to dissolve glues and plastics, paints, varnishes, textiles
Testred	Category X Drug—Do Not Use During Pregnancy or Breast-feeding; masculinization of female fetus	Male hormone; medical
Thalium	Risk of neurological impairment with accumulations, destroys myelin	Metal; pest control, rodenticides, fireworks, alloys
Toluene	Neurological impairment, growth retardation, facial and cranial abnormalities, attentional disorders, developmental delay, neural tube defects, endocrine effects	Solvent; paint, varnish, adhesives, cleaners, degreasers
Toxaphene	Reported endocrine disruptor	OC pesticide; pest control, banned in some nations
Transnonachlor	Reported endocrine disruptor	Pesticide; pest control

Chemical	Use	Developmental/Health Effect
Tributyltin oxide	Pesticide; pest control for fungus	Reported endocrine disruptor
Trichloroethane (Chlorothane)	Solvent; cleaning solvents	Risk of neurological impairment
Trichloroethylene (Trichloroethene)	Solvent; dry cleaning, lubricants, adhesives, degreasers, anesthetics	Risk of neurological impairment, cranial nerve damage, myelin degeneration
Trifluralin	Pesticide; pest control for weeds	Reported endocrine disruptor
Tri-Norinyl	Hormone/contraceptive; medical	Category X Drug—Do Not Use During Pregnancy
Triphasil-21	Hormone/contraceptive; medical	Category X Drug—Do Not Use During Pregnancy
Tungsten carbide	Metal; electric light filaments, drilling and cutting tools, pigments, electrodes	Risk of memory deficits
Vacor (Pyriminil, PNU, Lovastatin)	Rodenticide; rodent control	Neurological impairment, suspected endocrine disruptor
Vanadium	Metal; steel hardening, pesticides, photo processing	Suspected immunotoxin and neurotoxin
Vinclozolin	Pesticide; pest control for fungus	Reported endocrine disruptor
Vinyl Chloride	Solvent; fiber processing, pulp and paper manufacture, lab chemicals	Suspected developmental and reproductive toxin and neurotoxin
Virazole	Antiviral; medical	Category X Drug—Do Not Use During Pregnancy

Substance/(Related Substances/Other Names)	Developmental Effect or Risk	Classification; Common Use
Vivelle	Category X Drug—Do Not Use During Pregnancy	Hormone/estrogen; medical
Xylene	Risk of neurological impairment	Solvent; varnish, glue, rubber, leather, paint, solvent mixtures, polymers
Wigraine	Category X Drug—Do Not Use During Pregnancy	Headache RX; medical
Winstrol	Category X Drug—Do Not Use During Pregnancy	Synthetic testosterone; medical
Zinc	Suspected developmental and reproductive toxin	Metal; batteries, alloys, found in acid foods stored in galvanized metal
Zineb	Reported endocrine disruptor, carcinogen, suspected reproductive toxin and neurotoxin	Carbamate pesticide; pest control for fungus
Ziram	Reported endocrine disruptor, suspected neurotoxin	Pesticide; pest control for fungus
Zocor	Category X Drug—Do Not Use During Pregnancy	Cholesterol RX; medical
Zoladex (Zoladex 3-month)	Category X Drug—Do Not Use During Pregnancy or Breast-feeding	Hormone inhibitor; medical

Appendix

These organizations can test carpet, water, and other materials for toxins:

American Environmental Health Foundation; 8345 Walnut Hill Lane; Suite 225; Dallas, TX 75231; 800-428-2343. (Also a source for environmentally safe products.)

Citizens Environmental Laboratory; 160 Second Street; Cambridge, MA 02142; 617-876-6505.

Laboratories that provide blood, urine, breast milk, and water testing:

AccuChem Laboratories; 990 North Bowser; Suite 800; Richardson, TX 75081; 214-234-5412.

Internet Chemical Information Sources

Best Sources for chemical evaluation:

Scorecard—About the Chemicals, Environmental Defense Fund
http://www.scorecard.org/chemical-profiles/index.tcl

EDIS, University of Florida Food and Agricultural Sciences
Information on chemicals and agriculture
http://edis.ifas.ufl.edu/

Medscape (includes toxline, medline, and full text articles)
Journal articles on toxins, medical conditions, and medications
http://www.medscape.com/Home/Topics/multispecialty/
multispecialty.html

Chemfinder
Gives some chemical information
http://www.chemfinder.com/

National MS Foundation information on preservatives
Great source for additives
http://aspin.asu.edu/msnews/preserv.htm

Oxybusters
Good site for chemical and environmental issues
http://www.oxybusters.com/mtbe_lay.htm

Sources for nontoxic tampons and other hygiene products:

Terrafemme
Long-fiber cotton and peroxide bleached tampons
http://www.web.net/terrafemme/

Bio Business International
78 Hallam Street; Toronto, Canada M6H 1W8; 416-539-8548
Fax: 416-539-9784

Natracare
Oxygen bleached and all-cotton tampons:
http://www.indra.com/natracare/
Or order from these catalogs:
1-800-869-3446: Seventh Generation (Now "Harmony")
1-800-475-3663: Goldmine Natural Foods
1-800-643-3909: Mt. Ark Catalog

Organic Essentials
Organic cotton hygienic products:
http://www.feminist.com/orgessen.htm
822 Baldridge Street; O'Donnell, Texas 79351; 800-765-6491;
806-428-3486; Fax: 806-428-3475

Safe Products

EcoMall
Gives links to all kinds of safe products. It is found at the bottom of the Organic Essentials page at the following address:
http://www.ecomall.com/orgessen.htm

Help to Quit Smoking

Tobacco BBS
http://www.tobacco.org/

QuitNet
http://www.quitnet.org/

References

Agency for Toxic Substances and Disease Registry (ATSDR). 1996. (Web site): (http://atsdr1.atdr.cdc.gov:8080/atsdrhome.html); Division of Toxicology , 1600 Clifton Road NE, Mailstop E-29, Atlanta, GA 30333 (888-422-8737); email ASTDRIC@cdc.gov.

Ainsworth, M. D. S. 1973. The development of infant-mother attachment. In *Review of Child Development Research*, edited by B. M. Caldwell and H. N. Ricciuti. Vol. 3. Chicago: Univ. of Chicago Press.

Akerstedt, T. 1990. Psychological and psychophysiological effect of shift work. *Scand J Work Environ Health* 16(Suppl 1):67.

American College of Obstetricians and Gynecologists. 1997. *Planning for Pregnancy, Birth, and Beyond*, Second Ed. N.Y.: Signet.

American Pharmaceutical Association. 1993. *Handbook of Nonprescription Drugs*. Washington, DC: American Pharmaceutical Association.

Annegers, J. F., W. A. Hauser, L. R. Elveback, V. E. Anderson, and L. T. Kurland. 1978. Congenital malformations and seizure disorders in the offspring of parents with epilepsy. *Int J Epidemiol* 7:241.

Anselmo, Sandra. 1987. *Early Childhood Development: Prenatal Through Age Eight*. Columbus, OH: Merrill Publishing Company.

Aranda, J., and Stern, L. 1983. Clinical Aspects of developmental pharmacology and toxicology. *Pharmacol Ther* 20:1-51.

Ashley, S. J., and R. E. Little. 1990. Maternal marijuana use during lactation and infant development at one year. *Neurotoxicology and Teratology* 12:161-168.

Bauman, M., and T. L. Kemper. 1985. Histoanatomic observations of the brain in early infantile autism. *Neurology* 35(6):866-874.

Benfenati, E., M. Natangelo, E. Davoli, and R. Fanelli. 1991. Migration of vinyl chloride into PVC-bottled drinking water assessed by gas chromatography-mass spectrometry. *Food Chem Toxicol* 29(2):131-134.

Bernsen J. J., W. I. Verhagen, M. A. de Bijl, and A. Heerschap. 1992. Magnetic resonance studies on brain dysfunction induced by organic solvents. *Acta Neurol Belg* 92(4):207-214.

Bogerts, B. 1997. The temporolimbic system theory of positive schizophrenic symptoms. *Schizophrenia Bulletin* 23(3):423-435.

Boris, M. and F. S. Mandel. 1994. Foods and additives are common causes of attention deficit hyperactive disorder in children. *Ann Allergy* 72:462–468.

Breecher, M. M., and S. Linde. 1992. *Healthy Homes in a Toxic World*. NY: John Wiley & Sons, Inc.

Brennan, P., E. Grekin, and S. Mednick. 1999. Maternal smoking during pregnancy and adult male criminal outcomes. *Arcj general Psyciatry* 56:215–219.

Briggs, G., R. Freeman, and S. Yaffe. 1994. *Drugs in Pregnancy and Lactation*. Baltimore: Williams & Wilkins.

Brown, C. C., ed. 1983. *Childhood Learning Disabilities and Prenatal Risk: An Interdisciplinary Data Review for Health Care Professionals and Parents*. Skillman, N. J.: Johnson and Johnson.

Camfield, P. R., C. S. Camfield, J. M. Dooley, K. Gordon, S. Jollymore, and D. F. Weaver. 1992. Aspartame exacerbates EEG spike-wave discharge in children with generalized absence epilepsy: a double-blind controlled study. *Neurology* 42(5):1000-1003.

Carr, A., M. E. Chauner, W. H. Hylton, S. W. Smyser, C. Stoner, M. Stoner, R. B. Y. Epsen, eds. 1978. *The Encyclopedia of Organic Gardening*. Emmaus, PA: Rodale Press.

Carson, Rachel. 1962. *Silent Spring*. Boston: Houghton-Mifflin.

Case Studies in Environmental Medicine. 1993. *Reproductive and Developmental Hazards*. September. U.S. Dept. of Health and Human Services, Agency for Toxic Substances and Disease Registry.

Cherry, N., F. Labreche, and J. McDonald. 1992. Organic brain damage and occupational solvent exposure. *Br J Ind Med* 49(11): 776-781.

Chua, S. E., and P. J. McKenna. 1995. Schizophrenia—A brain disease? A critical review of structural and functional cerebral abnormality in the disorder. *Brit J Psych* 166:563-582.

Colborn, T., D. Dumanoski, and J. P. Myers. 1996. *Our Stolen Future: Are We Threatening Our Fertility, Intelligence, and Survival?* N.Y.: Dutton.

Committee on Government Operations, Washington, D.C. 1985. Review of ground water contamination and depletion problems in the Northwest. Hearing before a subcommittee of the Committee on Government Operation, House of Representatives, First Session. Washington, DC: Government Printing Office.

Consumer Reports. 1998. Greener greens? The truth about organic foods. January. 63:13-18.

Coveny, J. 1985. Is breast milk the best food for all infants? *Hum Nutr Appl Nutr* 39(3):179-188.

Cummings, A. J. 1983. A survey of pharmacokinetic data from pregnant women. *Clin. Pharmacokinet* 8:344-345.

Cunningham, F. G., P. C. MacDonald, N. F. Gant, K. J. Leveno, L. C. Gilstrap, G. D. V. Hankins, and S. L. Clark. 1997. *Williams Obstetrics,* Twentieth Edition. Stamford, CA: Appleton & Lange.

Davis, L., M. Gottlieb, and J. Stampnitzky. 1998. Reduced ratio of male to female births in several industrial countries: A sentinel health indicator? *JAMA* 279:1018-1023.

Dawson, G., H. Panagiotides, L. G. Klinger, and S. Spieker. 1997. Infants of depressed and nondepressed mother exhibit differences in frontal brain electrical activity during the expression of negative emotions. *Dev Psychol* 33(4):650–656.

Deckel, A. W., V. Hesselbrock, and L. Bauer. 1996. Antisocial personality disorder, childhood delinquency, and frontal brain functioning: EEG and neuropsychological findings. *J Clin Psychol* 51(6):639-650.

Dencker, L., and B. Danielsson. 1987. Transfer of drugs to the embryo and fetus after placentation. In *Pharmacokinetics in Teratogenesis,* edited by H. Nau and W.J. Scott, Jr. Vol. 1. 55-69. Boca Raton, FL: CRC Press, Inc.

Dobbing, J. 1968. Vulnerable periods in the developing brain. In *Applied Neurochemistry,* edited by A. N. Davison and J. Dobbing. Oxford: Blackwell.

Dogheim, S. M., el-Z. Mohamed, S. A. Gad All, S. el-Saied, S. Y. Emel, A. M. Mohsen, and S. M. Fahmy. 1996. Monitoring of pesticide residues in human milk, soil, water, and food samples collected from Kafr El-Zayat Governorate. *J AOAC Int* 79(1):111–116.

Dowty, B. J., J. Storer, and J. L. Laseter. 1976. The transplacental migration and accumulation in blood of volatile organic constituents. *J Ped Res* 10:696.

Ducatman, A., and D. Haes, Jr. 1994. Nonionizing radiation. In *Textbook of Clinical Occupational and Environmental Medicine,* edited by L. Rosenstockand M. Cullen. Philadelphia: W. B Saunders Co.

Elia, J., T. Katz, and G. M. Simpson. 1987. Teratogenicity of psychotherapeutic medications. *Psychopharmacol Bull* 23:531.

Environmental Defense Fund. 1998. *Scorecard: About the Chemicals.* NY, NY (http://www.scorecard.org/chemical-profiles/index.tel)

Environmental Protection Agency (EPA). 1995. *Citizen's Guide to Pest Control and Pesticide Safety.* September. Washington, DC: Environmental Protection Agency (EPA).

Essen, B. 1977. Intramuscular substrate utilization during prolonged exercise. *Ann N Y Acad Sci* 301:30-44.

Fried, P. A. 1992. Clinical implications of smoking: determining long-term teratogenicity. In *Maternal Substance Abuse and the Developing Nervous System,* edited by J. S. Zagorand and T. A. Slotkin. NY: Academic Press, Inc.

———. 1980. Marijuana use by pregnant women. Neurobehavioral effects in neonates. *Drug and Alcohol Dependence* 6:415-425.

Garnier, R., J. Bedouin, G. Pepin, and Y. Gaillard. 1996. Coin-operated dry cleaning machine may be responsible for acute tetrachloroethylene poisoning. *J. Toxicol Clin Toxicol* 34:191–197.

Glanz, J. C. 1994. Reproductive toxicology of alkylating agents. *Obstet Gynecol Surv* 49:704.

Griffith, H. W. 1997. *Complete Guide to Prescription & Nonprescription Drugs.* NY: The Body Press/Perigee.

Gunzenhauser, N., ed. 1987. *Infant Stimulation: For Whom, What Kind, and How Much?* Pediatric Round Table 13: Johnson and Johnson.

Guyton, A. 1981. *Textbook of Medical Physiology.* Philadelphia: W. B. Saunders Company.

Haley, R. W. 1998. Point: Bias: From the "Healthy Warrior Effect" and unequal follow-up in the government studies of health effects of the Gulf War. *Am J Epidemiology* 148 (4):315:323.

Hamosh, M. 1996. Breast-feeding: Unraveling the mysteries of mother's milk. *Medscape Women's Health* 1(9):1-15 (http://www.medscape.com/Medscape/women's health/1996/v01.n09/w120. hamosh/w120.hamosh.html)

Handbook of Nonprescription Drugs. 1993. Washington DC: American Pharmaceutical Association.

Harbison, R., ed. 1998. *Hamilton and Hardy's Industrial Toxicology.* New York: Mosby.

Harland, E. 1993. *Eco-Renovation: The Ecological Home Improvement Guide.* Post Mills, VT: Chelsea Green Publishing Company.

Harlow, B. L., D. W. Cramer, D. A. Bell, and W. R. Welch. 1992. Perineal exposure to talc and ovarian cancer risk. July. *Obstet Gynecol* 80:19-26.

Hart, B., and T. Risley. 1995. Meaningful differences in the everyday experiences of young American children. In *Developmental Toxicology: Risk Assessment and the Future,* edited by P. H. Brooks and R. D. Hood. NY:Van Nostrand Reingold.

Hartman, D. E. 1995. *Neuropsychological Toxicology: Identification and Assessment of Human Neurotoxic Syndromes.* Second Edition. New York: Plenum Press.

Havery, D. C., and T. J. Fazio. 1983. Survey of baby bottle rubber nipples for volatile N-nitrosamines. *Assoc Off Anal Chem* 66(6):1500-1503.

Holzman, C., and N. Paneth. 1994. Maternal cocaine use during pregnancy and perinatal outcomes. *Epidemiol Rev* 16:315-334.

Hood, R. D. 1990. Paternally Mediated Effects. In *Developmental Toxicology: Risk Assessment and the Future,* edited by R. D. Hood. NewYork: Van Nostrand Reinhold.

Hyyten, F. E. 1980. Weight gain in pregnancy. In *Clinical Physiology in Obstetrics,* edited by F. E. Hytten and G. Chamberlain. 147-162. Oxford: Blackwell Scientific Publications, Ltd.

ICRF Newsletter. 1995. *Fluoride.* November. P.O. Box 97, Ardsley, N.Y. 10502.

International Labour Office. 1986. Protection of workers against radiofrequency and microwave radiation: a technical review. *Occupational Safety and Health Series.* Report No. 57. Geneve: International Labour Office.

Isaacson, R. L., and K. F. Jenson, eds. 1992. *The Vulnerable Brain and Environmental Risks.* Vol I. N. Y.:Plenum Press.

Jacobson, J. L., S. W. Jacobson, and H. E. Humphrey. 1990. Effects of exposure to PCBs and related compounds on growth and activity in children. *Neurotoxicology and Teratology* 12:319-326.

Jick, S. S., B. Z. Terris, and H. Jick. 1993. First trimester topical tretinoin and congenital disorders. *Lancet* 341:1664.

Joseph, P. M. 1997. Health effects from MTBE in gasoline. Educational materials. Philadelphia: University of Pennsylvania School of Medicine. (Contact Dr. Joseph at 215-662-6679).

Kacew, S. 1993. Adverse effects of drugs and chemicals in breast milk on the nursing infant. *J Clin Pharmacol* 33(3):213-21.

Kelmanson, I. A. 1995. Brain stem gliosis in the victims of sudden infant death syndrome (SIDS): A sign of retarded maturation? *Zentralbl Pathol* 140(6):449-452.

Kinlen, L. J., R. Harris, A. Garrod, and K. Rodriguez. 1977. Use of hair dyes by patients with breast cancer. A case-control study. *Brit Med J* 2(6083):368.

Kipen, H., and J. Stellman. 1985. *Core Curriculum: Reproductive Hazards in the Workplace.* White Plains, N.Y.: March of Dimes.

Kirchengast, S., and B. Hartman. 1998. Maternal prepregnancy weight status and pregnancy weight gain as major determinants for newborn weight and size. *Ann Hum Biol* 25(1):17-28.

Klein, J., B. Levin, Z. Stein, M. Susser, and D. Warburton. 1981. Epidemiological detection of low dose effects on the developing fetus. *Environmental Health Perspectives* 42:119-126.

Krauer, B. 1987. Physiological changes and drug disposition during pregnancy. In *Pharmacokinetics in Teratogenesis*, edited by H. Nau and W. J. Scott, Jr. Vol. 1. 3-12. Boca Raton, FL: CRC Press, Inc.

Kuruøglu, A. C., Z. Arikan, G. Vural, M. Karataê, M. Ara, and E. Iêik. 1996. Single photon emission computerised tomography in chronic alcoholism: Antisocial personality disorder may be associated with decreased frontal perfusion. *Br J Psychiatry* 169(3):348-354.

Kyrklund, T., P. Kjellstrand, and K. Haglid. 1990. Long-term exposure of rats to perchloroethylene, with and without a post-exposure solvent-free recovery period: effects on brain lipids. *Toxicol Lett* 52(3):279-285.

LaDou, J., ed. 1997. *Occupational and Environmental Medicine.* Stamford, CT: Appleton & Lange.

Lanski, V. 1986. *Feed Me, I'm Yours.* Deephave, MN: Meadowbrook, Inc.

Laseter, John. 1998. Personal communication.

Lee, M., 1985. Potentiations of chemically induced cleft palate by ethanol ingestion during gestation in the mouse. *Teratogenesis Carcinog Mutagen* 5:433-440.

Lerner, H. M. 1997. Prepregnancy counseling for primary care physicians. *Hospital Medicine* 33(6):28-40.

Levin, J. J. and N. T. Ilowite. 1994. Sclerodermalike esophageal disease in children breast-fed by mothers with silicone breast implants. *JAMA* 272(10):770

Levy, B. S., and D. Wegman., eds. 1995. *Occupational Health: Recognizing and Preventing Work-Related Disease.* Boston: Little, Brown and company

Little, R. E., K. W. Anderson, C. H. Ervin, B. Worthington-Roberts, and S. K. Clarren. 1989. Maternal alcohol use during breast-feeding and infant mental and motor development at one year. *N Engl J Med* 321:425–430.

Loftus, M., and M. B. Marcus. 1998. Hold the chemicals. *U.S. News and World Report* 124:74-76.

Marbury, M. C. 1992. Relationship of ergonomic stressors to birth weight and gestational age. *Scand J Work Environ Health* 18:73-83.

Mast, T. J., et al. 1989. Developmental toxicity studey of acetone in mice and rats. *Teratology* 39:468–476.

Matthews, M. S. and K. S. Devi. 1994. Effect of chronic exposure of pregnant rats to malathion and/or estrogen and/or progesterone on xenobiotic metabolizing enzymes. *Pestic Biochem Physiol* 48(2): 110–122.

Mattison, D. 1990. Fetal pharmacokinetic and physiological models. In *Developmental Toxicology: Risk Assessment and the Future*, edited by R. Hood. 137-154. New York: Van Nostrand Reinhold.

Mikkelsen, S., M. Jorgensen, E. Browne, and C. Gyldensted. 1988. Mixed solvent exposure and organic brain damage: A study of painters. *Acta Neurol Scand* Suppl 118:1-143.

Miller, C. J. W. Hare, J. P. Cloherty, P. J. Dunn, R. E Gleason, J. S. Soeldner, and J. L. Kitzmiller. 1981. Elevated maternal hemoglobin A, C in early pregnancy and major congenital anomalies in infants of diabetic mothers. *N Engl J Med* 304:1331

Millichap, J. G. 1993. *Environmental Poisons in Our Food*. Chicago: PNB Publisher.

Moller, S. E., E. L. Mortensen, L. Breum, C. Alling, O. G. Larsen, T. Boge-Rasmussen, C. Jensen, and K. Bennicke. 1996. Aggression and personality: Association with amino acids and monoamine metabolites. *Psychol Med* 26(2):323-331.

Moore, H. L., and T. V. N. Persaud. 1998. *The Developing Human*. Philadelphia: W. B. Saunders.

Morgane, P. J., R. L. Austin-LaFrance, J. Bronzino, J. Tonkiss, and J. Galler. 1992. Malnutrition and the developing nervous system. In *The Vulnerable Brain and Environmental Risks*, edited by R. L. Issacson and K. F. Jenson. Vol I. New York: Plenum Press.

Mountz, J. M., L. C. Tolbert, D. W. Lill, C. R. Katholi, and H. G. Liu. 1995. Functional deficits in autistic disorder: Characterization by technetium–99m-HMPAO and SPECT. *J Nucl Med* 36(7):1156-1162.

National Institute for Occupational Safety and Health. Research Report. 1977. Guidelines on pregnancy and work. The Amercan College of Obstetricians and Gynecologists, U.S. Department of Health, Education and Welfare. Rockville, MD: NIOSH.

National Institutes of Health. 1998. Don't take it easy—Exercise. National Institute on Aging: AgePage NIA Information Center. P. O. Box 8057, Gaithersburg, MD 20892-8057 (800-222-2225).

National Research Council. 1993. *Pesticides in the Diets of Infants and Children.* Washington, D.C.: National Academy Press.

Nau, H. 1986. Species differences in pharmacokinetics and drug teratogenesis. *Environ Health Perspect* 70:113-129.

O'Rahilly, R., and F. Muller. 1996. *Human Embryology and Teratology.* New York: John Wiley and Sons.

Olney, J. W., N. B. Farber, E. Spitznagel, and L. N Robbins. 1996. Increasing brain tumor rates: Is there a link to aspartame? *J Neuropathol Exp Neurol* 50: 1115-1123.

Paitrast, B. J., W. C. Keller, and R. G. Elves. 1998. Estimation of chemical hazards in breast milk. *Aviat Space Environ Med* 59(11, pt. 2): 87-92.

Paul, M. 1995. Reproductive disorders. In *Occupational Health: Recognizing and Preventing Work-Related Disease,* edited by B. S. Levy and D. Wegman. Boston: Little, Brown, and company

PDR *(Physicians' Desk Reference).* 1997. Montvale, NJ: Medical Economics Company.

Pellizzari, E., T. Hartwell, C. M. Sparacinio, et al. 1985. Interim report on the total exposure assessment methodology (TEAM) study: First Season. Northern Jersey. Research Triangle Institute, Report No. RTI/2392/03-035.

Physicians Family Guide to Prescription Drugs. 1996. Montvale, N.J.: Medical Economics Company.

Pinto, J. M., and T. J. Maher. 1988. Administration of aspartame potentiates pentylenetetrazole- and fluorothyl-induced seizures in mice. *Neuropharmacology* 27(1):51-55.

Pope, A. M. and D. P. Rall, eds. 1995. *Environmental Medicine.* Washinton, D.C.: National Academy Press.

Pottkotter, L. 1994. *The Natural Nursery: The Parent's Guide to Ecologically Sound, Nontoxic, Safe, and Healthy Baby Care.* Chicago: Contemporary Books.

Pratt, R. M., E. H. Goulding, and B. D. Abbott. 1987. Retinoic acid inhibits migration of cranial neural crest cells in the cultured mouse embryo. *J Craniofacial Genet Develop Biol* 7: 205-217.

Punnett, L. 1995. The strength of women. In *Occupational Health: Recognizing and Preventing Work-Related Disease,* edited by B. S. Levy and D. Wegman. 626. Boston,: Little, Brown, and Co.

Quinn, M., S. Woskie, and B. Rosenburg. 1995. Women and work. In *Occupational Health: Recognizing and Preventing Work-Related Disease,* edited by B. Levy and and D. Wegman. Boston: Little, Brown, and Co.

Raine, A., D. Phil, J. Stoddard, S. Bihrle, and M. Buchsbaum. 1998. Prefrontal glucose deficits in murderers lacking psychosocial deprivation. *Neuropsychiatry Neuropsychol Behav Neurol* 11(1):1-7.

Ramey, C. T., D. M. Bryant, and T. M. Suarez. 1987. Early intervention: Why, for whom, how, at what cost: In *Infant Stimulation: For Whom, What Kind, When, and How Much?* edited by N. Gunezenhauser. *Pediatric Round Table* 13: Johnson and Johnson.

Rantakallio, P., E. Laara, M. Isohanni, and I. Moilanen. 1992. Maternal smoking during pregnancy and delinquency of the offspring: An association without causation. *Int J Epidemiol* 21:1106–1113.

Rapp, D. 1996. *Is This Your Child's World?* New York: Bantam Books.

Raz, S., N. Raz, D. R. Weinberger, J. Boronow, D. Pickar, E. D. Bigler, and E. Turkheimer. 1987. Morphological brain abnormalities in schizophrenia by computed tomography: A problem of measurement? *Psychiatric Res* 22:91.

Reggiani, G. R., and R. Bruppacher. 1985. Symptoms, signs, and findings in humans exposed to PCBs and their derivatives. *Environmental Health Perspectives* 60:25-232.

Riley, E., and C. Vorhees, eds. 1986. *Handbook of Behavioral Teratology.* N.Y.: Plenum Press.

Rogan W. J., P. J. Blauton, C. J. Portier, and E. Stallard. 1991. Should the presence of carcinogens in breast milk discourage breast-feeding? *Regul Toxicol Pharmacol* 13(3)228-240.

Rogan, W. J., andB. C. Gladen. 1991. PCBs, DDE, and child development at 18 and 24 months. *Ann Epidemiol* 5:407–413.

Rom, W., ed. 1998. *Environmental and Occupational Medicine.* Boston: Little, Brown, and Co.

Rosengren, L. and K. Haglid. 1989. Longer-term neurotoxicity of styrene. *Br J Ind Med* 46(5):316-320.

Rosenstock, L., and M. Cullen. 1994. Fluorine and related compounds. In *Rosenstock and Cullen's Textbook of Clinical, Occupational, and Environmental Medicine.* Philadelphia: W. B Saunders Company.

Rutter, M., P. Graham, and W. Yule. 1970. In *Developmental Neuropsychology,* edited by O. Spreen, A. Risser, and D. Edgall. New York: Oxford University Press.

Samuels, M., and N. Samuels. 1996. *The New Well Pregnancy Book.* New York: Fireside, Simon & Schuster.

Santrock, J. W., 1992. *Life-Span Development,* Fourth Edition, Dubuque, IA: William. C. Brown.

Schlaud, M., A. Seidler, A. Salje, W. Behrendt, F. W. Schwartz, M. Ende, A. Knoll, and C. Grugel. 1995. Organochlorine residues in human breast milk: Analysis through a sentinel practice network. *J of Epidemiology and Community Health* 49(Suppl 1)17-21.

Schulte-Hobein, B., D. Schwartz-Bickenbach, S. Abt, C. Plum, and H. Nau. 1992. Cigarette smoke exposure and development of infants throughout the first year of life: Influence of passive smoking and nursing on cotinine levels in breast milk and infants' urine. *Acta Paediatr* 81(8):380-382.

Scott, Jr., W. J., and H. Nau. 1987. Accumulation of weak acids in the young mannalian embryo. In *Pharmacokinetics in Teratogenesis,* edited by H. Nau and W. J. Scott, Jr. Vol. 1. 71-77. Boca Raton, FL: CRC Press, Inc.

Seidman, L. J. 1983. Schizophrenia and brain dysfunction: An integration of recent neurodiagnostic findings. *Psych Bull* 94:563.

Setchell, K. D. R., L. Zimmer-Nechemias, J. Cai, and J. E. Heubi. 1997. Exposure of infants to phyto-oestrogens from soy-based infant formula. *The Lancet* (July 5) 350:23-27.

Seward, J. 1997. Occupational stress. In *Occupational and Environmental Medicine,* edited by J. LaDou. Stamford, CT: Appleton & Lange.

Shannon, M., and J. W. Graef. 1989. Lead intoxication from lead-contaminated water used to reconstitute infant formula. *Clin Pediatr* 28(8):380-382.

Shaw, G. M., and L. A. Croen. 1993. Human adverse reproductive outcomes and electromagnetic field exposures: Review of epidemiologic studies. *Environ Health Perspect* Suppl 101:107.

Shephard, S. E., K. Wakabayashi, and M. Nagao. 1993. Mutagenic acticity of peptides and the artificial sweetener aspartame after nitrosation. *Food Chem Toxicol* 31(5):323-329.

Shields, J., R. Varley, P. Broks, and A. Simpson. 1996. Hemispheric function in developmental language disorders and high-level autism. *Dev Med Child Neurol* 38(6):473-486.

Shulman, J. D., and L. M. Wells. 1997. Acute ethanol toxicity from ingesting mouthwash in children younger than six years of age. *Pediatric Dentistry* 19:404-408.

Spangler, E. 1992. Sexual harassment: Labor relations by other means. *New Solutions* 3:24-29.

Spinelli, N. 1987. Plasticity triggering experiences, nature, and the dual genesis of brains structure and function. In *Infant Stimulation: For Whom, What Kind, When, and How Much*, edited by N. Guzenhauser. *Pediatric Round Table* 13: Johnson and Johnson.

Spreen, O., A. Risser, and D. Edgall. 1995. *Developmental Neuropsychology*. New York: Oxford University Press.

Srisuphan W., and M. B. Bracken. 1986. Caffeine consumption during pregnancy and association with late spontaneous abortion. *Am J Obst Gynecol* 154:14-20.

Stegink, L. D., M. C. Brummel, G. McMartin-Amat, L. J. Filer, Jr., G. L. Baker, and T. R. Tephly. 1981. Blood methanol concentrations in normal adult subjects administered abuse doses of aspartame. *J Toxicol Environ Health* 7(2):281-290.

Stein, Z., and J. Kline. 1983. Smoking, alcohol, and reproduction. *Am J Public Health* 73:1154.

Steinman, D., and S. Epstein. 1995. *The Safe Shopper's Bible: A Consumer's Guide to Nontoxic Household Products, Cosmetics, and Food*. New York: MacMillan.

Stenchever, M. A., T. J. Kunysz, and M. A. Allen. 1974. Chromosome breakage in users of marijuana. *American J Obst Gynecol* 118: 106-113.

Swanson, L., and T. Byrd. 1996. Insect repellents. *U.S. Pharmacist* 21(8):16-31.

Szmigielski, S. 1996. Cancer morbidity in subjects occupationally exposed to high frequency (radiofrequency and microwave) electromagnetic radiation. *Sci Total Environ* 180(1):9–17.

Tabacova, S., B. Nikiforov, and L. Balabaeva. 1983. Carbon disulphide intrauterine sensitization. *J Appl Toxicol* 3:223-229.

Tzonou, A., A. Polychronopoulou, C. C. Hsieh, A. Rebelakos, A. Karakatsani, and D. Trichopoulos. 1993. Hair dyes, analgesics, tranquilizers and perineal talc application as risk factors for ovarian cancer. Sept. 30. *Int J Cancer* 55:408-410.

United States Food and Drug Administration. 1998. Pregnancy Category X Drugs. Washington, DC.

Upledger, John, 1996. *A Brain Is Born.* Berkeley, CA.: North Atlantic Books.

Wadhwa, P. 1998. High levels of prenatal stress associated with behavioral problems and temperamental dispositions in infants. 19th Annual Meeting of the Society of Behavioral Medicine. New Orleans, LA.

Waterhouse, L., D. Fein, and C. Modahl. 1996. Neurofunctional mechanisms in autism. *Psychol Rev* 103(3):457-489.

Wertheimer, N., and E. Leeper. 1982. Adult cancer related to electrical wires near the home. *Int J Epidemiol* 11: 345-355.

———. 1979. Electrical wiring configurations and childhood cancer. *Am J Epidemiol* 109:273-284.

Welch, L. S. 1986. Decision making about reproductive hazards. *Semin Occup Med* 1:97-106.

Welch, L. S. 1993. Reproductive and developmental hazards. *Case Studies in Environmental Medicine.* September. U.S. Dept. of Health and Human Services, Agency for Toxic Substances and Disease Registry.

Whaley, L. F., and D. L. Wong. 1989. *Essentials of Pediatric Nursing.* St. Louis: Mosby.

White, B. 1985. *The First Three Years of Life.* New York: Prentice Hall Press.

WHO. 1990. *Public Health Impact of Pesticides used in Agriculture.* Geneva: World Health Organization in collaboration with the United Nations Environment Programme.

Williams, R. 1996. Decreasing the chance of birth defects. *FDA Consumer Magazine,* November, 1998.

Wolff, M. S. 1983. Occupationally derived chemicals in breast milk. *Am J Ind Med* 4:259.

Wolverton, B. 1997. *How to Grow Fresh Air: Fifty Houseplants That Purify Your Home or Office.* New York: Penguin.

World Health Organization (WHO). 1993. *Benzene: Environmental Health Criteria* 150:156.

Yamanouchi, N., S. Okada, K. Kodama, S. Hirai, H. Sekine, A. Murakame, N. Kamatsu, T. Sakamoto, and T. Sato. 1995. White matter changes caused by chronic solvent abuse. *Am J Neuroradiol* 16(8):1643-1649.

Zacharias, J. 1983. A rational approach to drug use in pregnancy. *JOGN Nursing.* May 184.

Zhang, J., and K. R. Smith. 1996. Hydrocarbon emissions and health risks from cookstoves in developing countries. *J Expo Anal Environ Epidemiol* 6:147-161.

Zorumski, C. F., and J. Olney. 1992. Acute and chronic neurodegenerative disorders by dietary excitotoxins. In *The Vulnerable Brain and Environmental Risks,* edited by R. L. Issaacson and K. F. Jenson. Vol. I. New York: Plenum Press.

Index

reproductive damage caused by, 51–52; organizations for testing, 277; protecting your baby from, 236–237; reducing in home environments, 110–112; reducing your baby's total load of, 27–28; research on negative effects of, 30–31; stress-related, 174–175. *See also* chemicals
toxoplasmosis, 170
toys, 215
tranquilizers, 168
transnonachlor, 274
Tretinoin, 169
tributyltin oxide, 275
trichloroethane, 275
trichloroethylene, 275
triclosan, 208
triethanolamine (TEA), 210
trifluralin, 275
Tri-Levlen, 261
Tri-Norinyl, 275
Triphasil-21, 275
tungsten carbide, 275
2,4,5-T, 246
2,4- dichlorophenol, 246
Tylenol. *See* acetaminophen
U.S. Food Quality Protection Act (1996), 144
Upledger, John, 39
urine tests: biological monitoring through, 243; for evaluating toxic load, 56; organizational resource for, 277
vaccinations, 70
vacor, 275
vanadium, 275
vegetarians: sources of protein for, 25; supplemental nutrients for, 187
video display terminals (VDTs), 125–126
vinclozolin, 275
vinegar, as cleaning agent, 109, 110
vinyl chloride, 92, 275
Virazole, 275
viruses, 165–166
Vitamin A, 178
Vitamin C, 77
Vitamin D, 186
vitamins: as antioxidants, 65; overconsumption of, 178; pregnancy and importance of, 26

Vivelle, 276
volatile organic compounds (VOCs), 89, 95–97; biological monitoring of, 243; reducing with plants, 111–112
water, 83–93; bottled, 92–93; chlorine in, 85–86; as cleaning agent, 109, 110; contaminants in, 84–85; filtration systems for, 93–94; fluoride in, 86–87; importance of drinking, 63; lead in, 87; metals in, 91; microbes in, 91–92; MTBE in, 89–90; nitrates in, 87–88; pesticides in, 90–91, 144; plasticizers in, 90; testing, 85
water filters, 93–94
weight: detoxification through losing, 65; gained during pregnancy, 26; lactation and loss of, 197
Wigraine, 276
windows, developmental. *See* developmental windows
Winstrol, 276
women: feminine hygiene products for, 210–211, 278–279; fertility problems in, 49. *See also* mothers
wool fabrics, 220
work environment, 113–134; anesthetic gases in, 122; antineoplastic agents in, 121–122; biological agents in, 126; controlling occupational effects in, 132–134; developmental disorders related to, 114–115; emotional stress in, 126–127; fetal risk factors in, 115–132; heavy metals in, 120–121; household toxins and, 130; list of agents with teratogenic effects in, 123–124; neurotoxins in, 117–118; office equipment toxins in, 129–130; PCBs in, 122; pesticides and fertilizers in, 119–120; petrochemicals in, 118–119; physical stress in, 127–129; radiation effects in, 124–126; reducing chemical exposure in, 116–117; solvents in, 118–119
work schedule, 128, 133
World Health Organization (WHO), 142
xylene, 276
zinc, 218, 276
zineb, 276
ziram, 276
Zocor, 276
Zoladex, 276

More New Harbinger Titles for Parents and Families

DR. CARL ROBINSON'S BASIC BABY CARE
A Guide for New Parents for the First Year

Covers all the basics, through childbirth and the first days at home to questions about bathing diapers, dealing with sleep problems and crying, making decsions about feeding, and the many other concerns that new parents have. *Item DRR $12.95*

THE TEN THINGS EVERY PARENT NEEDS TO KNOW

Ten warm and straightforward chapters offer advice on how to nurture a child emotionally, listen and foster self-esteem, solve problems and handle discipline issues, and take care of yourself as well as your child. *Item KNOW $12.95*

KID COOPERATION
How to Stop Yelling, Nagging, and Pleading and Get Kids to Cooperate

There really is a way to talk so that kids will listen and be reinforced to be helping, responsive members of the family. This is an empowering work, filled with practical skills. *Item COOP $13.95*

WHY CHILDREN MISBEHAVE
And What to Do About It

This text offers practical strategies for dealing with common behavior problems in a concise, easy-to-use format. Beautifully illustrated by over 100 photographs. *Item BEHV $14.95*

WHEN ANGER HURTS YOUR KIDS
A Parent's Guide

Learn how to combat the mistaken beliefs that fuel anger and how to practice the art of problem-solving communication—skills that will let you feel more effective as a parent and let your kids grow up free of anger's damaging effects. *Item HURT $12.95*

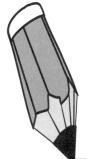

Some Other New Harbinger Self-Help Titles

Claiming Your Creative Self: True Stories from the Everyday Lives of Women, $15.95
Six Keys to Creating the Life You Desire, $19.95
Taking Control of TMJ, $13.95
What You Need to Know About Alzheimer's, $15.95
Winning Against Relapse: A Workbook of Action Plans for Recurring Health and Emotional Problems, $14.95
Facing 30: Women Talk About Constructing a Real Life and Other Scary Rites of Passage, $12.95
The Worry Control Workbook, $15.95
Wanting What You Have: A Self-Discovery Workbook, $18.95
When Perfect Isn't Good Enough: Strategies for Coping with Perfectionism, $13.95
The Endometriosis Survival Guide, $13.95
Earning Your Own Respect: A Handbook of Personal Responsibility, $12.95
High on Stress: A Woman's Guide to Optimizing the Stress in Her Life, $13.95
Infidelity: A Survival Guide, $13.95
Stop Walking on Eggshells, $14.95
Consumer's Guide to Psychiatric Drugs, $16.95
The Fibromyalgia Advocate: Getting the Support You Need to Cope with Fibromyalgia and Myofascial Pain, $18.95
Healing Fear: New Approaches to Overcoming Anxiety, $16.95
Working Anger: Preventing and Resolving Conflict on the Job, $12.95
Sex Smart: How Your Childhood Shaped Your Sexual Life and What to Do About It, $14.95
You Can Free Yourself From Alcohol & Drugs, $13.95
Amongst Ourselves: A Self-Help Guide to Living with Dissociative Identity Disorder, $14.95
Healthy Living with Diabetes, $13.95
Dr. Carl Robinson's Basic Baby Care, $10.95
Better Boundries: Owning and Treasuring Your Life, $13.95
Goodbye Good Girl, $12.95
Being, Belonging, Doing, $10.95
Thoughts & Feelings, Second Edition, $18.95
Depression: How It Happens, How It's Healed, $14.95
Trust After Trauma, $15.95
The Chemotherapy & Radiation Survival Guide, Second Edition, $14.95
Surviving Childhood Cancer, $12.95
The Headache & Neck Pain Workbook, $14.95
Perimenopause, $16.95
The Self-Forgiveness Handbook, $12.95
A Woman's Guide to Overcoming Sexual Fear and Pain, $14.95
Don't Take It Personally, $12.95
Becoming a Wise Parent For Your Grown Child, $12.95
Clear Your Past, Change Your Future, $13.95
Preparing for Surgery, $17.95
The Power of Two, $15.95
It's Not OK Anymore, $13.95
The Daily Relaxer, $12.95
The Body Image Workbook, $17.95
Living with ADD, $17.95
When Anger Hurts Your Kids, $12.95
The Chronic Pain Control Workbook, Second Edition, $17.95
Fibromyalgia & Chronic Myofascial Pain Syndrome, $19.95
Kid Cooperation: How to Stop Yelling, Nagging & Pleading and Get Kids to Cooperate, $13.95
The Stop Smoking Workbook: Your Guide to Healthy Quitting, $17.95
Conquering Carpal Tunnel Syndrome and Other Repetitive Strain Injuries, $17.95
An End to Panic: Breakthrough Techniques for Overcoming Panic Disorder, Second Edition, $18.95
Letting Go of Anger: The 10 Most Common Anger Styles and What to Do About Them, $12.95
Messages: The Communication Skills Workbook, Second Edition, $15.95
Coping With Chronic Fatigue Syndrome: Nine Things You Can Do, $13.95
The Anxiety & Phobia Workbook, Second Edition, $18.95
The Relaxation & Stress Reduction Workbook, Fourth Edition, $17.95
Living Without Depression & Manic Depression: A Workbook for Maintaining Mood Stability, $18.95
Coping With Schizophrenia: A Guide For Families, $15.95
Visualization for Change, Second Edition, $15.95
Angry All the Time: An Emergency Guide to Anger Control, $12.95
Couple Skills: Making Your Relationship Work, $14.95
Self-Esteem, Second Edition, $13.95
I Can't Get Over It, A Handbook for Trauma Survivors, Second Edition, $16.95
Dying of Embarrassment: Help for Social Anxiety and Social Phobia, $13.95
The Depression Workbook: Living With Depression and Manic Depression, $17.95
Men & Grief: A Guide for Men Surviving the Death of a Loved One, $14.95
When Once Is Not Enough: Help for Obsessive Compulsives, $14.95
Beyond Grief: A Guide for Recovering from the Death of a Loved One, $14.95
Hypnosis for Change: A Manual of Proven Techniques, Third Edition, $15.95
When Anger Hurts, $13.95

Call **toll free, 1-800-748-6273,** to order. Have your Visa or Mastercard number ready. Or send a check for the titles you want to New Harbinger Publications, Inc., 5674 Shattuck Ave., Oakland, CA 94609. Include $3.80 for the first book and 75¢ for each additional book, to cover shipping and handling. (California residents please include appropriate sales tax.) Allow two to five weeks for delivery.

Prices subject to change without notice.